Howard and Cynthia

A LOVE STORY

YYYYY YYYYY
YYYY YYYY
YYYY YYYY
YYY
YY
YY
Y
YYY YYY
YYY YYY
YYYYY
YYY
Y

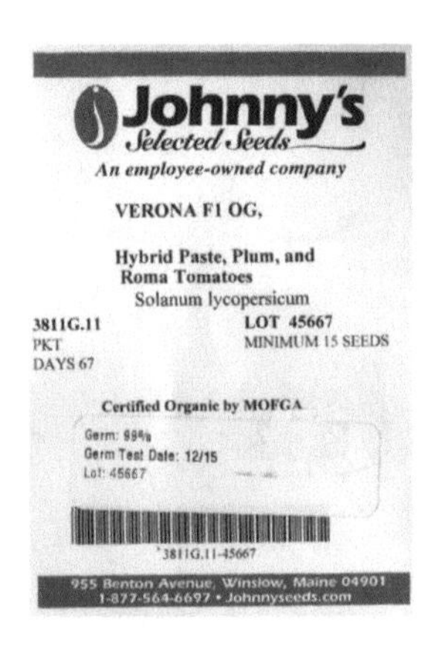

Y y
yyyy yyyyy
yyyyyyyy y yyyyyyyy
yyyyyyyyyyyyyyyyyyyy
yyyyyyyyyyyyyyy
yyyyyyy
yyy
y

HOWARD AND CYNTHIA

A LOVE STORY

HOWARD ATTEBERY & CYNTHIA RIGGS

MMXVI

ACKNOWLEDGEMENTS

We want to acknowledge Jay Ellison of *The Moth*, Lynn Christoffers, photographer; Susanna Sturgis, editor; Janet Holladay, designer; Chris Decker, delivery man; and Tisbury Printer.

Cleaveland House Books
P.O. Box 723 · West Tisbury, MA 02575
www.cynthiariggs.com

Designed by Janet Holladay
Tisbury Printer, Vineyard Haven, Massachusetts

ISBN-13: 978-1535189361 · ISBN-10: 1535189363

CONTENTS

To

The Wednesday Writers

and

The Moth

PART 1: GETTING IN TOUCH

Chapter 1. Coded Messages

The package arrived in early February.

As usual, I had driven the two-and-a-half miles to the post office to pick up my mail, not expecting anything special. A raw and chilly southwest wind carried the sound and salt smell of the sea, and I was in a hurry to get home to the comforting fire in the parlor fireplace. My sister, Ann Fielder, and a photographer friend, Lynn Christoffers, were coming for lunch. I was working on my latest mystery, *Bloodroot,* about murder in a dental office, and I was eager to finish lunch and get back to my writing to find out what would happen next. I had no idea the package would prove more intriguing than anything my imagination could conjure up.

The package was addressed to Cynner, a nickname that I'd stopped using after I graduated from college. The sender was H. Attebery.

My first reaction when I saw the sender's name was "Of course. I spelled it wrong."

Two weeks earlier, Howard Attebery, a man I'd met in San Diego, California, during a four-month college internship, had popped into my mind and I'd Googled his name. Nothing came of it and I thought no more about it until the morning the package arrived and I saw the correct spelling.

My second reaction was astonishment. "There's no way on earth he could possibly have known I was thinking about him."

The return address on the package was 32.7°N 117.12°W. No street address. The package was postmarked San Diego, CA, and it had been mailed on January 30, 2012.

The package of paper towels with its return address

I'd cut my time close, and couldn't open the package before lunch. When we'd finished dessert, I reached for it from the nearby telephone table. "Look what arrived in today's mail," I said, showing it to them. Ann took the thick envelope and studied the address. "Cynner?"

I'm the youngest of three sisters. All of us, Alvida, Ann, and I, live on Martha's Vineyard on the same property that's been in our family for several hundred years.

"Cynner?" she repeated. "We haven't called you that for a long time."

"I met this guy a long time ago," I said.

Lynn pointed to the upper left corner. "What kind of address is this?"

She passed the package back to me. Lynn, in her late forties, is much younger than Ann and me. She was sitting with her back to the window and her stunning silver hair formed a bright halo around her face.

I shrugged. "I guess that's where he was when he sent it."

Ann passed me the letter opener. "Don't keep us in suspense any longer."

The padded package was white, about eight inches by ten inches. I opened it carefully. Inside was a plastic archival envelope. When I opened that, I found a handful of yellowed paper towels on which were penciled what looked like gibberish. I was every bit as mystified as my luncheon guests.

"I have no idea what this is," I said, putting the envelope back into the package and setting it aside.

Coded messages on paper towels that Howard kept for 62 years

"We'll help you clear the table. " Ann folded her napkin neatly and stood. "I've got to run. Let us know when you solve this mystery."

"I've got to run, too," said Lynn, looking at her watch. "I have a shoot in Chilmark." Lynn specializes in photographing cats and children. "I hate to leave without knowing what this is all about."

Left to myself, I opened the package

again, took out the archival envelope, removed the paper towels and stared at them. I drew a total blank. The writing seemed to be in some kind of code. Enclosed along with the towels was a new white three-by-five-inch card, also written in code. When I sorted through the paper towels, I found the writing was a series of cryptograms with solutions to the puzzles written above in a different hand.

The first one I looked at read "Yippee! I can hardly wait until Friday!"

The second one, which must have been the first written, said, when translated, "Dear Howard; How are you at solving cryptograms which involve the use of simple substitution? . ." The message went on and on in an obnoxiously condescending way.

I set the paper towels aside and stared at the coded message on the white card. I knew the code. I remembered it from years back. Letter by letter I translated it.

The message read, "I have never stopped loving you. Howord." He'd misspelled Howard, his own name.

With a hot sense of embarrassment it all came back to me.

• • • • •

Most eighteen-year-olds are clueless. I was an especially clueless eighteen-year-old, a second-year student at Antioch College in Yellow Springs, Ohio, a college noted for its co-op work/study program. Both of my sisters had graduated from Antioch. I'd been an indifferent high school student, drifting through subjects that didn't interest me. I intended to be an artist and would never need science. However, Antioch required its students to take a broad range of courses. The easiest science course, I'd heard, was Introduction to Earth Science, so I enrolled.

I will never forget the effect the course had on me. It opened a door into knowledge that allowed me to read the history of the Earth in road cuts. A course that introduced me

A sketch of 28-year-old Howard and a new note

to fossils hundreds of millions of years old that I could actually touch and that I could search for in Ohio's limestone cliffs.

Around the same time, I read an article in the *National Geographic* about sea-going geologists. That night I woke up from a deep sleep in my dorm room, lights flashing through my mind. I would switch my major from art to marine geology. I come from a long line of seafarers so the sea is in my blood. No matter that the college of my choice was in Ohio and the geology department consisted of one professor and five geology majors, if I were to be included. This meant catching up with the science and math courses I'd faked my way through in high school. Now the incentive was there.

Antioch found a four-month-long job for their new and only marine geology major starting in April 1950. The job was in San Diego, sorting plankton for the U.S. Fish and Wildlife Service at a Scripps Institution of Oceanography laboratory at Point Loma.

Ohio was as far west as I'd ever been. I was about to travel all the way across the country to work in a real research laboratory. I arrived at the laboratory, a temporary wooden build-

Howard's honorary PhD awarded by Plankton Pickers of Point Loma

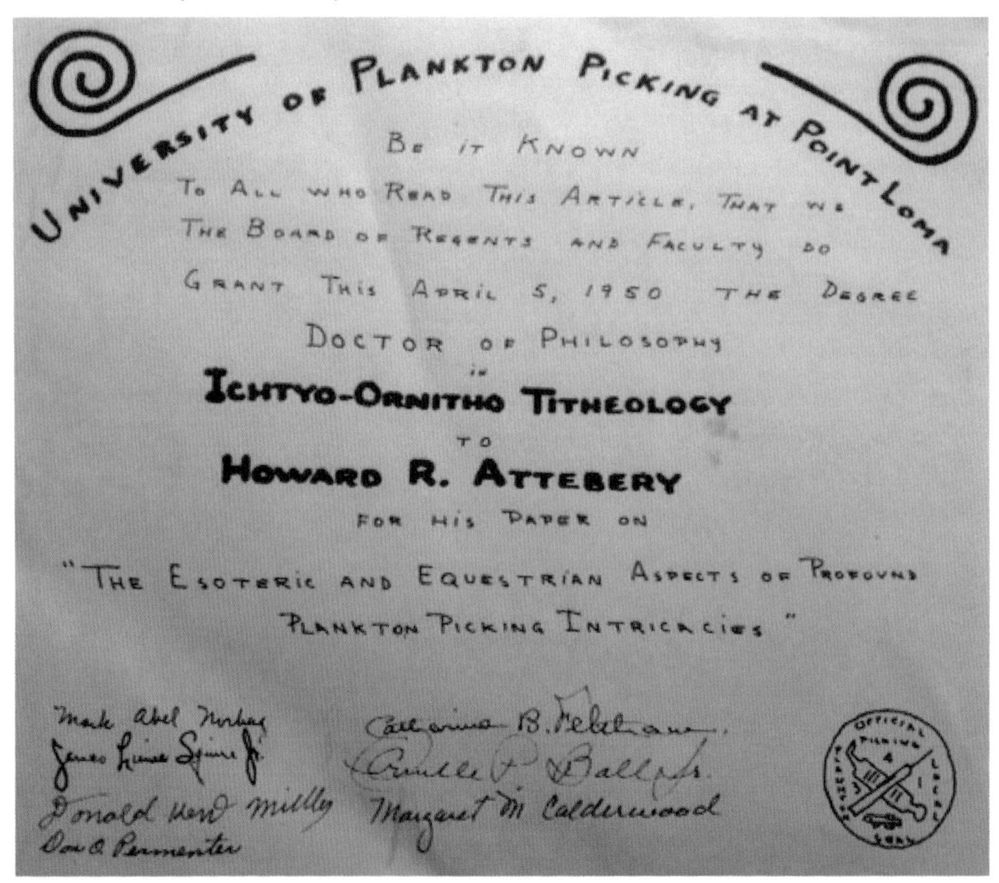
UNIVERSITY OF PLANKTON PICKING AT POINT LOMA

BE IT KNOWN

TO ALL WHO READ THIS ARTICLE, THAT WE THE BOARD OF REGENTS AND FACULTY DO GRANT THIS APRIL 5, 1950 THE DEGREE

DOCTOR OF PHILOSOPHY

IN

ICHTYO-ORNITHO TITHEOLOGY

TO

HOWARD R. ATTEBERY

FOR HIS PAPER ON

"THE ESOTERIC AND EQUESTRIAN ASPECTS OF PROFOUND PLANKTON PICKING INTRICACIES"

Margaret M Calderwood

ing that belonged to the Navy and overlooked San Diego Bay. At the lab I had a desk and a real microscope, and I was introduced to plankton, microscopic organisms that drift in the sea. On my lab desk were a pair of forceps, a petri dish, a form on which to list my findings, a jar of plankton preserved in formalin, and a pile of paper towels. I had become part of a group that called itself the "Plankton Pickers of Point Loma," assigned to sort out fish eggs and larvae from the plankton as part of a sardine research program.

I was a gawky, long-legged, six-foot-tall teenager with thick glasses and straight hair that I made some effort to curl the way my grandmother had taught me, by winding it up in rags at night. My co-workers, mostly men, had been sorting plankton for a long time and needed a distraction. I was it. Ingenious and sophomoric practical jokes were played on me, like nailing my lab drawers shut, or putting some kind of slimy stuff on my bicycle seat, and I had no idea what it was all about.

The plankton pickers had their own code words, their own secret jokes, their own agonizing stories. The worst story was Don P.'s. He had survived the Bataan Death March of 1942. They were a strange, intelligent, clever bunch, and I was no match for them.

But one plankton picker, Howard Attebery, took pity on me. Like my father, he'd served in the Army in World War II. The war had ended only five years before. To me, Howard seemed almost as old as my father. He was 28. A microbiologist with a degree in dentistry, he was tall, quiet, and clean-cut, with light brown hair worn short, blue eyes that saw through me and beyond, a broad chest, and huge hands that he could use to make the most delicate of adjustments. Unlike our slovenly co-workers, he was always neat, with sharply pressed tan trousers and polished ankle-high leather boots.

Somehow Howard got my tormenters off my back without making matters worse for me. They had enormous respect for him and had even awarded him a "PhD" in "Ichtyo-Ornitho Titheology" from the "University of Plankton Picking at Point Loma," citing a paper he'd written and circulated among them called "The Esoteric and Equestrian Aspects of Profound Plankton Picking Intricacies." The certificate was signed by seven of the plankton pickers. I recognized a friend, and began to write him notes in code on the paper towels beside my microscope. During the war, my father taught me about cryptograms, so I was full of myself and my knowledge of secret codes. The notes I wrote to Howard were merely friendly, although most of them were signed "YY," code for "XX." The code was simple — A equals B, B equals C, C equals D, and so forth.

On lunch breaks we'd sometimes sit outside and talk, with me talking and Howard listening. I told him about the courses I was taking at Antioch, the boy named George I was dating, the books that I liked.

My job as a Scripps Oceanographic plankton picker started in April 1950 and ended that August, in time for me to get home to Martha's Vineyard for my mother's 52nd birthday, August 6.

Chapter 2. Every Woman's Fantasy

The day after I got the package was a Wednesday. Every Wednesday night, from 7 to 9 pm, the Wednesday Writers meet at my home, the Cleaveland House.

The group consists of eight or nine women, all young enough to be my children, some even my grandchildren. We are serious writers and over the six or more years we've met have become as close as family. Although we concentrate on writing, we are always ready to share relationship problems. That Wednesday, I showed the writers' group the package containing the coded paper towel messages I'd written 62 years earlier. I wasn't sure how I felt about the whole thing.

"What do you make of this?" I asked. "I have to say, I'm a bit uncomfortable." I was sitting in the wing chair in the parlor where we meet. The fire was blazing, the popcorn bowl had started out full, and Cat had poured me a glass of wine.

"Uncomfortable!" said Lisa, sitting forward. "Are you crazy? It's every woman's fantasy, having a man come back into her life like this and saying he loves her."

"It's so romantic, Cynthia," said Cat, who was sitting on the uncomfortable Victorian sofa to my left. "Lisa's right."

"I don't know," said Amy, from the rocking chair. "I can see why Cynthia feels uneasy." Amy comes to the Wednesday meetings from the barn where she keeps her horse and we tease her about the aroma. "Maybe he's a stalker."

Lisa refilled her own small bowl with popcorn. "You have to be kidding!" She laughed, spilling some on the floor. "Stalker? Cynthia hasn't heard from this guy for 62 years. Some stalker!" Lisa is running a marathon in every state in the United States, and at that time had only five more states to go. "She's 80 and he must be around 90 now." She bent down, still laughing, and picked up the spilled popcorn.

I looked from one to the other. Emily, Sarah, Cat, Mary Lou, Valerie, Amy, Lisa. Nods all around.

"You've got to get in touch with him," said Lisa, sitting up straight again.

"No way," I responded, taking a sip of wine. Because she's always training, Lisa won't drink wine, only water. "Yes, you do," she said.

"Look, you guys," I said holding up the package so they could see the return address. "Latitude and longitude. How am I supposed to find him?"

"You can find him," said Lisa, and that was that.

• • • • •

I'm a published mystery writer. Over the course of the next week, instead of writing about it, I turned sleuth. I tried to track down the location of 32.47° N, 117.12° W. Google put it somewhere around the coast of Baja California, Mexico. With a further search, I found a golf resort in that general area.

I recalled that he'd told me, way back when, that during World War II he'd gotten a dental degree. Aha, I thought. Perhaps he had a career in dentistry and is now a retired golfer.

I got the resort's toll free number and called. "Is Dr. Attebery registered there?"

A long wait. "I'm sorry, madam, no guest here by that name."

"Has he been there in the recent past?"

"No, ma'am. I'm so sorry. Would you like us to contact you if he should register?"

"No, thank you," I said, and spent some time thinking about another explanation of the geographic coordinates, which covered some distance offshore as well as on.

Aha! I thought. He's on a cruise ship in that area.

I found a cruise ship tracking site on the Internet. Checking dates a couple of weeks on either side of the time the package was mailed, found no cruise ships in that area. None at all.

So my thinking went like this: He's a rich retired dentist. He's on his yacht cruising the Pacific. He's sitting on his deck chair drinking margaritas and his captain comes down from the bridge, salutes him, and says, "Dr. Attebery, sir, your latitude and longitude is . . ."

But that was a dead end.

The postmark on the package was San Diego. Maybe he was living there?

I tried 411, the information number for the phone company, but that, too, was a dead end. No one I called in the San Diego metropolitan area listings named Attebery, or a close approximation of the name, knew of a Dr. Howard Attebery.

"You've simply got to find him," insisted Lisa on Wednesday when I gave my report. "He's somewhere, and you have to find him."

Nods around the group. Even Amy had come around. "It's too romantic to drop," she said. "You can do it, Cynthia."

I found his name on a register of Army enlistees in 1942, but that led nowhere. I knew he'd been interested in ornithology, and found his name in an article in *The Condor,* a scientific journal dedicated to ornithological research. The quote was brief, and it had to do with willets: "Eats jack mackerel eggs."

That, too, led nowhere.

My next thought and the only other possible clue I could follow up was to try the California Dental Association, and, at last, I found his name, an address, and a telephone number. The listing showed he'd been the public health dentist for two California counties, Sonoma and Santa Cruz, an area of more than two thousand square miles, which shot down the idea of a wealthy dentist with a yacht. He'd given up his dental certification in 1988, and his address dated from then, 25 years before.

The chance of his still being in the same place was slim. I tried the phone number and got a weird robotic message. I learned later that sometime during those intervening 25 years the area code had been changed.

As a last resort I wrote a short, non-committal note to the only address I had, saying I got the package, thank you. Perhaps, I thought, someone will forward the letter. "Good girl!" was the consensus of the Wednesday Writers.

OAK CREEK - SEDONA, AZ
THIS SCENE IS NEAR THE
LODGE AND WAS [illegible]
AFTER BKFST ON A NIPPY
BUT DELIGHTFUL MORNING
IT WAS GREAT LIVING HERE
FOR 3 DAYS.

DEAR CYUNER - Better THAN
NICE - HEARING FROM YOU -
COORDINATES ARE FROM MY
HOME - 307 FT ABOVE SEA LEVEL
AM COOL, SELFPROPELLED,
SEEKING WISDOM AND TRY-
ING TO RAIN COMPASSION AND
WANTING All TO BE FED,
LOVED AND AIMED IN THE RIGHT
DIRECTION. I DO POSTCARDS AND
WILL SEND YOU MORE IF YOU DO NOT
MIND. Do well, MPWF XY
Howard

C. RIGGS
P.O. BOX 723
WEST TISBURY
MA
02575

ROSEMARY ESSENCE FROM MY GARDEN

ALOHA

Howard's postcard photo and message from Sedona, Arizona

"We'll drink to some great detective work," which they did, toasting me with wine and, in Lisa's case, with water.

"I haven't found him," I protested. "No one lives in the same house for 25 years anymore." Amy laughed. "Look at you. Eight generations in this same house?"

• • • • •

That week I got a postcard, a photograph of a rocky stream in Sedona, Arizona. "Better than nice — hearing from you . . ." the card read, and it was signed "Howard." What was he doing in Sedona? The postmark was blurred and the mystery was not entirely solved. But apparently mail to the address I'd used was getting through.

"You've got to follow up," insisted the Wednesday Writers. "Now you know where he lives. You've got to write back."

"No," I said.

"Yes," they said.

I thought about that for a while.

Sedona.

The middle one of my five children, Mary Wilder, had written a powerful and angry poem called "Meeting My Father in Sedona." In 2007, when she was not yet 50, she died of a sudden heart attack. Her husband, Doug Green, and I put together a collection of her poetry, including the poem about Sedona, and published a slim volume we titled "Unknown Territory," the title of one of her poems. I sent a copy to Howard at the San Diego address.

Meeting My Father in Sedona

Mary Wilder Stoertz

What wise fools we are to laugh:
This New Age Mecca gathering place!
But what celestial harmonies
Converged so unexpectedly

To draw us here? Beyond divorce
The frazzled father-daughter cords
Vibrate in pain. Each airy note I send
Conciliatory in intent

Conceals a rock. The truth is I
Am angry; the red sandstoned sky

Indifferent. We survey shelved
Minerals, geologists ourselves

Assaying crystal symmetries
Disparaging the promises:
"To heal the broken heart." But at
A price! And knowing gems we do not

Credit it. We are, in fact, unmoved;
Unchanging as the cliffs themselves.
A fortitude rebuked by weathering,
And sympathetic faces. Even

As I steeped in anger, you grew old.
I comprehend a million cold
Years: A blink of time that our
Sands run!
Dissolved, I let the anger go.

• • • • •

Howard's next letter was written entirely in capital letters.

Hello Cynthia —

Your last handwritten letter is at hand. You write with such clarity and beautiful phrasing. I feel so small in my writings. The few good words that I know get stuck somewhere in my head and do not want to come out. Writing in capitals may be easier for me but they are not meant to convey shouting but a whisper, something up close. You referenced page 39 ["Meeting My Father in Sedona"] which I read and I felt the anguish and release. I flipped through the pages looking for my next and it was easy to decide on "Yeast," it being of microbiological nature, and used in my cooking of mini-loaves of bread. I treasure this poem for the humor and passion and I now know who put the music in the words. I will be thinking about it when I am baking and maybe even when I am looking at flours.

Yeast

Mary Wilder Stoertz

To sell a house, they say
Bake bread. I know I'd buy

That argument. I'll take
The man who bakes the bread
As well: his sinewed back
Reveals his kneads (or mine)
Muscle tapering to denim
Waist, arched over in profound
Embrace with stretchy dough
Shaping rye loaves buttocks
Firm. Lazing on the couch
I gaze, then drowse, and wake
From sensuous sleep, a yeasty
Revelation: Here he sits
Hot buttered bread before
My lips. The things we do
For love! The loaf he hands me--
Darling! Fresh-cut flours.

I then went to the start of the book and I was surprised for the moment and then all was clearer to me. I feel for your loss of such a beautiful, truth-seeking, talented daughter, and named Mary. I had a son, named Paul, who died two years before Mary. They were about the same age. Paul fought a non-operable brain tumor for a number of years but it won.

Son Mark is the flutist and is now the music director at the Fieldston School in New York. Paul was the cellist and later turned to keyboards, drums and guitars and played in blues bands most of his life. Their mother passed due to a fatal coronary.

I remember your long strides and it was challenging for me to keep up with your pace. What you have done with your life and are doing speaks to me and I am thankfully impressed. You are the one. You are so precious. Your total package is so overwhelming that you can only be compared to yourself. You have an upwelling of imagination. I like what you are. What I feel is unmistakable.

Thank you for the "Guide Book"* — a splendor on a paradise. I feel such a strong attachment to the scenes. I know why!

I am mailing you one of my books. I did most of the photographs. The book was published to give the medical profession an insight into the diagnosis and treatment of anaerobic infections. It was published in several languages. Some of the pictures may be disturbing.

Love, Howard YY

---

* *Victoria Trumbull's Martha's Vineyard,* written by Cynthia with photographs by Lynn Christoffers and maps by Stephen Wesley (Cleaveland House Books, 2011, 2016)

Here is the beginning of the real story of this empowering love in my life.

I was seated in the laboratory using a microscope to sort plankton when the lab's white, tight-fitting double doors opened wide and Margaret Calderwood came in with a young girl and introduced her to all the lab workers as Cynthia Riggs. It was at that moment when the doors opened and Cynthia appeared that I got that so-called tingle. Perhaps it was a moment of respiratory distress, but it certainly was a new wave of sensation for me. Hers was such a beautiful face, short dark hair to frame it, and she was adorned with a pair of long sensual legs that were obvious through her jeans.

This happened in April of 1950 at the Scripps Institution of Oceanography lab located at what was then called the Naval Electronics Laboratory in Point Loma. April is a good month in San Diego, as most of the others are also, and there is usually a gentle and satisfying breeze from the ocean on the west that goes over the thin strip of land to the San Diego Bay side. It was good to sit on the steps at the side of the building and enjoy the sun and the breeze and talk and become acquainted with Cynthia.

I learned that she was a student at Antioch College, that this was her first four-month student work program, and that she was a geology major, came from some island off the east coast, and was dating, I thought seriously, a fellow student named George. I thought personally that I should not interfere. I did enjoy listening to stories of their canoe portages and adventures, but most of all I was overtaken by other things she talked about and how she spoke. I had never heard such a distinguished sound from a voice. She pronounced "aunt" in a way I had never heard before, and I liked to hear it again and again.

I have these remembrances of time segments that are so clear they could have happened yesterday. One was on the breakwater wall at Mission Bay. We were there watching the fireworks and C was telling me in her delightful way about Winnie-the-Pooh and the adventures of Pooh Bear and the bees. She would talk lovingly about her parents, and she told me about one sister who was a chemist and another — I remembered her name because it was simply Ann — who played the cello.

It was a delight being with Cynthia those four months: I was delivered those most beautiful thoughts and ideas and prose and so much that she had read and experienced and it all seemed to have remained there ready to be recalled. What a gift. In comparison I am mostly blunt, but I hold on to what is beautiful and what I love. I have never let go of Cynthia. She has steadfastly remained somehow near over the decades. I am so thankful for all that.

Work as a plankton picker started with an announcement for Biological Aides that I saw at the bulletin board of a local post office. I applied and was accepted. I began working at the lab as a

Biological Science Aide, GS-2, then went from GS-3 to 4 when I became sort of the chief plankton picker. After that I had other government service jobs, ending up as a Research Microbiologist GS-9. In many ways the tour at the Point Loma Lab was the most memorable position I was favored to obtain.

Number 314 was the name of the building that housed the Fish and Wildlife Service laboratory where Cynthia and I became known to each other. The lab was on the first floor, occupying a large room on the north side. It contained four lab benches in a row, four workers to each bench. Each had a drawer, a low-power stereo microscope, numerous dishes in which to place sorted material, and the ever handy forceps used for specimen removal. Cynthia was placed in the first row by the entrance. I was in the fourth row, as far from her as it was possible to be. However, I was fortunate in that I was facing her, which I appreciated.

Our lab occupied half of the room. The remainder was for storage of glass bottles containing plankton preserved in formalin. Plankton consists of algae and protozoans drifting together with fish eggs and larval fish and on occasion a water insect called *Halobates.*

A large piece of metallic electrical equipment, with chains, levers, buckets, and paddles, had been designed to sort plankton. It went unused in one corner of the space. I was told it did not work, hence the number of individuals hired to do the sorting. If it had worked, I would not be writing my love story here today.

I realized later, much later, that it was a life changing position. I met my love and held on. It is said a mulberry leaf can turn to silk if you have patience. I have had patience and it is more than silk. It is all that a man could want. A wise man dreams of happiness, a fool dreams of wealth. A heart in love never grows old. I am young in heart. I met Cynthia there. What a wonderful, beautiful event that was not in my job description, but thank you, U.S. Fish and Wildlife Service.

The lab building where Howard and Cynthia met 62 years earlier

Chapter 3. Seeking Wisdom

By mid-March, less than two months after Howard sent the package, they were writing regularly, letters at first, emails later. Not all had dates. Howard filled Cynthia in on some of the doings of their former colleagues, the Plankton Pickers of Point Loma. He also explained the puzzling coordinates that had baffled Cynthia in the return address of the very first package he sent her: "To clear up some items that you bought up in your letter — geographic coordinates must have been misread by me as they were taken in my backyard, but I sure like the spin you put on it with the yacht off Baja. I owned a Sabot, an 8-foot-long sailing dinghy, but it never got out of Mission Bay." Shortly afterward he wrote:

> Well here we are and it is about 62 years since you left San Diego. In a short time period I was surprised to find that I missed you no more, as you were with me. How can I explain this when I do not know the explanation. It is like an ESSENCE OF YOU is with me. I am not alone — you are here. You have been here — you have not left. No, I do not have a mental condition or if I do — please, no cure is wanted. You have given me so much happiness without you even knowing — perhaps this is a secret I should not share — no, I should tell you and should graciously thank you for your unknown participation. The music of principally Alexandre Scriabin and then of Rachmaninoff enhances your presence. I am so profoundly thankful for you at West Tisbury and you here.
>
> A toast to your Health, Wealth and Wisdom, and may all be assured. As for me, my health is compromised, am comfortable and wisdom is in doubt. I am physically limited due to my many medical conditions and cannot travel. I send postcards from past trips to keep in touch with friends. So at 90 and under the circumstances of poor health and my reclusive behavior — time has nearly run out. However, with my Buddhist philosophy I have every hope that on one of my go-arounds that I will meet with you on one of your trips and that meeting will start the most beautiful and eternal togetherness.
>
> Some books from my Library:
> *Reversing Heart Disease,* Ornish
> *The Art of Cooking for the Diabetic,* Hess
> *The Healing Power of Herbal Teas,* Ceres
> *Microwave Cooking for One,* Smith
> *Vitamix 5200c Owner's Manual*
> *The 120 Year Diet,* Walford
> *What the Buddha Taught,* Rahula
> *English Renaissance Poetry,* Williams
> *Notes of an Alchemist,* Eisely
>
> Love, H yy

Chapter 4. A Bit More Than That...

"It's amazing how well he got to know you just from the plankton-picking job," said Lisa one Wednesday at the writers' group meeting.

"Well," I said, looking down into the wine Cat had just poured for me, "there was a bit more than that."

Cat put the wine bottle back on the coffee table and glanced over at me.

"Cynthia!"

"More than what?" asked Amy, leaning forward in the rocker.

I shook my head. "I've never told anyone. "

"You can tell us," said Amy. "After all . . ."

"No," I said. "I've never told a soul."

Lisa said, "She doesn't have to tell us if she doesn't want to."

"She wants to," said Amy.

I had to laugh. This was, after all, more than a half-century ago. "Okay, you guys." I set my wine glass on the end table and sat back. "We went on a camping trip together."

"Cynthia!" said Cat.

"Is that all!" said Amy.

"Let her finish," said Lisa.

"Howie had a Jeep and we went on a two-week camping trip up into the high country of California," I said. "The year before, California had named a road that ran through the Gold Rush country Highway 49, in honor of the '49ers."

"My fifth grade students are studying the California Gold Rush," said Amy. "Where did you sleep?"

"In pastures and fields. One night we camped in an orange grove."

"How romantic," said Cat with a sigh.

"We had separate sleeping bags, of course," said I.

"Oh, Cynthia!" said Cat.

"Of course," said Amy, laughing. "That was 1950."

"The smell of the orange blossoms . . ." I continued.

They all sat forward. I could hear them take in breaths.

"Around three in the morning . . ."

"Yes?" said Amy.

" . . . the irrigation channels flooded and our sleeping bags got soaked," I said. "We gathered up our gear and left."

"Oh." A collective sigh.

HOWARD'S STORY

I was not really sure that Cynner was going to go with me on the trip, but I did know that she really wanted to see the wonders of Yosemite National Park. I asked her the evening before the planned trip and she said, "Yes, I want to go." To myself I gave a sigh of relief.

We left San Diego in my 1950 Willys Jeep, grey, canvas top, air conditioned by the breeze blowing thru. We left our jobs a few hours early (with permission of course) around 3 and headed with only minimum stops to Sequoia National Park 340 miles away — it took us about 7 hours and we arrived around 10 pm to find the eateries and camp store closed. I was hungry, and all I had in my pocket was a Mars chocolate bar which was shared. Cynner did not utter hungry complaints but seemed to enjoy what she had. We had the evening coolness together.

We took a short drive and found a meadow surrounded by redwood trees and scooped up sequoia leaves to make a ground mattress upon which we placed our sleeping bags close together.

One of the cars near our Jeep was not occupied but the headlights were on, so we used those lights to guide us to our camping location — but away from the lights. I was comfortable sleeping there in the now cool morning. But then I heard snorting and sounds and most of all a foul odor. Yes it was a black bear and very close — I woke Cynner and we ran to the Jeep and spent the remaining dark there. The headlights of the unoccupied car went off as the battery depleted.

We refueled with a hearty breakfast at the Watch Tower Diner and then hiked and drove around to see the signature trees like the drive-thru tree. We found a meadow and rested there with walking paths circling our spot. But no one should have seen us there.

PART 2: BY EMAIL

Chapter 5. A Great Invention

On March 21, 2012, Howard sent two photos, one "at my prime," the other "now and on decline." The latter was upside-down.

Cynthia replied the same day, via email: "Once I righted your upside-down picture, I was delighted to see you've worn well. You look every bit as well put together as I remember, with the added grace of a few years."

She attached two photos of herself. The second, she noted, "is of me this past summer trying to thin out the ever expanding number of books that accumulate in this house. I was trying to decide what could be given to the West Tisbury Library book sale. I'll send you a copy of an article I wrote called 'Maybe I Should Buy a Kindle.'"

"Thanks for the catch-up with the Plankton Pickers of Point Loma," she continued. "I remembered quite a few of them, surprisingly, since my tour at Scripps was only four months. It was an important part of my life. One of my first real jobs, after the youngest of my children was in pre-school, was sorting plankton at the Smithsonian Oceanographic Sorting Center in Washington, DC. We sorted one batch of plankton preserved in whiskey, not formalin, a century before."

Howard, upside-down, in decline

Howard, at his prime

Cynthia in Santa Barbara visiting her daughter Ann

Sorting books for the library's book sale

MARTHA'S VINEYARD

Dear Howard:

Thanks to Google, I found a photo of the cul-de-sac on Piper Street where you must live. I could see a number painted on the curb close to your address, but couldn't figure out exactly which house was yours. There was a place that looked as though it might be a house of worship, with what looked like a cross in front, the whole painted black. I decided that must be your house and, naturally, wove a fantastic tale about your life since 1950. Private yachts and a black house.

It was an honor to know that you thought about me for such a long time. What a clueless kid I was. I'm not sure I've changed much. I don't feel much older than 18. It surprises me when I find I can't haul 50-pound bags of mulch around and get out of breath climbing stairs. More exercise, I figure. Certainly not one year piling on top of another. When I look in the mirror I see my mother. Was it the same for her, seeing not the 99-year-old she was, but her mother?

That hurt over losing a child never goes away, does it? It gets diluted with time, but there is always that thought that your child had so much to offer that hadn't yet been realized. I am so sorry for your loss of your Paul. And losing your wife, as well.

The Wednesday Writers, all young women, meet here tonight, and I haven't written my daily quota yet. They are charmed by the fact that you remembered me all those years. They think this is a terribly romantic story. I must say, I think so, too.

Love, Cynthia

CALIFORNIA

Dear Cynner March 22nd, 2012

This is the front of my house. I must have designed it after a restless night. Anyway, it is sort of on a minimalist Asiatic theme. It looks better viewed in person but not that much better. A forest is in the backyard, the dominant tree is the Torrey Pine.

Thank you for your photographs. You are splendid. You will never be unbeautiful. I am a mnemelist (sp?), anyway I am one who has recurrent effects from past experiences — you are the past experience. Life is good. I have been favoritized. I am sailing.

Love, Howard yy

The entrance to Howard's house in San Diego and Cynthia's house on Martha's Vineyard

Cynthia aboard her land-based yacht

MARTHA'S VINEYARD

Dear Howard: March 23rd, 2012

Here's my house — wish it were a bit more minimalist. However, it's dear to me and worth the hassle of upkeep. It does its best to support itself by housing my B&B guests — poets, writers, artists, musicians, and other creative people.

The other picture is of me on my "yacht," which was named *Miss June* on the Egg Harbor Owners Calendar of 2011. A 1968 Egg Harbor Sport fisherman, 38 feet. No engines, no generator, no water tanks, no nothing. Leaks terrifically from the top down, which I'm fixing, the bottom can leak all it wants to let the rainwater out. It was a wreck I located in New Hampshire. Had it trucked to New Bedford, barged over to the Vineyard (no way she could float), and then trucked to my west pasture.

She's been renamed *Victorious* (formerly *Poseidon*). I figured since she is not likely to go to sea in the foreseeable future it would hardly be bad luck to rename her. In the meantime, a Newfoundlander named Chris Cull lives on her in the summer and is charged with making her leak-proof. Everyone should have a lawn ornament on her lawn.

Love, Cynner
yy

CALIFORNIA

Dear Cynner: March 24th, 2012

Wow! What a woman you are. That is not surprising to me as from our moments together I knew you were destined to continue to be grand and I surely thought you would be on island where you belonged. You have done very well.

Your house is the most beautiful home of a princess.

You mentioned New Bedford and I recalled doing a genealogy research and I was derived from a Captain Attebury whose ship called on Atlantic ports and New Bedford most likely. His ship was registered from England. His name was changed to Attebery after some time.

The left photograph was taken from the entrance gate and shows the building that houses

Howard's glass-working shop

Shop (right), entrance to house (left), Toyon Canyon (ahead)

what is left of my glass-working shop. After my coronary I stopped the activities of glass etching, casting and slumping — all that is left now is one kiln, a compressor and a sandblast cabinet.

The right photo is the breeze-way (the house entrance to the left and shop to the right). Then a view facing west and then the view facing east. I can do little gardening now but did manage to put in some sweet alyssum.

Love, Howard yy

Facing west, bench and swing overlook the canyon

Facing east, Toyon Canyon to the right

Dear Howard: March 24th, 2012

Tell me about the glass works. I know what etching is, but what is casting and slumping, and what sorts of things did you make? We have a glass works here in the Vineyard where they melt blobs of glass on the ends of pipes and blow it into fantastic shapes, everything from simple vases to complicated artwork. Do you have any pictures of you at work or pictures of your finished glass? I love seeing your pictures.

Attached is a photo of Quansoo, my favorite beach on earth, where the Atlantic has pounded, is pounding, and will pound forever (well, for a long time more), shaping the south shore of the Island.

I have a guest staying at my B&B, Eleonore Biber (the "o" is correct), from Vienna, Austria. The chairman of our West Tisbury Board of Selectmen, Richard Knabel, is of Austrian descent, so he invited Eleonore and me to dinner tonight. Wow! All Austrian, and if you are concerned about heart healthy diets, this was not it. Hungarian goulash (spicy paprika), spaetzle he'd made himself, a sort of spinach soufflé, asparagus, lots of different cheeses, salad, and finished off with strudel he'd made himself. All delish, and the company was nice, about eight of us altogether.

Murder is extraordinarily rare on Martha's Vineyard. The last unsolved murder took place in 1940. I was telling Eleonore how New York City is nice to visit for a very short time, three days or less, because of the constant sound of sirens, and how quiet and peaceful it is in West Tisbury with nary a siren. Ever. Whereupon, sirens burst forth from every direction — from Edgartown to the east, Chilmark to the west, Vineyard Haven and Oak Bluffs to the north. Turns out that we Islanders just had the first murder in 120 years, although Richard Knabel (as head of the board of selectmen he was one of the first people in town notified) says it appears to be a killing in self-defense and technically is not murder. A man broke into his estranged wife's house with a shotgun and allegedly (one has to say allegedly) shot her. She, in turn, allegedly shot him fatally with her pistol. She's in the hospital, his corpse is on its way off-Island for autopsy. At dinner tonight, everyone was saying, "Cynthia, this is your cup of tea!" but since, according to Richard, it isn't considered murder, and since it's (allegedly) solved already, I'm not interested.

Once we discussed the alleged murder at length, the conversation turned to Austrian food, derivations of words for food, Eleonore's schedule in the US, the unseasonably warm weather, the fact that you had contacted me after 62 years, and underground oil tank removal.

You realize, no U.S. politics. The mainland might as well be on a far planet. Someone did ask "Is Mitt his real name?" and someone else said, "No, his first name is something like Alphonso," which began and ended that, and was the total extent of the political discussion.

Enough. With that, goodnight, Howard.

Love, Cynner

ps I did ask the group, if someone were to mention Scriabin and Rachmaninoff as bringing one to mind, was that a compliment? And was assured it was the highest possible compliment anyone could ever be given. Thank you yy

Quansoo, a wild beach on the south shore of Martha's Vineyard

Chapter 6. The Fire Is Laid

CALIFORNIA

Dear Cynner, March 26th, 2012

My glass castings were done by using various frits (small pieces of colored glass or my favorite PB-83 frit which gives a heavy laden lead glass that gives a sparkling clear rendition with a beautiful ring when sounded) that were heated to 1050 degrees F. and then poured into molds of different subjects that I constructed. The kiln was gradually cooled down to prevent stress fractures in the glass. This is a very old process that I latched on to. I do not have any existent pieces or photographs. Slumping consists of heating a panel of glass until it is soft and then placing it over a mold of the desired shape that you want the glass to form and gravity does the trick and then one continues with the cool-down functions. The etchings that I have done were sand blasted in a cabinet. I do have a simple piece that I constructed and it is my interpretation of Kokopelli. I use it as a paperweight in my office and I am delighted in that I am going to send it to you. Kokopelli figures are seen in rock carvings and on cave walls in the Southwest region and date back 3000 years.

The photograph of Quansoo is beautiful, peaceful — thank you!

Love from Howard and may the mystical music of Kokopelli surround you and bring you all that is offered — Good Night Cynthia.

• • • • •

Cynthia looked up Kokopelli. According to legend, he was a wandering hunchbacked musician who played a magical flute. He brought good luck and prosperity to anyone who listened to him. When he played his flute, "the sun came out, the snow melted, grass began to grow, birds began to sing, and all the animals gathered around to hear his songs." His music prepared the Earth to receive his seed.

• • • • •

MARTHA'S VINEYARD

Dear Howard: March 27th, 2012

Right now I'm drinking yesterday's warmed-over coffee in a mug printed with vessels from New Bedford. I wonder if your Capt. Attebury's ship is one of them. I like to think so.

I am delighted to know about your Kokopelli and will treasure it. My father, around

1934–35, was adopted into the Hopi tribe, and given the name, I think this is right, of Quaquatka, at least that's how it sounded. He said it meant "Eagle's Nest," because he towered over the much shorter Hopis. A traveling group of Hopis had come to the elementary school where he was principal, to perform, and ran into some serious problem; I never knew what, and my father, who could fix anything, whether it was mechanical, bureaucratic, or psychological, somehow saved the group. I can vaguely remember the leader in full Indian regalia giving me a beautiful necklace made of colored rice grains, and I, being three or four, ate the delicate necklace. I can remember the nice taste of it and the way it crunched in my teeth. I can remember distinctly my father's appalled reaction when he saw what I'd done, and I can distinctly recall the reaction of the chief, who reassured my father that nothing could have been more of an honor than to have a child consume that necklace.

My father was proud of his new Indian roots and in 1962 published a young adult book called *Arrows and Snakeskin.* I had the book reprinted year before last and it's being used as a textbook for a class in Colonial American History at Westchester County (NY) Community College. I'll send you a copy.

Tell me about your dental career. The internet is quite remarkable, and I did learn that you (at least, I'm pretty sure it was you) were the public health dentist for two counties, which nixed, in my mind, the idea that your latitude and longitude were from your private yacht off the coast of Baja with you reclining in a deck chair, minions bringing you bouillon, your captain, in full-dress uniform, reporting your geographic coordinates to you on a regular basis. Oh, well!

Bunch of Grapes, our Island's bookstore, just called in an order for six copies of our tour book, *Victoria Trumbull's Martha's Vineyard.* Besides the tour book, the bookstore ordered some of my mysteries, and told me to hurry up — they've sold out. Nice.

My career as mystery writer is new, dating back to 2001, when my first book was published. After my mother died in 1997, I was disoriented. I'd lived with her for the last ten years of her life and we were close. Arlene Silva, a B&B guest, urged me to go back to school for my MFA in creative writing, and after trying to fend off her suggestion (NOT school at 68!) I finally yielded and here I am, a mystery writer with an MFA. My 11th book is *Poison Ivy.*

Gotta rush off to the bookstore.

Love, Cynner yy

CALIFORNIA

Hello Cynthia, March 27th, 2012

I mailed the Kokopelli etched rock — a simple piece — I picked up the rock on one of my trips — it has a hard surface — much harder than glass so I did not do a deep etch on the surface. Perhaps you can identify the rock.

My first job after dental school was with the State of California Health Department, Dental Division and I was sent to Santa Cruz where I spent a year visiting rural schools in the mountains with a trailer equipped with a dental office.

I packed my lunch and always ate with the students in the school yards. I remember trading sandwiches, cookies and stuff — and one time I traded for a hard-boiled turkey egg. It was a fun job talking to the students and instructing them in dental health. I also operated the dental office in the county hospital on Saturday for children of indigent parents. I was paid $400/month. I was then transferred to Sonoma County with a trailer and a dental office in the county hospital — that was for a year and $599/month. Next dental job was the school dentist for the San Diego Unified School District. Then I was awarded a National Institute of Health Post Doctoral Fellowship to UCLA and an appointment to the School of Dentistry Pediatric Department. Later I left clinical dentistry and emphasized microbiological research at VA hospitals in Los Angeles and San Diego.

Thank you for doing what you are doing — you are on a great path — maybe you can squeeze in another book to make it 21. Thank you for writing to me amidst all the other things that you are doing. Good night Cynthia — if you are awake.

Love, Howard

MARTHA'S VINEYARD

Dear Howard: March 29th, 2012

I loved knowing about your trailer dental office. Dozens of the students you worked with in those rural areas must be passing on to their own kids good things about dentists and dental care as a result. Astonishing what a difference one person can make in one year. In just a short paragraph you conveyed a lifetime of information. I suspect you could easily write a book about that one year in the mountains and another one on showing kids how important dental care is. Do you ever hear from any of them? Horace Mann, the educator, admonished students to "be ashamed to die until you've won some victory for humanity." You won't need to be ashamed when the time comes.

The book I'm working on now, number 12, is called *Bloodroot* and deals with murder in a dental office. Funny timing, isn't it. I'm about two-thirds of the way through. All my books have plant names. If I were to send you excerpts that deal with the dental office, might you be willing to critique them ? You can say no, and I won't be offended.

This old house got oil hot water heat, first floor only, somewhere between 1975, when my father died, and 1978. My two big sisters, who live on the same property, decided my mother needed something better than the fireplaces to stay warm. No snow to speak of this winter, but attached is what the place looked like after the last big snow. The first picture is from the west step and you can see the prow of my boat in the background.

The second is the fish pond to the east of the house right now.

Love, Cynner yy

Winter view from west step, with prow of boat in the background

The fish pond near Cynthia's house in late March surrounded by chionodoxa and daffodils

CALIFORNIA

Dearest Cynner:

I would be pleased to receive excerpts of your writings about the scenes in the dental office and give you my opinion about them. I am of the old school and a revolution has since taken place in dental care since I graduated from dental school and I did post-graduate training. I used to work standing up or sitting on a swivel base stool — patients sitting slightly reclining. Now the patients are usually supine with the dentist comfortably seated. X-rays are now done digitally instead of with film. Dentists now use latex gloves or plastics and wear face masks and eye protection or even full-face shields, an apparel suitable for robbing banks. Yes, I did hear from one of my school patients who went into dentistry and is now limiting his practice to surgery. I received letters of thanks from families, especially of Japanese descent, who were most appreciative of my services.

My eyes are doing well. Next month I am due for an exam and a photo of my retinas. Going for a wraparound pair of sun glasses. Last time the optometrist wrote me a prescription for glasses that were optimal for work with the computer screen. They have worked quite well.

The photographs that you send are very professional. The glory-of-the-snow lilies around your pond are spectacular. Glad to hear that your hot water and heating things are soon to be concluded and that you will be assured of these comforts.

Yesterday I was sitting on my bench in the backyard watching a female Anna's hummingbird going around my cedar tree picking off little spiders supplementing her diet with protein and she came down to the bench 18 inches away and gave me a good stair [sic] and I said "nothing here to eat" and she flew away but then I gave two audible kisses from my lips and she returned maybe 12 inches from my face and then departed.

Cynthia, you write so beautifully, so alive, so optimistically. You make me feel so good. You are so loved.

Howard YY

Chapter 7. Please Note

MARTHA'S VINEYARD

Dear Howard: March 31, 2012

I look forward to your address showing up on my screen. It probably would be more intimate to hand-write letters, but there's something wonderful about the immediacy of e-mail. Unlike phone calls, which are so ephemeral, I can save and re-read our messages.

I hope you understand what you've committed yourself to by agreeing to advise me on my book's dentistry segments. There are quite a few of them. Thanks so much. Tomorrow, I'll send you the first several chapters. You don't need to read all of them, unless you want to. I'll mark the parts that I need help with, but please note anything at all that's confusing or doesn't ring true — I take that back. The entire book is untrue. Philosophically, not untrue, but fictionally. I'm trying for True in my writing.

Do you have access to a DVD player? If you do, I'll send you a couple of DVDs. One is of the text of some of my mother's poetry scrolling down while she reads. My brother-in-law had taped her reading on his home machine, and an electronic whiz here on the Island cleaned up the odd scratchy sounds and clicks, and a friend who knew my mother put the DVD together. Also, I had a TV show on our local community-access cable, actually two shows — one was called *On Island Writing,* and I interviewed people who wrote, not necessarily published writers, just interesting people. One interview was of my doctor, Gerry Yukevich, whose business card has, under his name, *Theater, Writing, Poetry, Medicine.* Perfect combination. He's writing a screenplay and a musical, and whenever I go to the walk-in clinic we talk about writing and usually forget any ailments I might have. The other show was a one-year snapshot of West Tisbury called *Our Town — 2007.* The first show is one of my favorites, and is of winding the town clock. The cameraman and I climbed up a rickety ladder from the choir loft and through a small trap door into the church steeple and filmed the Winder of the Town Clock at work. He's a town employee and gets a handsome $250 a year stipend. We got there just short of 12 noon, so we saw and heard and recorded the clock getting ready to strike, and then it chimed out. You can hear it all over town.

Mind you, I don't have and never have had a television set. I've never viewed most of the shows. The Cleaveland House B&B is TV-free.

I am typing this with a serious handicap. Daphne, the cat, is on my lap trying to clean me as though I'm in need of a good licking. My left wrist now, and I have to type with the wrist within her reach. Ouch! It's like being sandpapered.

Goodnight, Howard,

Love, Cynner

yy

MARTHA'S VINEYARD

Dear Howard: April 1st, 2012

Happy April 1st . It's already tomorrow on the East Coast. Your birthday must be soon and, by my reckoning, you'll be a nonagenarian. That used to seem ancient to me. It doesn't seem so anymore. A friend up Island just celebrated her 104th birthday and is still driving.

Here it is, Chapters 1 through 4 of *Bloodroot.* I didn't mark the dental sections because, well, just because I hoped you'd want to read it all. Any and all comments welcome. I want the writing to be clear and accurate (where accuracy is required) without any unnecessary verbiage. You're welcome to hack away. I don't take criticism personally, and I do appreciate it. Mark it up any way that is convenient for you.

Love, Cynner yy

CALIFORNIA

Dear Cynner, April 2nd, 2012

My usual routine is to arise around 7 am, step on the scale, dress warm, turn on the hall gas furnace then to the front-room furnace and turn that on then continuing my turn ons — this time the little Grundig radio near the kitchen sink for KPBS and last, the light above the kitchen table. Next I get the San Diego newspaper, return to the house, and prepare breakfast, return to the table to simultaneously eat and review the emails.

It was nice to get your two emails and I sent Chapters 1-4 to my printer in the office by wireless to print double sided to get the feel of a book. I took it in all at once and made a few notes on the margins.

I decided not to e-mail you right away but to sleep on it and let it all meld. My sincere, honest and unbiased conclusion: God you are good! To repeat: God you are good! You do not have to change anything. You brought me into the story by lightly describing the characters and immediately a mystery and then another mystery and then the intrigue of personal relationships that you set up with just a few words. I hope that the forensic team from off-Island checked the spit-bowl trap for clues. White booties sound better than shoe covers and shower caps sound better than bouffants. But shoe covers and bouffants are actually better. Operatory could be another substitution for cubicle. Sanitized areas might be more appropriate than sterilized areas. Bleach solutions are used commonly for sanitizing. Dr. Minnowfish is an unforgettable name. You are fun!

I have been fortunate that mysteries have been rare in my dental office. One time a 13-year-old girl fainted in my chair and I placed her head between her legs and rubbed her neck and she revived. I finished the procedure and told her father about it. His explanation was that his daughter was not eating much as she wanted to lose weight.

You do so well, Cynthia. You live life. You are so lausnes. Who am I with my mind substituting stair for stare. These homophones do creep in. Buy, By, Bye.

Love Howard yy

MARTHA'S VINEYARD

Dear Howard: April 2nd, 2012

I was going to ask, "What is your usual morning like?" You anticipated me!

Thank you. I like the suggested changes. They make it more authentic. Thank you, too, for liking the writing.

Five years ago when Massachusetts passed its same-sex marriage law, two B&B guests asked if I might consider having the ceremony near the fish pond (where the chionodoxa grows). Consider! I was more than delighted. The West Tisbury Congregational Church had voted that the minister was authorized to perform all marriages without regard to whatever. So the Cleaveland House was the setting for the first same-sex marriage on Martha's Vineyard. The two men were dressed up in suits with coats and ties, a rare sight here on the Island. The witnesses were a friend of the couple's, me, and a catbird. The minister came in full regalia. It seemed as though they ought to have a reception, which hadn't occurred to them, so I called up everyone I knew, baked a wedding cake, and about 50 people came to celebrate, including the catbird. Someone brought crackers and cream cheese with blackberries on it, and the catbird perched on the table, socialized, and dined on the berries.

The Wednesday Writers, all romantic young women, are utterly thrilled about our romance. Lisa Belcastro, just finished her 40th (that is fortieth!) marathon. The reason I mention this is I had told them about your Kokopelli etching and my father's Hopi adoption. Such a remarkable conjunction. Lisa won a medal, and what should it have on it but Kokopelli. It is so special to renew a relationship that had a gap of 62 years, to learn what you did in the meantime, and to tell you what I've done. I don't think I'm all that different from what I was at 18. Still fairly clueless about the world around me despite the passage of time and experiences of one sort and another that should have taught me something. Tell me more about what's happened to you. Marriage and children. I'd love to know more about your wife and your two boys and suffer with you about the loss of a child much, much too soon.

Love, Cynner yy

MARTHA'S VINEYARD

Dear Howard: April 2nd, 2012

Here's the next installment of *Bloodroot*. The pagination is off slightly from the first installment because I added a bit of stuff. The forensic team checks the spit-bowl trap, and while someone suggests they're donning booties and shower caps, the boss says it's really a bouffant scrub cap. They put on and take off their shoe covers, but I did leave in one mention of booties. And operatory sounds much better. I didn't use it all the time, just alternated that with cubicle. And sanitized — definitely changed from sterilized.

Many thanks.

If you happen to keep reading and notice anything confusing or repetitive or inaccurate, even if it's not dental, let me know. I've been over it so often it all sounds blah.

Love, Cynner yyy

MARTHA'S VINEYARD

April 2nd, 2012
What is "lausnes" ?

YY

CALIFORNIA

Dear Cynner, April 2nd, 2012

That word LAUSNES, I mean nothing but good by it. Please look at it backwords [sic].
I have this tune going around in my head — I'm ok — just want to keep happiness alive.

Unforgettable, that's what you are
Unforgettable, though near or far
Like a song of love that clings to me
How the thought of you does things to me

Never before has someone been more
Unforgettable, in every way
And forevermore, that's how you'll stay
(And forevermore, that's how you'll stay)

Love, Howard yy

MARTHA'S VINEYARD

Dear Howard: April 3rd, 2013

I must be slipping! I tried to decode it. I looked it up on Google, and got lausneselam, which turned out to be for gay men, and it never entered my feeble mind to read it backwards. Points for you!

(And thank you. Nice to be lausnes.)

Cynner yyy

Chapter 8. In the Right Direction

CALIFORNIA

Subject: NYCTEEWS April 3rd, 2012

Dear One,

Received *Arrows and Snakeskin.* Thank you! I very much like it. Will start Ch. 5–8 after I prepare pumpkin pudding and asparagus soup. Keep the questions coming — I will answer in time.

Love, Howard yy

MARTHA'S VINEYARD

Dear Howard: April 4th, 2012

I read it [NYCTEEWS] in the right direction this time. Ecin! You are raising my self-image to a very high pitch. The three DVDs went in the mail today. I'm glad you like *Arrows and Snakeskin.* The book has worn well. Still fresh, fair, and informative.

I planted peas about two weeks before the traditional planting time, which is St. Patrick's Day, and have been checking every day fearing I may have made a mistake by planting too early. But today they're up. It's like magic, this gardening. Peas are up, so are my spinach, lettuce, radishes, and beets. Tiny things. Less than a quarter inch tall, hard to see. Each is coming true to its ancestry with distinctive miniature leaves. The kale wintered over and is flourishing. In fact, I steamed kale with some chunks of kielbasa for supper. Steaming leaches the grease out of the kielbasa but leaves whatever is underneath with a good flavor. My rhubarb is just barely up, and I pulled three stalks, all there was, and stewed that with some orange chunks I'd had for decoration in the hot cider for the Sunday writers. I forgot to eat that because I got so wrapped up in the book I was reading, a mystery by Michael Connelly, so I'll have it for breakfast. Usually I take my supper on a tray into the parlor where I've laid a fire and read with the fire crackling. Especially wonderful if the wind is rattling the window panes and it's snowing. Cozy.

All that was an introduction to asparagus. My father planted a 35-foot-long narrow bed that's at least 35 years old. Every late April I start harvesting asparagus until it finally bolts around early June. By then, I've had almost enough of it. It doesn't freeze well, but I bet asparagus soup could be frozen. It grows so rapidly I can harvest it every day for that entire month-plus. A neighbor across New Lane has two horses, and I wheel my garden cart across the lane and bring back loads of manure. Asparagus just barely steamed, plain or with lemon butter. Or just lemon juice. Cold with salad dressing.

Good night, Howard

Cynner yyy

MARTHA'S VINEYARD

Dear Howard: April 4th, 2012

Kokopelli arrived safely in today's mail and is now holding down a list of chapters I'm going over before posting them off to you. What a wonderful rock. And what a perfect rock for the little hunch-back flute player and what a perfect time of year for the god of fertility to be spreading his seed. I know you'll miss him, but he's safe here, in good hands, and with lots and lots of paper to hold down. My best guess about rock type would be that it's an ultramafic rock, but I don't know which one it would be. Probably basalt. The ultramafics are dense, dark colored, low in silica, high in iron and magnesium. Where did you ever find such a beauty? Jupiter's moon, Io, has basalt.

And how did you manage to etch such a perfect image. It must have taken an extraordinarily steady hand plus a huge amount of patience.

Liza, the postal clerk, who changes her hair color weekly, including shades of green, blue, purple, and orange (she's also tattooed), was totally baffled by the weight of the package, and kept shifting it from hand to hand as she brought it to me. "I know exactly what it is," I said. "Like, you know, a rock?" she said. "Exactly," said I, and left her shaking her head of hair, black this week with scarlet streaks.

Thank you.

Love, yyy

Cynner

CALIFORNIA

Hello Cynthia, April 4th, 2012

Your communications to me — I am trying how to describe them — in one word they can be called "jewels" — you always add warming information, useful facts, interesting mini stories and they always bring a smile of happiness to my face and the good feelings. Thank you.

My process for sand etching was to combine three layers of sticky shelf-lining paper and adhere it to the rock, pencil in what I wanted to remove so that would allow the sand to penetrate that area and to protect the other area not removed. I would cut out this area with scalpel blades — then blasting was the easy part. So I did not do "free" blasting except on special occasions.

From what I can remember I picked up this rock from the bank of a rapidly moving stream near Aspen, Colorado. I was attending a conference in Aspen and my camper was parked by this mountain stream. I vividly remember the dippers, also called water ouzels, diving into the water and swimming about seeking aquatic insects for a meal.

NYC81OSRU You mentioned 18 a few times — it seems to me you have carried along those qualities which you had then and they are good and they are with you with the addition of accumulated wisdom, compassion and all those skills. You are a wonderful package.

Love, Howard yyy

CALIFORNIA

Dear Cynner, April 6th, 2012

I like your story. It is a good mix and my curiosity is up to know what is going to happen next.

My house is empty now. Mark and wife, Jennifer, were here for three days with Sophia and Luke, my two grandchildren. They took advantage of spring break and got away from Nyack, NY. All went well except Luke came down with strep throat and they placed him in a hotel to isolate him from the rest of us and give time for the antibiotic to work.

Love, Howard yyy

MARTHA'S VINEYARD

Dear Howard: April 7th, 2012

Again, thank you for reading the manuscript. In today's publishing world authors are essentially setting their own type, so it behooves us to send clean copy. I'm surprised there weren't more typos.

A favorite typo of mine that reached the published book stage was, well, I forget exactly what it was, but I got an e-mail from a Bruce Steinbicker who wrote, "on page 179 [or whatever] you have a typo. And furthermore, you didn't have the Greek chorus sitting on the porch of Alley's Store and I would like to see them back." So I e-mailed him, thanked him, and sent him a new section in the book I was working on with the three characters again sitting on the porch of Alley's Store, musing on the goings-on about town. A Porsche drives up, a handsome young man gets out, locks the door (which we Islanders never do) and comes up the steps of the store, nodding to the three regulars. He goes into the store. Joe, the plumber, says to Sarah Germaine, who works at Wampanoag tribal headquarters, "Hey, you know who that is?" Sarah says, "No, who?" Joe says, "That was Bruce Steinbicker, the famous TV star." I sent that off to the real Bruce Steinbicker along with my thanks for picking up the typo. He wrote back, "I'll have to find some more typos."

Now the fictional Bruce Steinbicker was supposed to make a cameo appearance, never to be seen again. But you've probably heard writers say how their characters take over and they, the authors, have little control over their characters' actions? Well, fictional Bruce Steinbicker turned out to be having an extramarital affair. He traded his yacht, temporarily, to a student friend in exchange for a cozy nest for his dalliance with a married woman. The friend he'd loaned his yacht to has kidnapped his professor and has imprisoned her on Steinbicker's yacht. The professor had stolen her student's research work and has submitted it to a prestigious journal under her own name. The student plans to keep her on the yacht until the publication deadline for the stolen research paper has passed.

I realize all this is implausible, but so are all my books.

After the plot thickened, I had a sick feeling that the real Bruce Steinbicker might not like having his name attached to a fictional character running around behind his wife's back. So I e-mailed the real Steinbicker asking if this might give him problems in his personal life. He wrote back, "I showed your message to my wife of 49 years and she just laughed."

I'll write more later, but this is such a glorious day I should be outside. Must be outside. The peas are about an inch tall now. I dug up two more rows this morning and planted broccoli in one, radishes and parsnips in the other. Parsnips are slow to germinate and radishes come up in a few days, so the radishes will act as markers.

Your going over my work helps me more than you can know. Not only for accuracy and picking up on typos but for keeping me writing. I was stuck, and now that I realize you're actually reading what I've written, and reading it critically, I've got a burst of creative energy.

Kokopelli is now watching over me from a 3-inch stack of paper. Sowing seeds is good, I think he's saying.

Love, Cynner yyy

MARTHA'S VINEYARD

Dear Howard: April 7th, 2012

Tomorrow my sister Ann is having the family over for Easter dinner, and there'll probably be about 15 of us. A noisy, rambunctious mob. If the weather is like today's, I'll celebrate Easter by digging and planting.

Almost 9 pm and I haven't fixed supper yet. I'll dine in front of the fire with a book.

Love, Cynner yyy

CALIFORNIA

Hello Cynner, April 8th, 2012

Sorry, but I do not have much criticism of the book at the present point. I think it flows well from scene to scene, no boredom, some humor, great rendition of words from numbed oral areas, a villain appears now with the possibility of two sub-villains from recent chapters. The story deepens. Arsenic, is there a garlic smell? I seem a kindergartner correcting a PhD's work but I am trying and it is good for me and it makes me happy and that is what life should be about.

I was out back watering this afternoon and the peach tree is in full bloom, the pear is just starting and the apple — no signs. All in good time as they dictate. The birds are acting silly. The meadowlarks are establishing territories and singing up the decibels for a mate. While watering, a white-crowned sparrow came for a bath.

More tomorrow so I can tell you about my grandmother and other things.

Goodnight, Cynner

Love, Howard YY=

MARTHA'S VINEYARD

Dear Howard: April 9th, 2012

You are right about the large cast of characters. It might be a good idea for me to combine some of the characters to shorten the list. There seem to be more and more characters appearing all the time. This is one of those things about which writers have little control. You counted 15 characters before this latest episode. In subsequent chapters there are 18 or more, probably a bit much for the reader who is simply hoping for a non-challenging book to read. Or I could handle the multitude of characters by redefining them as they reappear. It's a nuisance for a reader to have to look up some character who appeared so many pages earlier, the reader's forgotten who it is. I would like my writing to be transparent, so a reader is getting the story directly from my mind without noticing the printed words. The writers I admire most can do that, where I get so involved in the story I forget I'm reading.

The writing doesn't get easier. I'm learning how to get certain effects that I didn't know when I first started. That means my standards are getting tougher and the writing is more difficult. I like to tuck phrases from my mother's poetry into the books, and toy with anagrams, and sneak in bits from mythology. I'm not really aiming at great literature, but am hoping for something more than dismissal as simply a work of genre fiction.

Re-reading your list of books from your library, I like *The 120 Year Diet.* I think we need a good healthy 30 years of catching up.

Love, Cynner yyy

Chapter 9: Love of Life

CALIFORNIA

Howard's 90th birthday

Hello Cynner: April 9th, 2012

Good day! It is a warm, very beautiful spring time in San Diego. Had a senior moment yesterday when I typed meadowlarks, it should have been mockingbirds.

My grandmother, Kathleen Kearny, born in County Cork, Ireland, is remembered and loved for her love of life and the fellowship, kindness, friendliness and Irish wit that was in her nature. As I understand it she was a shop keeper in Dublin but due to the poor economics of the country (potato famine or otherwise) arrived in New York and worked in a candy factory for funds to allow her to get to her destination "California." To get to California she took a ship from New York to the Caribbean Sea and a port on the Isthmus and then walked on a trail some 40-50 miles to the Pacific side to pick up a ship to San Francisco. That must have been some adventure. She worked on a cattle ranch as a cook and it was there that she met Henry and they married and moved to Napa. She had seven children. Two died in childbirth. Of the five surviving one was my mother, Berniece. Grandma used to care for me as my mother worked as a clerk in a dry goods store. It was a happy time for me being with my grandmother, she knew all, they talked and talked and laughed, and could she cook — she taught me how to make ketchup gravy — the one thing I did not like was the parsnip soup — and you were the one who mentioned parsnips from your garden that got me started on this discourse. Nice how one word can lead to a bunch of other words.

May all be fed, loved, and aimed in the right direction.

Love, Howard YYY

MARTHA'S VINEYARD

Dear Howard: April 10th, 2012

What a remarkable woman your grandmother was. What a privilege for you to have known her. I was trying to figure out when she must have been born, and came up with around 1855, which is about when my grandmother was born. She must have been a teenager when she came to New York. Imagine a teenager now, male or female, with the fortitude to leave her family and country and with incredible determination, intelligence, and ambition, figure out a way to get to California. Her life is an inspiration. I'm glad I mentioned parsnips.

Her story got me to look up the Irish Potato Famine. There's a fascinating account on Wikipedia that told about the deplorable conditions in Ireland, and the horrible exploitation by the British. My great-grandmother was Irish, too, by way of Australia, a convict's daughter.

I'll write more later. I don't want to dilute the thoughts of a young girl somehow getting passage to New York, somehow finding a job that paid almost nothing, bearing the prejudice that came with being Irish, saving enough out of a bare living wage to pay for passage to the Isthmus, hiking 50 miles, when the area must have been rife with snakes, insects, yellow fever, heat, and rude and rough people. Don't you wonder where she slept along the way. The trek must have taken three or four days. And she still had ahead of her passage to San Francisco. Do you know where the cattle ranch was? What a wonderful story. And to think that was just the early part of her life.

All I can say is Wow. Aren't you glad you have some of her genes.

Love, Cynner yyy

MARTHA'S VINEYARD

Dear Howard: April 10th, 2012

The cast of characters has topped 20 and is heading toward 30, and I'm not sure that's all of them. My first thought was to combine, in several places, a couple of characters into one, but that didn't seem to work. So current thinking is to make sure each time a character appears in a scene, s/he is identified in some not too obvious way so the reader remembers how the character fits into the story.

You have hit on the key to good writing — "just get the facts together and use the least amount of accurate words to get the message across." That applies, whether it's science writing or fiction. I tell the writers' groups they need only three elements to have a good piece of writing: (1) know the audience they're writing for; (2) know the subject they're writing about; and (3) know how to put words together. The fourth, and the most important, now is (4) use the least amount of accurate words to get the message across.

Love, Cynner yyy

Chapter 10. *Cactus on Mars*

Cynthia found and purchased a DVD titled *Cactus on Mars*, a selection of musical pieces that Howard's son, Mark Attebery, had composed.

• • • • •

MARTHA'S VINEYARD

Dear Howard: April 14th, 2012

Your Mark's music is terrific. Incredible. I was listening to *Cactus on Mars* this afternoon, exactly the right name for the work. Ethereal, a hint of Western Desert, a feeling of antiquity, a sound of Plains Indians. All that was going through my mind. I love the music. I was sorting seeds at the cookroom table while I listened.

Next time you talk to Mark, tell him how much I like his music.

Love,Cynner

yyy

MARTHA'S VINEYARD

Dear Howard: April 14th, 2012

I looked up the smell of arsenic and found this, thanks to Google: You're right about the garlic smell, so I'll be sure the villain is using arsenic trioxide.

"Arsenic trioxide, remains odorless when exposed to air, and thus it is frequently a poison of choice due to its toxicity (thus unfortunately you won't be able to smell it), However, other forms of Arsenic, particularly organo-arsenicals, have a distinct garlic smell."

Love, yyy
Cynner

CALIFORNIA

Dear Cynthia, April 15th, 2012

Yes, arsenious oxide (arsenic trioxide) is without odor and taste and is fatal in small quantities. It is not obtainable without ID and verification for its pure form. I wonder how the villain obtained his/her amount and what source? Anti-fouling substance? Pesticide? Jugs of water from Austria for concentrating? Please, I cannot wait to finish reading the book to find out!

More tomorrow.
Love, Howard yyy

MARTHA'S VINEYARD

Dear Howard: April 15th, 2012

The DVDs I sent you got returned to me saying wrong zip code. Someone in the San Diego PO must have read my 9 as a 7. I took it to Liza, our multi-colored-hair West Tisbury PO clerk — green and purple this time — and she shook her head at the stupidity of it all. She blacked out the "return to sender, no such zip," blacked out my correct zip, and re-wrote what I'd had in the first place. So this time it may actually get to you.

Arsenic: got any thoughts about how the villain might obtain it? I suppose I can fake my way out of that, however, I want to be sparing of my fakery. Phil Craig, a fellow mystery writer and Vineyarder, said of writing mysteries, "You've got to be accurate. Tell the truth, the truth, the truth, the truth — then you can lie."

Did you tell Mark how we re-connected, despite your latitude and longitude putting you in your private yacht off the coast of Baja?

Love, Cynner
yyy

CALIFORNIA

Dear Cynthia: April 16th, 2012

Mark has known back so many years about you and my utterings about Martha's Vineyard. Since you have the *Cactus on Mars* CD I am sending you the *Burnt Earth Ensemble* CD which is music performed on clay instruments. Mark plays flute and triple-chambered ocarina on this CD.

I have no doubt that you will find a remarkable way that arsenic comes into service in *Bloodroot.* It is still used in some herbicides, insecticides and rodenticides. It is being phased out, but will continue to be used in the future in cotton fields and sod farms, so Google and its kins relate.

For relaxation, enjoyment and learning experiences I am getting to be a familiar user of The Great Courses, www.thegreatcourses.com. I started with "My Favorite Universe," by Degrasse Tyson, then to "Museum Masterpieces: The Louvre" by Brettell, which is excellent. I am now going through for the second time "The World's Greatest Paintings" by Kloss, also excellent. They offer a course on "Masterpieces of Short Fiction" by Krasney, which I am not interested in obtaining, but I am using the reading list to my advantage and started with Kafka's parable — *A Hunger Artist,* almost devoid of dialog but a haunting tale. I am now with and my Kindle Fire points out that I am 6% through Chekhov's *The Lady and the Dog,* which is very enticing and an easy read. I do a lot of Pandora. Do you do Pandora music?

Love, Howard YYY

MARTHA'S VINEYARD

Dear Howard: April 17th, 2012

I don't know what Pandora is. Most electronic wizardry is waaay beyond me including cell phone (none). iPad and iPod (none), Kindle and Nook (none) and television (none). My computer is a fancy typewriter, an amazing research tool, and a great way to communicate. Aside from that, I'm pretty much a Luddite.

I listened to Mark's *Cactus on Mars* again tonight, and it's wonderful. I noticed the publisher is "Piper Street Music." You? Good job. It seems almost insulting for me to be listening to his music on my tiny DVD player, where three-quarters of the effects he's worked so hard to get are lost. I can imagine his music in live performance with dancers. Even with the book-size player, the color and motion and the musicians and the audience are there. The "Emperor and the Nightingale" is poignant. The bird song is sweet and touching. The gong announcing the emperor's appearance is magisterial. After the last note, I shut down the little player. Turned it off completely. But the four note theme of "Cactus on Mars" was echoing off the walls. Really. The effect lasted for a good ten minutes. All day long the sea has been pounding. You can feel and hear it from here. Tonight it provided a mysterious obbligato to those four notes.

Back to mundane stuff. Would this work: (If) An old apothecary and ice cream parlor dating from the mid-1800s and abandoned around the Second World War is being converted into a dwelling by the descendants of the original owners, and they've been selling off the contents of the store. Might the contents have included arsenic powders used for all those things you mentioned, cosmetics and breathing enhancers? If so, might the villain — as yet unknown, even to me — at some time have acquired bottles or packets or tins of arsenic trioxide from one of the several closing-out sales?

Today I got zero writing done. The day was just too beautiful to be inside. In the upper 60s with a fluorescent blue sky and birds singing at full voice. You would know what they are. I recognize cardinals, blue jays, chickadees, robins, doves, and flickers. And redwing blackbirds. Crows. That's about it. Where the grass was all dug up from the propane tank exercise, I scattered grass seed and then, because I could see the birds hovering in anticipation, shoveled compost on top of the seed and then watered it for a good two hours. Filled the bird feeder so they might not be tempted to eat the grass-to-be. Then I dug in the vegetable garden until it was too dark to see, and I'd forgotten both lunch and supper. With my late-late supper I listened to Mark's music, the fire humming, the sea pounding.

Good night, Howard.

Love, Cynner

yyy

Chapter 11. Spring! Joy!

MARTHA'S VINEYARD

Dear Howard: April 17th, 2012

The seeds arrived today, the most beautiful day yet, and what a delight to go through them and plan where they'll go and what time is right. Joy! The only packet in the entire collection that duplicates what I already have is kale, and since kale lasts through our winters into early spring, one can't have too much. All the rest are new and interesting, like the Asian he-shi-ko bunching onion and the long slender beans. The cover crop will be perfect for this fall when the garden has given up, and I'll be able to spade it into the soil next spring. The butterfly weed packet says it's deer resistant, a big plus around here. The cut flower garden and the songbird garden can be planted right now. Our last frost is usually around May 15th, but I think it will be earlier this year. The packets say two weeks before the last frost, so I'll take a chance. The corn will have to wait until after all danger of frost is past. I've never grown corn before. This will be fun.

That leaves the first two packets, lovage and love-lies-bleeding. You are a dear. The challenge you set for me in trying to locate you, given only those mysterious geographic coordinates, was worth every second of head scratching and Internet searching.

Enough — I'm off to dig.

Love, Cynner

yyy

MARTHA'S VINEYARD

Dear Howard: April 17th, 2012

While I was digging places for my new seeds, I got to thinking. Perhaps you had sent me a coded message having to do with the seeds. So I took the first letters of all the seed packets and tried to work out your presumed message. A challenge, because there was a dearth of vowels. Only an O for onion. But I've figured out what the message was, allowing the one vowel to be used repeatedly and using a bit of creativity. But I worked in all the plant seed initials. The message goes like this: "Folks: Clock blocks Glock. Loss. Skoll." The minute I found the Glock, I was pretty sure I'd gotten it right.

F = flower, butterfly
O = onion
L = lovage/Love Lies Bleeding
K = kale
S = songbird delight
C = corn/cover crop
B = beans
G = grandmother's cut flower garden

Much love, Cynner yyy

CALIFORNIA

Dear Cynthia, April 18th, 2012

The once misdirected package arrived yesterday and I then viewed two DVD's leaving *Circle of Years,* until I give you some words, as I feel I am getting behind in communicating. I was well pleased with the presentations, sure there were some technical stuff that could have been improved but your personal presence, style and performance was "right on." Nice meeting Daphne and Lynn Christoffers. I perked up a little when you said Stephen [Wesley, who drew the maps for *Victoria Trumbull's Martha's Vineyard]* lived in the United States, but I understand that must be island talk distinguishing the Island from the mainland. You show nice control in public speaking and you improvise, show restraint, are courteous — have the whole package. What am I doing? I just want to enjoy your offerings and not look for holes or bumps. So there! What I like for myself I will tell you. I like the way you do your hair, your posture and your white coat is fabulous. Thank you for your presence.

That was an admirable way you solution-ed the arsenic presence. Reminded me of the time I was with the VA and we ordered all our supplies from the store room office and then they changed the procedure to order directly from suppliers — they closed the store room and put out a notice to empty the store room of supplies — I did not take any poisons but did remove all the Platinum salts as I was doing Platinum photo printing.

Yesterday I did a shopping at the Fresh and Easy Market at Point Loma. I stopped and photographed Bldg 341. Do you remember you were doing some salinity titrations on the second floor and that your pipetting was not going well because your fingers were too dry and when moistened all went well.

For now and love,
Howard yyy

MARTHA'S VINEYARD

Dear Howard: April 19th, 2012

Burnt Earth arrived, and the Wednesday Writers spent the first half hour of our precious two-hour evening listening to it. Cat, especially, the one who's been through chemo and radiation and feels as though she's been to hell and back, loved the music.

She's an architectural designer and uses feng shui. She's walked on fire and had a Scottish sword crafted for her. She kept saying, about the music, How beautiful. How spiritual. How passionate.

Love, Cynner YYPY

CALIFORNIA

Dear Cynner, April 21st, 2012

I like the feel of the *Vineyard Gazette*, and wish that the *San Diego Union* would take on most of its characteristics. Nice to see the mostly senior audience doing what is right. The large paper size reminds me of the time when I was a carrier for the *Vallejo Evening News* and the pressmen used to manually feed this sheet size paper into the press. The men used to make themselves a hat out of newsprint and rarely a carrier was given one of these hats. I was never the lucky one. I was issued my first Social Security Card and number on 5/28/37 and I still have the original. However, my first job was selling *LIBERTY MAGAZINE*, 5 cents each. I was paid in script for prizes but I could never accumulate enough to get a harmonica. I had an interesting newspaper route which included all the whore houses on Georgia Street. I remember three names: Rex Rooms,

Howard Rooms, and Yosemite Rooms. Without exception a one-door entrance, long hall leading upstairs and a bar underneath. I soon discovered upon my once-a-month bill collection calls that the stairs were rigged so that customers' order of steps on the stairs showed if they were coming or going by bell signals in the office where I did my collections. I was treated well by the attendant and a few times offered a snack (food that is).

LOVE, Howard yyy

CALIFORNIA

Dear Cynner, April 21st, 2012

You have introduced me to some unusual women on your island, the last being Cat, and I hope for her continued success in her battles. I should have hired an architectural designer specializing in Feng Shui when I built my vacation home in Idyllwild but I did not know about it then as I do now. I live in a house in San Diego that is completely adverse to good feng shui. The entire ceilings are beamed which hinders the smooth energy flow which I have somewhat counteracted by placing bamboo flutes in each room, mouthpieces upright. I have a long hall and I placed a mirror at the end of the hall above the door as is recommended. The bedroom should be devoid of electronic stuff, but if it is so I would not be wording you with this computer.

Love, Howie

MARTHA'S VINEYARD

Dear Howard: April 21st, 2012

I love reading about your early days and imagining what you were like as a little kid. I loved, too, getting the picture of the building at Point Loma. Somehow, I'd imagined that it had vanished in the mist, like Brigadoon, not to be seen for another hundred years. It was an odd feeling to see it almost as I'd remembered it but with vehicles that were unthought-of then. I'm continually astonished at the things you remember from that very short blip of time, from April to August 1950, only four months. I hadn't recalled the titration episode. That trip to the West Coast was the first time I'd been west of Ohio, and everything was new and exciting. The first glimpse from the train window of real palm trees — wow!

Much excitement last night and this morning. My cat, Daphne, a tortoise-shell tabby, named for the wood nymph who was turned into a laurel tree, disappeared several weeks ago. I'd taken her to the vet and when I opened the car door at home she scooted off into the woods. When she didn't come home that night, I was concerned. Three days later, I was worried. Lynn Christoffers and I called the animal control officer — everyone we knew. Lynn scouted most of the houses and sheds in West Tisbury, with no luck. I'd decided, finally, that she'd been attacked by a raccoon or an owl or a hawk or had found a home better

Daphne bringing home the evening meal, ***photo by Lynn Christoffers***

to her liking. In the meantime, Lynn, who is a cat magnet, was driving down a back road to the high school and saw a Siamese cat sitting at the edge of the pine forest (the aforementioned cat just jumped up onto my computer keyboard).

Immediately after I wrote that, she did something that made my priceless prose vanish. I've kicked her off my desk and off my lap now.

Lynn stopped to photograph the cat, and it leapt into her car through her open window and stretched out on the dashboard. After some adventures trying to find its owner, Lynn learned that the cat had belonged to a family that had six cats and had decamped in the middle of the night, without paying owed rent, leaving two of the cats behind. So the Siamese, now named Diana, the goddess associated with woodland and wild animals, is now Lynn's, but when she's out of town, Diana boards here at the Cleaveland House.

Last night, Lynn called to say that Daphne had appeared. She was bedraggled, gaunt, filthy, smelly, and covered with ticks, and her leg had a bandage on it that was tight and smelled horrible. Lynn brought her over here, and we ran warm water in the bathtub, and together cleaned her as best we could. She didn't protest until we came to the leg, when we discovered the bandage. Lynn cut it off, we dried her, put antiseptic cream on her leg, and called the animal control officer, who soothed us, said we'd done the right thing, and made an appointment for Daphne at the vet's for today, Saturday. She's there now. She had been 10 pounds at her last checkup. Today she was 6.8 pounds. We're curious to know where she's been all that time. Another mystery.

What triggered your getting in touch with me after such a long time? I think I told you that two weeks prior to receiving your package I'd been thinking about you and wondered what you were doing, and Googled "Howard Attebury" in San Diego, with no results. So when your packet arrived my reaction was, "Of course." I had expected to hear from you.

Your (my) Kokopelli is holding down a three-inch stack of my manuscript pages that I really should go over because they have comments from the two writers' groups. But I want to rush off into this beautiful spring weather and listen to the flutes of the birds and sow my seeds. He's been luring me away from this desk. Fortunately, it's too dark now to dig.

Diana, determined to go home with Lynn, ***photo by Lynn Christoffers***

The stream of life floats us off in such unexpected directions, I hope you haven't been holding on to an image of a goofy 18-year-old who may still be goofy but isn't the same otherwise.

Love, Cynner YYY

MARTHA'S VINEYARD

Dear Howie: April 21st, 2012

Here's Daphne in usual form carrying a mouse and Diana on the day Lynn saw her. She jumped into Lynn's car and settled on the dashboard..

Love, YPYYPP Cynner

Chapter 12. Seeds of Love

Seven seed packets came in the mail. Spread out they were, Hollyhocks (H for Howie) and Catnip (C for Cynthia). In between were Leeks, Okra, Vinca, Eggplant, and Spinach. Also included was a slip of paper with a quote by Marcus Aurelius: "When you arise in the morning, think of what a precious privilege it is to be alive — to breathe, to think, to enjoy, to love."

• • • • •

MARTHA'S VINEYARD

Dear Howie: April 23rd, 2012

The seeds arrived — Nifty!

Kokopelli is trying to entice me outside to sow my seeds, but it's raining. A lovely, gentle, much-needed rain. It started last night, and in the few hours between then and now there's a faint flush of green everywhere. Trees, shrubs, grass. Marcus Aurelius is right. It's a privilege to be alive to be able to see and smell and feel and hear the magic of growing things.

And love, Cynner YPYPYPY

CALIFORNIA

Hello Cynner, April 23rd, 2012

Hallmark BD'S are maybe 15, 18, 21, 40, 65, 90, so on 90 I did what I needed to do — that legal stuff — put me to rest, and things I should have donea long time ago. When you left, I kept your packet of gov't paper towel writings in a suitcase at my home in Point Loma and in the same suitcase when I moved to Ocean Beach. But then on to Piper St in Clairemont, where it was honorably kept in the next to the top drawer in a new chest of drawers. This was a precious package and it only belonged to Cynner and Howard, so I sent it to you without a return address, in so doing for you to take it further or not as you desired. I am more than pleased that you took the initiative and found me. I wanted to send a manganese nodule with the writings, but over time it has been misplaced but I am diligently looking for it.

Let me go back a bit. I was at the SIO [Scripps Institution of Oceanography] starting on the PhD in Marine Biology and one day I was in the store room for geology specimens and came upon a bin labeled "deep sea dredge — Mariana Trench" which contained hundreds of pounds of the manganese nodules, so I walked off with a small one suitable for mounting in a choker — that neck adornment — that was to be for you — a jewel from the deepest part of the ocean for you to wear or not — and I cannot find it, I will continue looking. So sorry.

Love, Howie yypp

MARTHA'S VINEYARD

Dear Howie: April 23rd, 2012

Suddenly, it's Spring.

I called Steve Atwood, Daphne's vet, and apparently she's eating well and behaving herself and not hurting too much. Steve is going to operate on her leg tomorrow, Tuesday, to see if the tendon can be repaired. He's a super vet and the Veterinary Library at the University of Pennsylvania has been named for him.

Which means I need to add a picture — Dr. Atwood checking Daphne when she was a mere kitten (photo by Lynn Christoffers, my resident photographer). I procrastinate. Back to my writing.

Love, Cynner YYYYPy

Dr. Steven Atwood checks young Daphne, ***photo by Lynn Christoffers***

CALIFORNIA

Dear Cynner: April 25th, 2012

I have made a change for the good in my habits. Now when I am at my eating table with the iPad I am looking at your photographs and the one most frequently on pause is the "extended woodshed." Such a beautiful room, full of light, and life is abundant, and it is all put together in a charming manner.

My first year of college was a good one for me. Milo Baker was my instructor for botany 1A. He gave an excellent course. He was an expert on violets and was the taxonomist for this group. I was attending Santa Rosa Junior College and the botany class would meet on occasion at the Luther Burbank Garden where the plant wizard did most of his work (he had passed by then). The most notable point in my lackluster gardening forays was that I grafted an apple cutting to the tree that he planted and that had numerous kinds of apples being produced.

My grandparents were really into gardening. I remember all the seed catalogs on the dining room table at night and after supper they would discuss the purchases. Grandpa selected the vegetables for the most part and Grandma the flowers. G'pa had horses, plows and wagons for rent. One year he had a big field of hops on poles. He had actually a farm in the city limits. Big orchard — my favorites were the cherry and apple and apricot trees. Least favorite, the olive trees that it seems I was underneath raking too often. They had a good well, two barns, raised chickens and when I was small they asked me for the first time to gather the eggs, so I did and got a full basket but I was not told about the glass 'sample' eggs and collected them as well. One day around noon — this was in Napa — Napa was in the line to be at the point of a total eclipse of the sun. It was so funny the chickens sensing the dark went to their chicken coops and we all laughed. It was not dark for very long. It was good being a child with loving grandparents and a farm to be at with all that life going on. It is good now even though I am not much of a writer, I am enjoying scratching out some words to a woman that has my heart.

Love, Howie YYppYP

MARTHA'S VINEYARD

Dear Howie: April 27th, 2012

You couldn't possibly have sent anything more appreciated, appropriate, and romantic than that envelope of seed packets. I'm plotting the best possible way to plant all seven seed types in (blush) one bed.

It's too wonderful not to share, so last night I spread the seven packets out on the coffee table in the parlor. Emily, whom you haven't yet met, solved it first, with, "Ooooh!" and clasped her hands under her chin. Lisa, the marathoner, said, "Seeds! Howard understands you! There's hope for us!" Cat came in late and Lisa and Emily stood watching her until Cat, too, got it and was almost in tears .

I need to tell you about the Wednesday Writers, who have adopted you on my behalf.

The group arose from a five-week adult ed course I give a couple of times a year at the high school called "Writing and Publishing Your Book." When the five weeks were up after the very first course ended, Amy said, "I wish we could keep going," Cat said, "I do, too," and Lisa said, "Why not!" I said, "Meet at my house where we're not sitting under fluorescent lights in uncomfortable plastic chairs having to see homework assignments on the board. We can eat popcorn and drink wine." That was three years ago, and we've been meeting every Wednesday night from 7 to 9 pm since then.

I loved hearing about your grandparents and the farm and the fruit trees and cleaning up after the olive trees. Was this the spunky Irish grandmother?

Doug Green, my son-in-law, Mary's husband, is from San Diego, where his parents had an avocado ranch. Doug tells about coming home from school and feasting on fallen avocados. He almost set fire to his hillside, when he was a kid. Then he learned that his father had done the same thing when he was a kid. His grandfather founded a company in the late 1920s called, Kelco, which harvested kelp for algin. My computer keeps changing "algin " to "align." I dislike inanimate things telling me what to do. My car has a gear shift and I can roll the windows down with a hand crank. But I do have Wi-Fi.

Daphne goes to the vet tomorrow to have her bandage changed. The vet's office left four messages on my answering machine telling me to bring her in today, and shamefully, I was digging in the dirt and didn't get upstairs to the machine. They made an appointment for her tomorrow morning. When I brought her back from the vet's yesterday after Steve Atwood, the vet, operated on her leg, the technician had put her in Lynn's cat carrier, a nice old-fashioned wicker contraption. I hadn't driven far before Daphne had worked her way out of the carrier and had gotten into the front seat of my car, even though her starboard aft leg is in a cast from hip to toes. She ate three small cans of cat food yesterday, and two today. When I went into the Woodshed, her temporary domicile, she had gotten up onto a chair, despite her leg. This is one very fine, gutsy cat.

I've been out in the garden all day instead of writing. The weather has been perfect. Dry for a while, then a perfect rainy day that's made the soil just right for planting. Can't resist!

There's so much more I want to talk about, to ask you, to tell you. Thank you so much for that package with its geographic coordinates and the challenge to find you, should I want to. I'm so glad.

Much love, Cynner yyyyppyy

CALIFORNIA

Dear Cynner, April 28th, 2012

Yes, the grandmother I mentioned was the spirited one on my mother's side. On my father's side, all that I know are in the few paragraphs I am now going to tell you. G-pa, I cannot remember meeting him, had a concert band which played in parks on the bandstands which were a part of the times — bring a picnic lunch, listen to the music, dance, talk, enjoy the outdoors with friends — sorry that this has gone kaput for the most part.

My father had a brother Harry, and two sisters, Lena and Mabel, who all lived in Napa. I remember one day my dad and mom with me along were in the car — a Hudson, I think, and headed for, if I remember correctly, Fairfield, to the pen as Harry was incarcerated for hauling, I was told, sugar (it was prohibition time). As we got to the pen, Harry was outside the walls washing a big beautiful car. It was the warden's and Harry was a trustee and right hand man of the warden. Some time later Harry was a policeman in the Napa police department — I could never figure it out — how a felon could be allowed to be policeman. Many years later I visited Napa and saw a beautiful house with a sign that stated, "Attebery house." I photographed the house but did not further investigate, but I had the feeling it belonged to Harry.

Lena was married to Harry Prosise and this Harry was one of the few persons that brought me comfort after my dad's passing. Harry was in the Navy and retired as a chief warrant officer. While serving on the *Langley,* the first aircraft carrier, he took me aboard and I had lunch in the officers mess and then a tour of the ship and that huge flight deck

LOVE, HOWIE YYYYYYPPP

MARTHA'S VINEYARD

Dear Howie: April 28th, 2012

Yesterday I took Daphne to the vet to have her bandage changed, then went to MVTV, the community access station, to be interviewed for *The Vineyard View* about the guide book. I asked for an extra DVD to send to you. Then I picked Lynn up at the Steamship Authority dock on her return from Florida, glad to be home where our major problems at the moment have to do with cats, raccoons, skunks, owls, hawks, and deer (and ticks).

Daphne with cumbersome leg cast, ***photo by Lynn Christoffers***

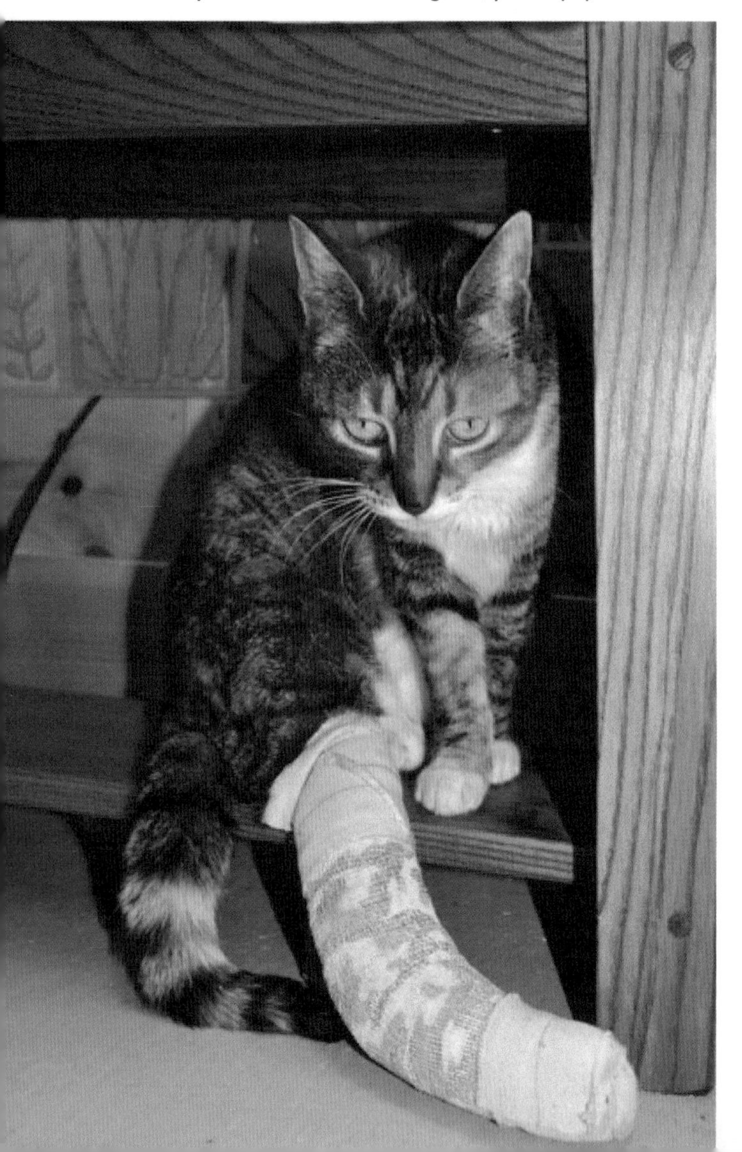

Daphne is mending rapidly. She's shut up in the Woodshed, which is not a bad place to be imprisoned, and gets around with that great leg cast on. She jumped up into my lap.

Diana, Lynn's Siamese, caught a rather large rabbit today, brought it into the house for my approval, and after I moved it to the step, ate much of it. Right now she's in my lap playing gentle, sweet kitty, not the mighty hunter she's turned out to be. I think of the highly bred animals as being wimpy. Like people. She's a pleasant surprise. Mongrels are the best, the strongest, the most comely, the brightest. British Royalty is a good example of the need for the benefits derived from a wide gene pool.

Much love, Cynner Yyyyypy

CALIFORNIA

Dear Cynner, April 29th, 2012

The *Langley* was berthed at Mare Island and I lived in Vallejo, which is across the widened portion of the Napa River. When Harry Prosise lived on the ship he visited me and on one occasion I mentioned that I was saving up to buy a typewriter and he suggested that he would get one for me at the post exchange for a better price than the local stores — so that is how I got my first typewriter, a Royal Portable in a nice carrying case. In his travels around the world he would send me short notes but lots of stamps as he knew i was a collector. He retired to Napa and owned and operated a dairy farm. That is all I know about my dad's family.

True story: Male broke up with his lover, a female dentist. He had a toothache and kept an appointment with her. She was really ticked from the separation — put him under sedation and separated him from all his teeth. His girlfriend would not date a toothless man so he was shut out of that romance. The dentist is in court facing a three-year sentence for her misbehavings.

Love, Howie YYYPPYYY

Chapter 13. The Manganese Nodule

Howard sent a small white pasteboard box with something heavy inside.

• • • • •

CALIFORNIA

Dear Cynner:

I found it! It was lodged in the corner of a drawer surrounded by books.

It was dredged by the Scripps Institution of Oceanography from the Mariana Trench — the deepest part of the ocean. The manganese nodule growth is said to be one of the slowest in geology — takes millions of years for just one centimeter.

I noticed a face on one side of the nodule and if it is turned over and upside down — you will see a heart. This nodule now belongs to you. — "A woman of the seas" — (and garden).

Tomorrow off to the "container" store for a case. If it is your taste to have it mounted on a gold chain or such, please take it to your jeweler and I will take care of the matter.

Love, Howard YYPPYY

Dear Howie: April 28th, 2012

The package came today with the jewel box inside, and is much too valuable a gift to be thanked simply by e-mail. A proper letter follows.

I want to say again how much the manganese nodule means to me. Thank you. It's got many depths and facets of meaning. Just wait until you see what I have to say in my letter!

Much love, Cynner YYYYpppY

• • • • •

In her letter, Cynthia thanked him for the manganese nodule and said she would treasure it. She puzzled over telling or not telling him, not wanting to one-up him, that she owned a sack full of manganese nodules. In 1963 she had gone on a two-month-long research cruise to the Antarctic aboard the R/V *Eltanin* as the lowest kind of flunky, collecting specimens for the Smithsonian. The extra nodules were about to be shoveled overboard, so she retrieved some for herself.

She conferred with the Wednesday Writers: "Do I tell him about my manganese nodules or not?" Lisa's response was, "If this relationship should go any further, you can't have held back such an important fact."

The best way to mount the precious nodule from the Mariana Trench took up a lot of space in the e-mail correspondence over the next several days. Cynthia wrote, "Dozens and dozens of boxes, glasses, caskets, baskets and who knows what all else in this house. No one's ever thrown anything out." At last it was decided — a little squarish box with an ivory-like lid carved with grapes.

• • • • •

Manganese nodule from the Mariana Trench

CALIFORNIA

Dear Cynner, May 3rd, 2012

Your house is full of treasure. I believe the squarish box with the grapes on the lid is a good choice, the nodule should be very comfortable there if you decide on this one. Choices! Choices! Choices!

Ego amare Cynthia Latin

yyypyyy

Chapter 14. Pause in the Game

MARTHA'S VINEYARD

Dear Howie:

There can't be many people with California roots going back three or more generations like yours. How old were you when your father died? Did you have brothers or sisters?

John Alley, a local character who's a lot younger than me, says, "I used to talk about Island characters and now I find I am one."

Much love, Cynner yyyyppp

CALIFORNIA

Dear Cynner, May 1st, 2012

I was 12 when my dad died. I was playing kick-the-can on the street near my aunt's house and my dad came to a pause in the game and kneeled besides me, started talking, and I was either not paying much attention or I forgot what he said — but I do remember him clearly saying "take good care of your mother." It was my time to kick-the-can and I pulled away from my dad and he left. Later I went to my aunt's house and two MD's were working over him and one yelled "get that kid out of here." My dad died of self-inflicted strychnine poisoning.

I feel that somehow you, Cynthia, are the one I can talk to about my feelings and past events. That I can tell you anything and all — where did I get that provision and permission? I more than feel it — it is just there!

No brothers or sisters. Keep the news coming about Daphne, I am a cat fancier. I grew up with cats.

Love, Howiey yyy

MARTHA'S VINEYARD

Dear Howie: May 2nd, 2012

What a cruel and dreadful thing for a father to do to his young son. Twelve is such a vulnerable age. He must have known that. I'm so sorry. That must live with you always. I can imagine the unanswered questions to which you can only guess the answers. From everything I've read, strychnine is a particularly nasty death, both for the suicide and those witnessing the effects. You can understand why you were sent away summarily. Such a vivid memory, and so sad. My mother once scolded a niece who attempted to kill herself, "Suicide is the most selfish act you can do. You rid yourself of your problems, but leave a mess behind."

I wish I could comfort you.

Much love, Cynner

Chapter 15. Thoughts Are True

CALIFORNIA

Dear Cynner, May 2nd, 2012

I have been reading *Arrows and Snakeskin* in bed before I turn the lights out, for 15 minutes or so each night, leaving me with only three chapters left. It is an excellent bedtime story book for me as it covers many important areas dealing with human life. Your DAD did a masterful job weaving together a story that includes history, family responsibility, courage, survival skills, personal responsibility, respect, community (tribal) involvement and many other. I really like it, and could do with more.

ohcum uoy evol

Howie yyyppyyp

MARTHA'S VINEYARD

Dear Howie: May 3rd, 2012

This appeared on the port side of the *Shenandoah,* a topsail schooner that makes her home in the Vineyard Haven harbor.

Love, Cynner YYPYYPYY

It is so easy to love you.

MARTHA'S VINEYARD

Dear Howie: May 3rd, 2012

Weeding, oh joy! I'm here at my computer with damp and filthy (clean Vineyard dirt) knees and fingernails that won't release the dirt, and cracked skin around my thumbnails that hurt. But I've got Bert's Bees Hand Salve downstairs that smells like lavender and rosemary. The smell alone is enough to heal anything.

Daphne is recuperating amazingly well. Steve Atwood, her vet, says better than he expected. She limps over to the cat door that I've slid the cover on so she can't use it, and looks expectantly at me. Robins are nesting in the maple tree at the end of the drive, and I think the first chicks have hatched. I picked eight spears of asparagus this morning and had them for lunch, and just now, before starting this letter, I was weeding here and there and feeling happy, and checked the asparagus bed, and voila! Another eight spears for supper. I wish I could ship them to you so you could get them instantly. They are nothing at all like the canned/frozen/produce shelf asparagus. I snap them off at the lowest place that snaps easily, and the spears are tender and sweet. The flavor! It's such fun to go out into the garden and ponder on what's for supper. So much has wintered over that I don't have to wait for this year's crop to materialize. The mint is up. I've been putting that in salads, too. And a sprig of mint in a gin and tonic.

I'm delighted with the treasure from the Mariana Trench. The little box is just right.

Love, Cynner PyyyPyyyP

CALIFORNIA

Dear Cynner, May 4th, 2012

These are the lyrics that go with the message on the hull: So easy to love you Baby you're my everything You were my sunshine When I was walking through all this rain It's so easy to love you Baby you're my everything You were my sunshine (You were my sunshine) When I was walking through all this rain It's so easy to love you I woke up right beside you Head in my hand Staring at you while you sleep Oh God, sometimes it feels like God sent an angel to me I can't believe it No, I can't believe it I never want to wake up from this dream You and me Are meant to be together Forever and ever.

How nice.

My grandson, Luke, is going to China on an internship this summer and he is now renewing his passport.

我愛你辛西亞
Chinese for: I love you Cynthia pyyp

Chapter 16. High Country

MARTHA'S VINEYARD

Dear Howie: May 5th, 2012

I've thought often of the trip we made to Highway '49. That must have been the year after it was given the designation. It was a magical trip and I remember it in the most pleasant haze. Even the stop in San Jose and the stolen suitcase didn't mar the trip. I recall stopping to see my great uncle Eugene Perham, who was in his 90s at the time.

I loved camping out and remember that one field with hay stubble and the barbed wire fence. Climbing the fence — what timing! — I had that first seizure. After I returned to the Vineyard, you wrote to my mother telling of your concern. Aunt Nan (for Hannah), my mother's big sister and a nurse, was at the Vineyard for her yearly visit, and she, my mother, my father, and I conferred. I, of course, dismissed it as a fluke. Aunt Nan wasn't so sure. A few days later, I took the canoe out on Tisbury Great Pond by myself and spent the afternoon on the water. I returned home sunburned and nicely tired and was climbing the stairs to the second floor when I had the second seizure. My parents whisked me off to Boston for an electroencephalogram, and it was negative. But I had a third seizure. That got me started on Dilantin. Naturally, I didn't take it regularly, convinced that it didn't apply to me, and when I didn't take it, I'd have a seizure perhaps once every six weeks or so. One time I fell into the C&O Canal in Washington, DC, and, fortunately, got hauled out and sort of learned my lesson. In my late 30s, I stopped taking Dilantin, and have had no seizures since then. All puzzling. I never told anyone except my immediate family, never acknowledged on medical forms that I had epilepsy, and somehow managed to bury in my own consciousness that I ever had a problem. Such is the power of denial. Anyway, I thought you might have wondered how that worked out. I have a scar on my right forearm, not an obvious one, but one that reminds me of our time together. It's a good memory.

Around 1962, I got my first real job at the Smithsonian Oceanographic Sorting Center — sorting plankton, by gosh. You know about my cruise on the *Eltanin* where I was a supernumerary, happily watching everything that was going on and when the dredge came up with a load of manganese nodules, collected a sack full of them as they were shoveling the surplus overboard.

Later I went on the Antarctic continent as part of a group of journalists sponsored by the National Science Foundation and flew to South Pole Station. This was the era of bra-burning, and at the Pole, with Navy photographers around, I fished out from my parka a black lace bra, size 44 D, and asked if anyone had a match. The Navy was not amused.

Sack of manganese nodules from the Antarctic Ocean

After my divorce, I erupted into a new life. I had a few flings and avoided any commitments. I bought a boat, got my captain's license, did two trans-Atlantic crossings in a 32-foot sailboat, taught sailing at the Annapolis Sailing School, delivered a 40-foot boat for the Smithsonian to their research station in the Dominican Republic, stopping at the Turks and Caicos on the way. I started a ferry boat company on Chesapeake Bay, but since the company was built on a house of cards, it tumbled down after a year of operation. Great fun while it lasted — every once in a while I'd meet some boat captain who was aboard a container ship in a narrow Bay channel blasting its whistle at this boat that looked like a piece of furniture blocking the way. When the company failed, I ran home to mama, worked at the Martha's Vineyard Shipyard as a rigger, and ended up writing mysteries after my mother died in 1997. She wanted, very badly, to live in three centuries. She was born in 1898. She almost made it. I'm doing my best to keep her alive as the 92-year-old sleuth of my books.

Dear Howard, there you are. I live alone in this great and wonderful house. There's almost too much action around here — poets meet on alternate Wednesdays — I retreat upstairs when they come. Wednesday Writers , Sunday Writers. B&B guests will start coming soon.

I cherish our new relationship. I've had the intervening years to develop my cluelessness to a fine degree. I hope I am alert enough to make sure I don't lose sight of you this time.

Much love, CynnerYYYYYYYYYYYY

In 1952 I married George Stoertz, a brilliant, witty, but seriously disturbed fellow geology student. Being the clueless person I was and still am, I didn't recognize how troubled he was. We had five children, one right after the other. William, 1954; James, 1955; Mary Wilder, 1956; Ann, 1957; and Robert, 1960.

George worked for the U.S. Geological Survey, Military Geology Branch, and was part of a survey team identifying emergency landing sites for the X-15 in the playas of Nevada, Utah, parts of Oregon, and parts of California. We accompanied him out in the field, sleeping in a camping trailer that had drawers that pulled out and a tent that went over the top.

I can scarcely imagine, at this distance, five small kids on one side drawer, George and me in the other.

The fellow field-party geologists, all identifying themselves as He-Men (this was the early 1960s) were scornful of this not-so-little family, figuring the work would be held back because of us. However, they were staying in a motel and getting softer and softer, we were out in the desert determined to show them we weren't going to hold anything up, and getting stronger and stronger with all the good desert sun and air.

When the season ended, the field party returned to Washington, but George was asked to stay on, so we all did, for 14 months altogether, camping in sub-freezing weather. Ann and Robert were still in diapers. I'd put them to bed with three or four diapers on to get them through the night and until the sun rose. Rime frost would form on the tent ceiling.

William and James were school age at the time. I essentially home-schooled them for that year. We'd set up a folding table and the older kids would count up mileage, write letters back to school, send packets including such things as a horned toad, learned a lot of history and geography and geology.

We camped by hot springs at Gerlach, Nevada, on the edge of the Black Rock Desert, which hadn't been discovered by New Agers yet. The kids learned to swim in a seemingly bottomless warm pool, while I washed diapers in a hot pothole, and cooked hot dogs and potatoes in a canvas rock-sample bag suspended in a boiling pothole. At one point, a geyser erupted between the swimming hole and the cooking pool.

The father in *The Mosquito Coast,* a novel by Paul Theroux, describes George perfectly. Obsessed, driven, brilliant, unbelievably strong, frightening but compelling. I excused his eruptions of anger as understandable — young kids underfoot, settling himself in his job, financial problems. There was always a way I could excuse his behavior. Until finally, after we'd been married for 25 years, his violence escalated. We were okay financially, the kids had grown, and the USGS recognized him as a brilliant geologist. There was no excuse left.

This was 1978. When I ended up in the hospital, the police warned me to leave him, and I did. Feeling at the time that I'd failed. No one in my family had ever gotten a divorce.

George remarried a second and third time. His third wife moved out and, unbeknownst to George, moved in with another man. George by then was experimenting with drugs and seriously abusing his body. After our divorce, he stalked me by phone or appeared at the Vineyard suddenly. At one point Chief Toomey, the West Tisbury police chief, stationed one of her patrolmen where he could watch the drive after my son Robert called to warn me that George had obtained a gun and had plans to "take care of the matter."

Eventually, because he'd abused himself so badly, he was wheelchair-bound. The blackest blacknesses have light spots. Mary Wilder called me to inform me that George had asked her if the Cleaveland House was wheelchair accessible.

This saga ended in 2003 when George wrote a note to the wife who checked in on him daily, wrapped himself in a quilt so as to not leave too much of a mess, and shot himself. My reaction was relief, but a sadness that a mind was so horribly wasted. The kids and I got together to clean up his house in Reston, Virginia. It was a foul mess. Papers, food containers, stuff of every imaginable sort, that hoarding pathology, where everything was saved. Circulars, brochures, stuff, more stuff. The sunken living room had been turned into a rock storage area with rocks and minerals, all neatly identified, piled in box after box after box. He'd gotten interested in fluorescent minerals, and had made displays of rocks and posters that, under black lights, showed naked women in various unseemly poses.

We contacted the Geological Survey, which is headquartered in Reston, where we lived, and they sent a team over to see what might be salvageable. All of it, apparently. They returned with trucks and carted the collection off to the Survey building.

What seemed especially sad to me was that at the end of his life he was in such miserable shape that his next step was to be taken to a hospital where he'd be kept alive whether he wanted that or not. We understood his suicide. He was desperate and would have had no control over his end of life had he been taken to a hospital. This was unthinkable to him, a man who wanted to control everything and everybody. I wish the medical authorities would recognize that keeping a human being alive in intolerable circumstances deprives that human of his humanity.

Chapter 17. Coincidences

CALIFORNIA

Dear Cynner, May 6th, 2012

Rec'd your Life communication and I want to respond. Some things happened this morning that were rather unusual and that I cannot put off as coincidental. Why today did neighbors Fred and Dot want to come over for a rare visit? They called me first and I said OK. They came for a while with nothing important to say other than a friendly visit and giving me a slice of cake. Then a call from Mari next door asking me if I would like to come over for again a not too common a visit. She has a three-year old and prefers to keep her Annie confined to damaging her own home. Another friendly visit and another piece of cake, two oranges, and a DVD she made of her trip to Texas to see family. Some things I try, but I cannot figure out. Coincidences I know are a part of your concerns.

First, I hope to be here in San Diego for the coming years and am looking forward to Maya calendar end date, December 26 this year. I am living the life I accept and to make someone happy makes me happy too.

In truth I am not completely here in San Diego, you have cut me some sail with your photos, words and all, so if imagined or not — I am with you — you are not alone. I do not have a White Horse but am settled on a Red Wheeler which sees sunlight, does move, but has none of the expectations of that charging White Horse.

You know that you are loved, and this loving you then and now is no different — it the same. Knowing of the pain in your marriage has me wanting to hold you more than ever. PPPPPPPP

Scars on the heart are the most damaging and difficult to put aside but your NOW speaks well of how much you have recovered. You are precious. The world is not perfect. You did as right as could be done. You were thrown some curved balls, but the important thing, you did not strike out, you hit the damned things and are a winner as much as anyone can be.

Love always,

Howie PPPPPPPYYPPPPPPP

CALIFORNIA

Handwritten letter from Howard

Dear Cynner, May 8th, 2012

Yesterday when I wrote, I failed to mention the red-tailed hawk that sits on the scaffold of the bld'g across the canyon — it looks for rattlesnakes, cotton-tailed rabbits, jack rabbits and others.

Have you ever wondered why I worked at Point Loma? I will start at the front of the story. When I started dental school in San Francisco it was war time and the school was told to turn out dentists as fast as possible — so without breaks — I graduated in three years. I was in the army for the first two years — nice — all expenses paid. After license went to Santa Cruz for a year then Sonoma County for a year as the pay was $100 more a month. Work for me started out fine — children, PTA lectures, fluoride treatment for children, preventive dentistry at its fullest. Then the director asked me to change direction and do for some deserving pregnant girls & young women — so I did as directed. But all the time I was feeling I was getting away from the purpose of the program. So with two years' experience with the state I contacted the State Director of Public Health about the promise of sponsorship in the M.P.H. Degree at UC Berkeley. He stated that the program of sponsoring was discontinued. So in a job that I thought was going in the wrong direction, working hard for five years without stop, etc. I started looking in a new (any) direction. My mother had State of California Directives that I looked at one day and saw that they needed fishery aides in San Diego — I was hired — that was with the State of California Dept. of Fish & Game. Later the same position was changed to the Federal Fish & Wildlife Service. So in a sense I was then on a paid vacation — a no-stress job — in a beautiful city and met the love of my life — I would call that a good move.

So now I am placed at Lindbergh Field (now San Diego International Airport) saying goodbye to you — then with Mrs. Feltham went to a chain-link fence — watched the plane fly up and away. Mrs. Feltham said, "Do you love her?" Howie answered, "Yes" by nodding his head.

Howard drove Mrs. Feltham home and very few words were spoken. Mrs. F. sensed my deep loss and invited me to her home on several occasions for dinner — which was most appreciated. Side note: Mrs. F., I believe, loved her microbiologist employer — who named four species for her. They studied chromogenic bacteria of the ocean and the role of bacteria in geologic processes.

Double-stick tape on plaque — remove outer layer, please. I wanted HC touching and it's a mirror image or can be seen reversed. I like doing projects with you —

Much Love from

Howie YYY

PPP

YYY

MARTHA'S VINEYARD

Dear Howie: May 9th, 2012

Thank you for going over the latest in the serial installments of *Bloodroot.* I'm glad you picked up that the cowbird hatchlings kill the host bird's babies (instead of the cowbird itself). That makes the comment of the Alley's Store Greek chorus member more meaningful. I'm astonished that there weren't more typos, ambiguities, stuff needing clarification, etc. Many thanks.

I think this commonality of manganese nodules is the darnedest thing ever. How many private persons do you know who own manganese nodules? I tell people about this, and they have no idea what to say or think, knowing nothing about manganese nodules and where they fit in the great scheme of things. Mine came sort of legitimately, as the shipboard geologists had collected samples of all they needed that came up in the dredge and were shoveling the excess overboard. I've had the bag of them sitting on the floor under a bookcase in my study since 1963. I must have known they would be useful someday.

On Daphne's visit to Dr. Atwood, yesterday, Tuesday, he said her leg was recovering with remarkable speed and looked good. He took the stitches out, and at the next visit, Friday, he said he would do away with the cast and re-bandaging he's been doing twice a week. I brought Daphne home, tucked her safely into her suite in the Woodshed, turned out her nightlight, bid her goodnight. She curled up on the chair she was able to hop up onto, dragging that cast up. This morning, she was nowhere to be seen. Finally found her under the futon. She'd managed to slip her leg out of the cast, no easy task. I found it, intact, on the far side of the room. Called Dr. Atwood, who said, essentially, "Good for her." The leg, without its fur, looks awfully insubstantial. She spent much of the morning cleaning herself and her leg.

Much love, Cynner YyyPppYyy

MARTHA'S VINEYARD

Dear Howie: May 11, 2012

I'm listening to the *Burnt Earth Ensemble* as I write. I should be doing a task like sorting seeds or visiting Daphne in her Woodshed captivity instead of trying to write. The music is far more than background music. It's wonderful. I like all of it. It seems ancient. And yet modern. Strobes from one to the other in my mind. The voice on the Track 10 is so ethereal and clear and true. Beautiful.

The plaque came today, and it's perfect. It's now affixed on the nodule's box, just the right size. I'm glad you added SIO Deep Sea Dredge.

Track 18: Beautiful, eerie. Feels like travel through outer space with the sound of the craft's engine, the wind, bird whistles. Gives me wonderful chills. Still sounds ancient as though the flight is happening hundreds of millennia ago. Maybe bringing primordial consciousness to earth.

All right, Track 19 ended. Now I can concentrate on my e-mail to you.

Today started out as One of Those Days. Something broke on the downstairs toilet tank and flooded the bathroom floor. My car was making a strange and definitely wrong flapping sound. The lawnmower was not working and the grass over the propane tank was knee high. A black cat appeared from who knows where and was terrifying Diana, the

Siamese stray. When each of these catastrophes happens it seems like the end of the world. But I turned off the water and called the plumber. They promised to be here Monday and said I was their favorite customer, which was nice, and probably true after all the work they did with the propane switchover. Chris, the Newfoundlander who lives on my boat, accompanied me to Courtesy Motors, and drove me back when the car was fixed. Instead of the $350 bill I expected, it was $80. Some plastic flap had come unmoored and was flapping against the tire. Then Chris took the lawnmower apart and fixed it. And mowed the grass. Air filter and spark plug. I chased off the black cat. And finally, I went to the Post Office.

Today, Liza, the post office clerk, had orange hair in front, crimson in back, sort of under the top orange layers. I've started commenting on her hair after politely trying to ignore it, and she delights in telling me how she gets the effects she does. "What's your natural hair color?" I finally got up the nerve to ask. She shrugged. "Dirty blonde." Anyway, Liza said, as she scanned whatever it is the USPS needs scanned, "Hmmmm, you got two packages from your boyfriend."

One package contained the plaque.

Brass plaque on small box containing manganese nodule from Mariana Trench

I will write you a hand written letter about the second. Your mother's slim gold pencil. I am touched. I marvel at how well you understand me. You know, to the finest degree what will please me. I am humbled by the homage you pay me. I've got to say a lot more. All I can say here is thank you. I am honored to own the pencil. I treasure it. What a lovely Mother's Day gift.

Thank you for keeping those government paper towels in such good shape and sending them to me. And making me work to locate you.

Much love,
Cynner
Y and P to ∞

CALIFORNIA

Subject line: "JOKE/from Howard May 12th

Through a pitch-black night, a captain sees a light dead ahead on a collision course with his ship.

He sends a signal: "Change your course 10 degree east."

The light signals back: "Change yours, 10 degrees west."

Angry, the captain sends: "I'm a cruise ship captain! Change your course, sir!"

"I'm a seaman, second class, CG," comes the reply. "Change your course, sir."

Now the captain is furious. "I'm a large passenger loaded ship, I'm not changing course!"

There is one last reply. "I'm a lighthouse. Your call."

Chapter 18. Never Say Never

MARTHA'S VINEYARD

Dear Howie: May 14th, 2012

Got the postcard — that is one sensuous picture. My word! What a wonderful thing for your grandmother to influence her grandson with.

The asparagus is up and thriving. If I were to send a batch by overnight FedEx/UPS/USPS would it be easy for you to retrieve it? And which carrier would be best for you? I hope California agricultural laws don't prohibit such a transaction. I bet my day- or two-day-old or even three-day-old asparagus is better than the frozen kind you're eating. The only trouble is, a taste of my asparagus will spoil you forever, and the season is awfully short.

A good and full day. Brunch at Richard Knabel and Jim Osmundsen's with a dozen people, seven of us mothers, who were given small pots of roses to plant. Richard is one of our three selectmen, Jim is a diver and EMT, and at Christmas they decorate a tree that must be 15 feet tall. Then a housewarming dinner at sister Ann's son and daughter-in-law's new house, David and Libby Fielder. They've built what seems to me a gigantic house, because they're determined to entertain the entire immediate family at sit-down meals. Immediate family translates to this: Alvida and Ralph (Johnny) have three sons and a daughter; Ann and Bill (who died two years ago) have three sons and two daughters, and I have (had? Still hard to say) three sons, two daughters, a total of 14 grandchildren for my mother. Al and Johnny have seven grandchildren, Ann has eight, and I've got thirteen — seven boys, six

"Daybreak," a picture Howie remembers that hung in his grandparents' house

girls. David and Libby imagine all of the above fitting into their house, and I suspect we all could. I left early because Sunday night is the writers' group. I had nothing to read.

The Sunday Writers' group had eight members tonight, almost too many, but since two of us hadn't done our homework, we finished promptly at 9 pm. One new member — last week was his first time — is wheelchair bound, and this house is not really wheelchair accessible. However, he's got a portable ramp that we shoved his chair up the front steps last week, and this week I got Chris Cull, the boat dweller and a stocky brute, to shove the chair up, which he did essentially one-handed.

At some point we must get together. We have so much to talk about face to face. Are you able to travel? I checked flights from San Diego to the Vineyard, and it's possible without too much hassle. I can bed you down in the Woodshed with its large futon and private bath as soon as Daphne is freed from her captivity a few days from now. Might Mark and Jennifer come at the same time? That would be fun. If this is even vaguely possible, I'll send you a list of dates when there's no one staying at the B&B.

You understand exactly what touches me most. Diamonds, emeralds, and pearls are nothing compared to the love and thought you have put into the delightful surprises you've provided me.

Much love,

Cynner yyyyyyyyyyyyyyyyyyyyyyyyy (holding the key down on purpose)

CALIFORNIA

Dear Cynner, May 14th, 2012

I was reading in my Dad's *Encyclopedia of Food,* that asparagus patches go 100 years, but are at best the first 10 years and then should be heavily fertilized to maintain quality. In Napa and Vallejo, as a youth I remember only white asparagus being served. Now in San Diego I see only green except in specialty stores that have both. It is so sweet and thoughtful of you to offer me some of your garden-produced and personally tended asparagus. You are a wonderfully caring woman. If I have my rather's, it would be that you spend that time writing or sitting on your bench with Daphne and giving me a thought or two. Yes, you do things that continue deepening my love, if it could be any deeper.

I am doing better at keyboarding since I purchased a full-sized one that just plugs into the USB connection on the laptop, and then it is wireless. Before, my large hands with the big fingers would often strike two keys at the same time.

I cannot travel due to health reasons, and rightly so. I am never saying never however, and I like challenges.

Love, Howie

YPYp

YPPp. I know these meanings come alive, and are felt.

Chapter 19. Equipped for Anything

MARTHA'S VINEYARD

Dear Howie: May 15th, 2012

What kind of support would you need to make a visit to the Vineyard possible? We have one of the best hospitals in the state. I was born there, but now it's a brand new $45 million building. Food is easily tailored to any possible diet. Since the Island has a large over-70 population, we're equipped for pretty much anything. I even know someone in LA who has a home here on the Vineyard and a great big private airplane. I bet I could talk him into detouring to San Diego next time he comes to the Vineyard.

If a trip to the Vineyard doesn't work, next time I visit daughter Ann in Santa Barbara, I'll make a point of coming to San Diego. Ann graduated from UCSD in psychology and computer science. I would love to sit by my fish pond or in your backyard with a view over the canyon and converse. E-mail is pretty good, but it's still a bit one sided, like C: "... over." H. "...over and out."

I think I told you when I listened to *Cactus on Mars,* after the CD finished and the music stopped, I kept hearing the four notes of one of the themes. The same thing happened with *The Burnt Earth Ensemble.* I'm trying to figure this out.

I'm reading Mark Twain now. I acquired all the books he wrote. This August I'm scheduled for a week-long trip on the Mississippi from Nashville to St. Louis on a brand new paddle wheeler called *Queen of the Mississippi.* I'm about three- quarters of the way through *Innocents Abroad.* I used to think of Mark Twain in terms of being a Mississippi riverboat pilot, and it's almost disillusioning to see how much else he was besides that. I have his autobiography, a big thick tome. Not something to sit down and read, but something to nibble at occasionally. I've finished the obvious books, *Tom Sawyer, Huckleberry Finn, Life on the Mississippi, A Yankee in King Arthur's Court,* and others that I'd have to look at their titles again to remind me. At first, I thought *Innocents Abroad* was a lot of gushing about new sights, but now I've got into it his description of Pompeii makes me want to go see it for myself. He's visiting the Holy Land now, camping out, and he makes one feel right there. He's funny, of course, and perceptive, and not afraid to say what he thinks, and quite irreligious. He's very knowledgeable about Bible stories and how they compare with what he's seeing. For instance walking over ground Paul walked over and seeing people who look just the way they must have looked 1500 years ago and are probably descendants of people who talked to Paul.

Just looked at the time — done it again!

Much love,

YYppYYpp

Cynner PPyyPPyy

MARTHA'S VINEYARD

Dear Howie: May 15th, 2012

Andrew Nanaa, a friend who understood that I wanted to hear your video, installed two speakers on my computer, so I was able to hear your description of the new house going up across the canyon with its eight-car garage and yacht storage. Why do people want all this stuff! Stuff to take care of, stuff to worry about, stuff to protect against theft. Stuff to show off. The same sort of gross waste is happening here on the Vineyard. Trophy houses. "My name is Ozymandias, king of kings: Look on my works, ye Mighty, and despair!"

Your video came through loud and clear, and the image filled the screen, and there wasn't much wiggling around despite your camera being hand-held. You have a wonderful clear voice. This opens up another communication channel.

Love, Cynner YYPPYY

CALIFORNIA

Dear Cynner, May 15th, 2012

Please let us put my visit to the Vineyard on hold but I sure appreciate your sweet and innovative ideas on a visit. Your stay in San Diego would be most welcome after your visit to Santa Barbara. I also have room for a traveling companion if that is your need. I will not be able to meet you at the airport, and dining out is not in my favor as I Vitamix all my food. I am 90 and spurting, you are an octogenarian, consumed with the good things of life and you should not run out of room.

Love, Howie YYYYPPPPp

MARTHA'S VINEYARD

Dear Howie: May 16th, 2012

See what you're missing?

Picked these a few minutes ago in the rain. It's about four meals' worth, and tomorrow there'll be more. Each autumn I pile the asparagus bed with manure from across New Lane and compost from my compost bins. The white (bleached) asparagus used to be thought of as a delicacy. To get that pale color, they piled dirt around the growing stems to keep out the sunlight. Now the green ones are more desirable, as they have more flavor and probably more vitamins. As a child I didn't like asparagus, but now it's such a fleeting yet robust crop, I eat it every day. The way I like it best is to steam it just until it turns bright green, still crisp, but tender. With melted butter and lemon juice. Yum.

Lettuce is thriving, enough thinnings to give away. Spinach, too, and radishes. I planted the okra yesterday and the Love Lies Bleeding last week (I forgot to tell you that).

Nice rainy day. Everything turned green, quite suddenly after just a few days of rain. It's always miraculous, this spring greening.

Back to work.

Love,

Cynner yyyyyyy
pppppp

Asparagus, fresh from the garden, wet with rain, headed for the kitchen

PART 3: TO SAN DIEGO

Chapter 20. Living to 120

MARTHA'S VINEYARD

Dear Howie: May 17th, 2012

Funny that in 1950 I thought of you as quite an elderly man at 28. Now you seem considerably younger at 90. I was glad to see that in your library of reading matter, you have a book on living healthily to 120. I will definitely plan on getting to San Diego. You mention not dining out. I have always been such a slow eater, dining out is painful to me. I'd much rather eat in. My big sister, Alvida, and I, both pokey eaters, used to eat out once a month when we both lived in the Washington, DC, area, because we didn't feel rushed the way both of us did with normal diners.

Back to my writing.

Much love,

Cynner

Y y
yyyy yyyyy
yyyyyyyy y yyyyyyyy
yyyyyyyyyyyyyyyyyyy
yyyyyyyyyyyyyy
yyyyyyy
yyy
y

That wasn't easy!

CALIFORNIA

My Dear Cynner, May 18th, 2012

I would be more than glad to review C-Dock, and to become acquainted with your earlier writings.

Your letter ended with that beautiful heart. A SWEETHEART — and thank you for all that work you put in to make it just perfect. YOU MAKE ME FEEL SO GOOD!! I am off to bed now, but first I am thanking everyone that should be thanked for this wonderful, rare, beautiful woman, who is an unselfish thinker, compassionate, that lives life as I see you living.

You are deeply loved,

Howie YPYPYPQp

MARTHA'S VINEYARD

Dear Howie: May 18th, 2012

Now that I created it, I can cut and paste the heart, but that seems to lessen its impact, so I won't.

Love, YY

Cynner pp

Chapter 21. HLC In Every Tongue

MARTHA'S VINEYARD

Dear Howie: May 18th, 2012

I'm putting a hard copy of my manuscript, *Murder on C-Dock,* in the mail today. You can mark it up and send back pages that need, in your opinion, some kind of fixing. Please do critique big things like the protagonist — is she strong enough? And little things, like missing periods. And everything in between.

Love,

Cynner YYYYY

CALIFORNIA

Dear Cynner, May 21st, 2012

All those pages arrived with this afternoon's post and am raring to go but first, in time, is now andI will tell you about my marital stuff, which I will snail mail tomorrow.

Howard 하워드는 신시아를 사랑 (H L C Korean)

YYYpYYY

CALIFORNIA

Dear Cynner, May 25th, 2012

I finished *Murder on C-Dock*. Wondrous, beautifully done, words turned to video, a WINNER, BOOK — AUDIO BOOK — VIDEO. Give all to your guests — will write also after the holiday.

Much love, Howie YYYYPPPQ

HOWARD'S STORY

In got to know Dorothy Janette Stocker as we both attended the First Unitarian Church in San Diego. The church had many social events so we kept bumping into one another and somehow had a first date with a ride over to Coronado and down the Silver Strand and a walk on the beach. Over the course of several months she told me that she was recently divorced and when she was a teen she had been married and that she had it annulled — and she never again spoke of that matter. She was quiet about her divorce to E. Rhode who was from a prominent La Jolla family — but she did say he was an naval officer — an engineer — and that she was with him on his tour at Guam. In San Diego he had a dance band and she was the librarian.

Jan, as she liked to be called — she hated the Dorothy part of her name, worked for a time at the California Academy of Sciences as a Museum Preparator and when she was there a famous entomologist asked her for marriage but she said NO! — She did tell me she was molested as a young girl by the owner of a corner grocery store in San Francisco, when he would invite her behind the candy counter.

Her father worked for the *S.F. Chronicle* — as a pressman. Her mom ran a Jewish Foundation Rummage Store. Father died from pneumonia — mother after visiting us in S.D. had a coronary on way home to S.F. — and her automobile went over a cliff.

Jan it seemed did not have much love for her mother — but she spoke highly of her father. She had nothing to do with her mother's funeral — did not even attend. I took care of the proceedings.

Jan and I knew each other for only a short time and marriage was uppermost in her mind. She did not want to get married in San Diego as that would be in the newspapers and her ex and his family would discover it — so I obliged and went to Santa Ana in Orange County to Superior Court for the ceremony — this was on Friday the 13th of June 1952 — with an overtime parking ticket on the windshield after the ceremony. I remember the magnolias were in bloom.

After 22 years we divorced in Feb 28, 1974, She was an excellent cook (German food) and housekeeper (fanatic). Seems now that first she wanted to be a mother and then for someone to take care of her and that love was far down the list. Paul came 4/6/53, Mark 10/28/54. She liked to dominate and control and was a strident helicopter parent. All was perfect until the children were out of her sight — that is off to school. Then it was the kindergarten teacher who was inept, etc. She went to the principal's office and asked that she be made a school monitor — but they would not do it. She tired of San Diego Schools and then took the children to our mountain home in Idyllwild — and they were bussed down to San Jacinto for schooling. But activities on the bus were not to her liking so she moved down the valley to an apt. in the city of Hemet.

When I went to UCLA on the post-doctoral, Paul lived with me and he finished at Santa Monica High as star water polo player and then on to the community college. Mark finished H.S. with Jan and then came to Santa Monica. Then Jan moved to S.F. to her home which had been rented since her mother's death. Several times a year I would take the children to S.F. to see Jan and then to my mother in Napa. Jan died of a heart attack while taking groceries up the stairs. Mark sold the home that was in the Castro District. During Jan's last years she was a recluse — having nothing to do with anybody — no phones no nothing — except Mark would phone her at a scheduled time each week and only then would she answer the call. Mark distributed her ashes in the mountains as she requested.

On 4/24/1982 I married Sheri Martes, a native of the Dominican Republic. She was born on 8/15/1936 and passed on 6/10/1993. For eight years of our togetherness she suffered from multiple myeloma and passed due to that disease as chemo, blood transfusions, X-ray treatment and experimental means did not turn it around.

About Sheri — start with David an electronic engineer working for the Navy as a civilian and he being sent to the Dominican Republic to work there on a monitoring system. He meets Sheri, they are married and both return to the United States, have two children, Julie and John. David and Sheri divorce. I meet Julie working as a teller in my local bank and she introduces me to her Mother. However between David's and my marriage to Sheri she was wed to a Navy enlisted coxswain and the union conceived Susan. Her father had no use for Susan and I assumed the role of a father, and she is not looked upon by me or in my introductions to others, other than as my daughter.

Sheri had another daughter conceived by rape in the Dominican Republic and after six years the child was kidnapped by the male perpetrator. Sheri made contact with her lost daughter in New York and they continued communicating and seeing one another up until the time of Sheri's death. Sheri was known for her compassion — her life was dedicated to help the needy — in all ways. She was always good to and for me. Never once did she complain. She is at rest at Ft. Rosecrans National Cemetery at Point Loma.

• • • • •

Over the Memorial Day weekend, Cynthia invited her then agent, Christine Witthohn, and some of Christine's writers, to Martha's Vineyard.

• • • • •

MARTHA'S VINEYARD

Dear Howie: June 1st, 2012

It was a great weekend, stimulating, interesting, enjoyable, and great meeting new people. However . . . I'm glad to have my space back. Now comes the attempt to find things well-meaning people have put away in what they think is a logical place. How are they to know that I keep my mother's favorite spoon on a hook next to the sink, not in a pitcher with other spoons? All in all, they were well behaved. We ended up Monday night by doing a sort of summer girls' camp round-the-fire, made-up storytelling, accompanied by several bottles of red wine. One of us would throw out a starting sentence, then the next would add to it, and so forth. This was enhanced by the fact that none of us could understand more than one word out of three that our British publisher, who in true Brit fashion chewed and swallowed her words before they emerged, and her giggling didn't make what she said any clearer. And the two Italians, one a countess, the other a duchess, while pretty good at ordinary conversation, got utterly confused by some of the abstract turns the stories took. It must sound to you like *Alice in Wonderland*, which it was, in a way. Despite my caution about dress, namely jeans, T-shirts, and bare feet, the Italians started out with nicely done up hair and discreet makeup. By day three, they'd bought Martha's Vineyard sweatshirts and looked very much like the rest of us, including bare feet and uncombed hair.

The wisteria is now gone by, but the Siberian iris is in full rich purple bloom in the border. I uprooted last year's kale this morning. I hate to uproot plants after all the work they did to grow and survive. At least one of the hollyhock seeds has sprouted, but I haven't seen its catnip partner yet. I'll keep you informed. The peas are swelling and should be pickable tomorrow or the next day. The okra is up. I've never tried growing that before. Fun. Planted cantaloupe and eggplant and hot peppers this morning.

Tuesday, after everyone got off on planes or boats, my left leg, which has been bothering me for some time, started to really, really hurt. Nothing seemed to help. I lay down and raised it. Nope. Sat. Stood. Walked. Leaned on the kitchen counter. Nothing. I don't mind going to my doctor, Gerry Yukevich, whose card reads, "Writing, Theater, Poetry, Medicine," but I hate to bother him. But by yesterday enough was enough, so I eased my leg into my car and limped my way into the walk-in clinic, where Dr. Yukevich practices, and, worse luck, it was his day off. A knowledgeable nurse-practitioner thought the symptoms might be Lyme disease, which everyone on the Island including me has had at least once, but wanted to rule out blood clots and lower back nerves. So after an ultra-sound (all clear) and X-rays (all clear), we're back to "what next?" The nurse practitioner called to say stay off my feet (not likely), apply warm compresses, and take aspirin. They also gave me Percocet, and since I don't take any medications at all, they said to cut the pills in half and no more than a half every six hours. I took one half yesterday afternoon, and promptly fell sound asleep with Diana, the Siamese cat, curled up behind me and a book dropped onto the floor. I haven't dared take another half. Might be better to tough out the pain.

Anyway, I got up early this morning and went out to the garden, and invented a way to weed without having to bend my left knee. You're probably not wildly enthusiastic about hearing about other people's ailments, but I'll keep you informed anyway.

Out to take a photo of the Siberian iris, see if it comes out, then I'm going to take a quarter of a Percocet pill and zone out.

Much love

YYYYYYYYYYY

Y Cynner P

PPPPPPPPPPP

Chapter 22. A True Blessing

CALIFORNIA

Dear Cynner, June 3rd, 2012

I am thankful that you mentioned your left leg pain as I was having an uneasy feeling that something was going on that I could not explain to myself. This feeling started after the holiday and would not let go and was to the effect that you were in discomfort and I thought of an auto accident, a fall down the stairs, slipped on a rug, and things like that, so I was relieved when you described the mystery ailment. I hope that it is subsiding and that you are gaining comfort. You, not on previous medication and in such a wondrous state of health, have a true blessing. Yes, at any time keep me informed of your ailments or lack of them, I have a sympathetic ear.

Your round-the-fire storytelling sounded like fun. I had a wonderful ending to a spooky story I once told at a Boy Scout campfire. It happened at Dos Cabesos in the desert — a camp-out to test survival skills in an area with no facilities and the boys were tired and it was late and I was telling this tale of spooky things. It was at the end of the story and at the exact point as if I had ordered it, a coyote gave out a big, loud, howl.

You are such a busy lady! Summer must be the busiest of times for you!

You are loved by Howie. ppPPYYyy

MARTHA'S VINEYARD

Dear Howie: June 4th, 2012

We have a wireless communications system that beats all these electronic gadgets.

Went back to the walk-in clinic this morning for the follow-up to the ultra sound and lumbar X-rays — all digital now. Instant printouts of everything. Carol, the nurse practitioner, said the ultra sound ruled out any blood clots. The X-rays, however, showed (she told me the name and you'd probably know what she was talking about) a number of spiky protrusions near the base of my spine. When I overexert to an extreme, a swelling around the area of the protrusions affects nerves in my legs. When I'd limped in on Thursday and they asked me the pain level, one to ten, I mumbled "Ten!" Today I said "One." Between Gerry Yukevich and Carol, I had three bottles of Stuff to take — aspirin, Aleve, and Percocet. "What of this stuff do I have to take?" I asked. "Nothing, unless it hurts." So I'll continue

The drive and the Norway maple behind the car from the upstairs study window

to overdo, and if it gets too awful, I'll take a quarter of a Percocet pill and go to sleep. I tell you only because I suspect you know what I'm talking about and won't get unduly sympathetic.

I'm glad the camera is working okay. Everything is beautiful now. Actually, it's always beautiful. It's hard to say goodbye to the wisteria, but then comes the Siberian iris. Always a surprise to see what will happen next. It's been rainy for the past two days, and the garden is thriving. Attached is a picture from my study window.

The red car is Lynn's. The blurred image isn't the camera's fault. Jerome Gonsalves, who painted the trim last fall, keeps promising to return one of these days to scrape off the excess paint and clean the windows. On the Vineyard we talk about hundred-year plans.

I procrastinate. Kokopelli is trying to entice me to play outdoors and it's hard to resist, even though it's raining. The compost bucket needed to be emptied and, of course, I had to move uncooked grass and weeds from one heap to another and tidy them up. Came back in, soaking wet but fulfilled. Empty compost bucket in hand.

Much love,

Cynner **YYY**
PPP

ps I haven't been able to figure out what Q stands for, or should I stop trying?

CALIFORNIA

Dear Cynner June 6th, 2012

I have longed for two goals that were decidedly absent — to be surrounded by beauty and not be alone. I live in surroundings, clean, orderly, and functional but a long way from beautiful, but comfortable. Now comes Cynner and what does she give me — beautiful words and photographs of a magical garden on a magical island. No angst, at your timeline, my timeline, your words wondrous, mine unripe. I savor each letter, and punctuation mark that you send because they come from that unique, lovely, compassionate, knowing, beautiful, so thoughtful, seeker of peace and justice.

Love,

Howie **YYYpppY**

MARTHA'S VINEYARD

Dear Howie: June 7th, 2012

Funny weather — clear blue sky, then, suddenly, clouding over and showers. I was out picking my supper a few minutes ago with not a cloud in the sky, then suddenly had to rush in because I was getting soaked. Hadn't noticed the sky darkening. Here's what I harvested.

Vegetables from Cynthia's garden

Tiny beets with beet greens, tiny carrots, two little potatoes I found by scratching under one of the potato plants. Lettuce, parsley, peas, and mint for my gin and tonic. How I wish I could share this glorious feast with you. You'd have to break your diet, but I think this straight-from-the-earth stuff will add additional years. If you can hit a healthy 120 and I can hit a healthy 110, that would give us a good long 30-year relationship. Let's go for it.

I asked Lisa last night if she'd ever run a marathon in San Diego, and she said, "Yes." Then I said was she likely to run another in San Diego? She examined me carefully with that smile she has and said, "I'd even run a 2-K in San Diego if that will get you there."

I'm off downstairs to cook my repast. Definitely enough for leftovers.

Much love,

Cynner

Y y
yyyy yyyyy
yyyyyyyy y yyyyyyyy
yyyyyyyyyyyyyyyyyyy
ppppppppp yyyyyyyyyyyyyy pppppppp
yyyyyyy
yyy
y

CALIFORNIA

June 8th, 2012

Dear Cynner, Oh! Yes! I am for long life, togetherness and happiness. I am going for it!

Thank you for all the beautiful pictures. Your windswept photos are just what I needed — now I can retire the two I Googled of you from images. I like the way you present yourself — natural beauty, gorgeous hair, soft skin — you are a Wow!

I have a photo of your vegetable assemblage on the blue rimmed dish, that is now placed on my refrigerator door. You sure know how to make me happy and in so many ways — some even I had forgotten about.

The photo attached is my first attempt at HDR photography (high dynamic range) which means three photographs are taken of the scene, one correct exposure, one under exposed and one over exposed and then the photos are transferred to the computer to a program that fused them together into one. In the picture I am sending, if this were not done the brighter window area would be washed out.

LOVE, Howie YYYYPPP
CH
YYYYPPP

MARTHA'S VINEYARD

Dear Howie: June 9th, 2012

The HDR photo is remarkable, showing the bright outdoors just as clearly focused as the interior. Do you hand-hold the camera, or does your camera take the three different exposures automatically? Is that the interior of your house? Nifty, if so.

The asparagus is bolting. I weeded the bed, picked a couple of dozen spears for the last picking, and tried something different from my usual steaming. Sliced the ends crosswise to make fairly thin disks, a quarter inch or so, and while I was slicing them, sautéed chopped garlic in olive oil. Then dropped the asparagus in and stirred it around a bit, and Voila! Really good.

I've invited Mark to the Vineyard. I hope he and Jennifer can come. Next best to having you visit.

Much love, Cynner YYYPPPYYYPPP

Cynthia at Quansoo, ***photo by Lynn Christophers***

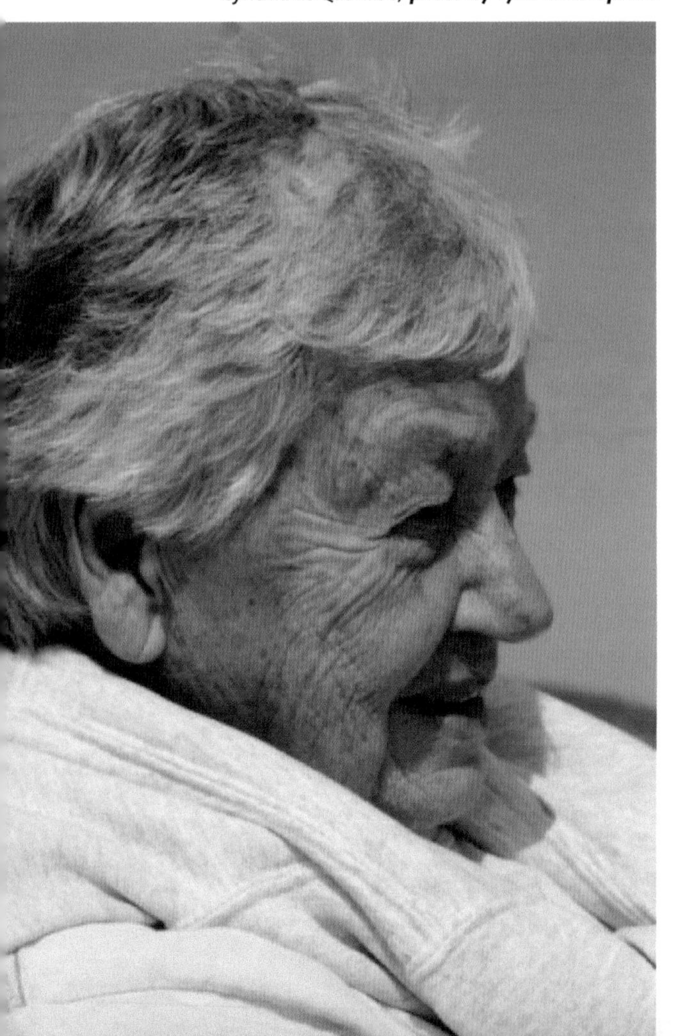

CALIFORNIA

Dear Cynner June 9th, 2012

The photograph is the NW corner of the house and shows what used to be a formal dining room that now holds a light-weight table that I use for eating, iPad, morning paper, and mail use. The director's chairs have replaced the heavy upholstered dining chairs. Two "money plants" and a fern by the window and benjamini plants are outside in front of a cement block fence. The blue bottle by the fireplace contains wheat stems that I picked on one of my camping trips.

On the left wall there is an art work that depicts two young boys surrounded by food and their mouths are full and the eyes of the boys express fulfillment (sorry that it is not displayed well). This is a picture that Sheri had to have because in her childhood and growing years in the Dominican Republic she was often without food and looking at this picture gave her some relief from the memories of her unfortunate days. One day Sheri asked me if she could go to New York to meet with a dear friend she had not seen since she was a child. I made arrangements for her for a three-week visit. About a year later she told me why the visit — it was her daughter that she found that she had not seen since the daughter was six years old. She was embarrassed to tell me that when she was a teen she was raped and gave birth to a girl and raised her until the sixth year and then the father kidnapped the little one and the father and the child disappeared.

I will do your crosscut asparagus recipe — it sounds delicious. Nice that you invited Mark and family to the Vineyard, I have a feeling that they will make it.

Good Night Cynner — I tell you this every night and love you,

Howie ypypypypy and YY

Chapter 23. Come Out And Play

MARTHA'S VINEYARD

Dear Howie: June 9th, 20112

My brother-in-law Johnny, who turned 89 last month, said I should have sent you a sexy picture, not the old lady ones, so here it is, the clueless kid at Antioch, age 18.

YYY Cynner

MARTHA'S VINEYARD

Dear Howie: June 10th, 2012

Very quick — my Sunday writers are about to descend, but this seems like hot news — all seven cygnets have survived the terrors and depredations of the snapping turtles in the Mill Pond. Only six in the picture, but there are seven.

YYYYYYYYYYYYYYYYYYYYYYYYYYYYYYYY
YYYYYYYYYYYYYYYYYYYYYYYY

Cynner

Cynthia, 18, by the Horace Mann monument at Antioch College

Mother swan with six of her seven half-grown cygnets, *photo by Lynn Christoffers*

MARTHA'S VINEYARD

Dear Howie: June 11th, 2012

Wild roses and honeysuckle are in bloom and the fragrance is magical. The trees' new leaves are perfect, not a bit of wilting or insect damage. We've had just the right amount of rain and just when needed, so everything is growing and thriving. Chris Cull, the boat dweller, planted two apple, two pear, and two walnut trees. He was commenting on how much cooler it is in the shade of the great maple trees around here, and he's optimistically thinking the trees he planted will give him shade next year.

Kokopelli is doing his usual enticement — "Come out and play!" I told him I'm resisting him long enough to write you a proper letter.

Your story of Sheri's lost daughter is touching. How sad to feel ashamed about a rape and pregnancy, events over which she had no control. Then to lose her child to a man she feared or despised. What a tragedy. She was fortunate to have found you and your capacity for understanding. You said she was good for you. I suspect you were a life saver for her.

The B&B season has started. Two women are coming this afternoon to stay for four days. I love the rhythm of the seasons, the weather, the flowering of everything, the solitude of winter, the frenzied pace of summer. I just got a call from the cruise director of the *American Star* asking me to talk next Wednesday when the vessel comes to the Vineyard. This will be the third year they've invited me. The passengers are always interested in hearing about the Vineyard and writing. Most have never been to the Island before. (We always capitalize "I" for Island when referring to Martha's Vineyard. Nantucket and Manhattan get a lower case "i.")

I keep meaning to ask, have you been to the Vineyard?

Much love,

YyYyY

Cynner

pPpPp

You didn't tell me what the Q stood for, or should I not ask?

CALIFORNIA

Dear Cynner: June 11th, 2012

You give me so many happy words that are ready to hop off the page. You have optimism and vitality, beautiful awareness of nature and your surroundings — you notice the sky, the surf, the sand, the earth, above and below — you know what is going on, seeds sprouting, fruition, decline, bucket for the compost pile, cycling. You feel life. You live life. You love life. You respect life. It is a privilege just to know you, and now I have one of the greatest gifts in that I can express my love for you and you take heart.

I have not been personally on the Vineyard soil or seen first-hand those brightly colored pebbles that the glaciers brought to your land from as far away as Canada. I first came to know of the Vineyard from a beautiful Lassie who in a very short time gave me a very adequate and loving description of West Tisbury and beyond. I subscribed to the *Vineyard Gazette* for a number of years and it was and is a delightful way to inform residents and others like me. I have been in a very unique position to learn from a loving expert on the Island thru personal words, photographs, and the flavor of local murder mysteries and most of all the fusion with feelings that I have about the Island.

The Q according to our code stands for P, and P offers me a way to relate to PASSION. The Yy's and Pp's are to me and you not just key strokes but meaningful symbols of a truly real Y and P. To me the "Q" means a combined YP, a passionate, respectful entwining.

Much love also,

Howie PPOOQ

MARTHA'S VINEYARD

Dear, dear Howie: June 12th, 2012

And here I thought my fires were banked. You've stirred the ashes and they're still glowing. Definitely add the Q to our lexicon.

Much love,

Cynner YyyPppQ
PDQ

MARTHA'S VINEYARD

Dear Howie: June 13th, 2012

When I presented the notice to Liza (today she has short blonde hair in front, crimson in back, dark roots) she presented me with a package and a knowing smile. "Something from your Man." I opened it carefully once back in the car. I love the wrapping paper — Bird News from the *Vineyard Gazette*. You do everything in the most wonderfully right way. Of all the wonderful scents, lavender is right at the top of my list. Thank you! And to be able to plant, not just one, but three varieties of lavender. My leg feels better already, just breathing it in.

Carol, the nurse practitioner in the walk-in clinic, knowing that I probably wouldn't make an appointment on my own to see another doctor, made an appointment for me at the Falmouth Hospital, which meant going off Island yesterday. The only boat I could get was 8:30 am and my appointment wasn't until 1:00 which meant a three and a half hour wait, but I had a book to read: *Disaster Off Martha's Vineyard* about the wreck of the *City of Columbus* in 1884. Aboard the ferry I held the book in such a way that other passengers could see the bold title and the distressing picture of a sinking ship without my being too obvious. Took my time about getting to the hospital, viewing the sights of America — traffic lights, shopping malls, honking horns, people.

Dr. Scudder met with me right away, before I'd even begun to fill out the voluminous forms, checked me over, said I was disgustingly healthy (not his words), that Carol was being overly protective, and for me to go home and dig in the garden. So I told him about our re-uniting. With your 120-year diet, he said, no reason why you couldn't make it, and despite my diet of toasted cheese sandwiches, butter, and steak, I would probably make it, he said, to 110, thereby allowing us a 30-year relationship. Good to have that confirmed. I made the 1:15 ferry back home. Driving down the hill into Woods Hole there's a first view of the Island off to the left, just a slim line of faint grayish-green. Such a good feeling to see it, even after having been gone only part of a day. My car was the very last one on the ferry and the crew could fit it aboard only because it's small.

There was a tiny bird, reddish brown with a perky tail, hopping around in the kitchen garden to the east this morning. Would you know, from that scanty description, what it might be? I know blue jays, cardinals, and chickadees that work the bird feeder, and crows. Robins and mourning doves and flickers. Red-tailed hawks. The catbirds are my favorites. But I hadn't seen this little brown bird before and didn't get a good look at him/her.

There's so much more to say, and I feel quite inadequate to say it, I, with all the words that are there at my disposal. I am deeply touched by your love for me and the great and small ways in which you express it. Thank you , dear Howie.

Much love,

Cynner YP Q PY You're right, they're more than keystrokes

CALIFORNIA

Dear Cynner, June 13th, 2012

Good to learn that you have passed medical inspection and that you're good to go with garden digging. Carol is to be complimented for her interest in your well-being, and shooing you off for a second opinion.

A tiny bird, reddish brown with a perky tail, hopping along in the garden is a perfect description of a wren. Wrens are very secretive and are more often heard than seen. It is likely to be a house wren or a winter wren, the house wren has no light streak above the eye. About names — my middle name sounds like "rabbit" down Ha-vad way. HA! HA!

Photo is from the front of 4352 Piper Street showing the Toyota camper and the Hyundai Shark with that big invasive Torrey pine in the background.

Love.

Howie Q ID Q

Howard's car and camper parked in front of his house

Chapter 24. Very Q-Ish

MARTHA'S VINEYARD

Dear Howie: June 15, 2012

The course on Mark Twain arrived just in time for my birthday. Thank you. I liked the wrapping paper with the reminder that if one Vineyarder can be writing books at 104, no reason why others can't. I've read almost all of the Mark Twain books mentioned. I've almost finished *Innocents Abroad.* I found a first edition of the book while trying to cull out enough old books from the upstairs bookcase to make room for ones I've acquired. I kept that.

Alvida, Johnny, and Ann are coming over tomorrow for drinks. Just the four of us. Since Mary Wilder died, I haven't wanted to celebrate my birthday, feeling that I'd gladly trade all my birthdays to have her alive to see her sons grow and marry and have their own children. My birthday and the anniversary of the day she died are quiet spots in my year. I suspect you feel the same about Paul. The totally wrong order of things.

I got the copy of *Murder on C-Dock* with your comments and should have told you right away when it came. You're too kind and too gentle. Lisa, the marathoner, also felt the ending should be different. When two critiquers whose opinions I respect are in accord about the ending, it behooves me to at least consider doing something about it.

Supper from the garden to be eaten in front of the parlor fire

I think of you when I go out to the garden. I think of you when I prepare my harvest. I think of you when I carry my tray into the parlor. Something about the digging in the soil around a potato plant and finding a perfect treasure is so sensuous. Thinning out the carrots and pulling up, not a scrawny thinning, but a robust and real carrot is magical. I found two four-leaf clovers and a five-leafer. To go off to San Diego. Year before last I found a four-leaf clover plant in the vegetable garden, and transplanted it to a safe patch. It's come up last year and this, true to form. I guess clover is a perennial. I don't know for sure. I'm wondering about its seeds. Might they produce one four-leaf plant out of X number of seeds?

I was in the garden until the mosquitoes chased me inside, and then it was almost 9 pm. What fun it would be to share the glorious night sky with you and the evening chill after a warm day. The stars are so close, so brilliant, right down to the horizon. To share the making of supper and arranging it to be a thing of beauty in your life. Fire in the fireplace. Well, here's tonight's supper.

Every single thing came from the garden except the chicken and the yogurt on the beets and beet greens. Peas with mint, potatoes with parsley. QQQQQ (Is that possible?)

Much love, and goodnight, Howie,

Cynner QQQQ
YPYPY

CALIFORNIA

My Dear Cynner, June 15th, 2012

You are unrepeatable, there is magic about you that is all your own. You give, and you do not know you are giving. I am going to have a quiet day thinking about you, and loving you — my love. I will also think about Mary Wilder and will read a selection of her poems and will hold her words.

This morning, in my state of half sleep, half awake, dream? imagination? wish? or whatever, this scene came upon me: You were at a distance and walking gently and quietly toward me. I was at a calm and waiting for you. Our eyes met, and nothing else seemed to matter — only this indescribable warmth that entered my body. Eye to eye. What is this soul to soul thru the eyes? Was this truly it? I cannot say how long this eye contact lasted, but it was going on when I raised my arms at waist height and toward you with my palms up and you then put forth your arms and placed both of your palms gently down on mine, and then I felt the endearing increase of pressure and what else but sounds of soft bells and whistles of the wind. More is happening now, the bell sounds are increasing in strength, there is an increasing moistness between palms. All is serene, comfortable, beautiful, a giving to one another (to be continued another day).

Cynthia you are beautifully loved,

Howie YP
QQ
Q+--Q
QQ

CALIFORNIA

Dear Cynner, June 16th, 2012

Today was my yard sale and it turned out to be fun with a good number of people coming by, and a cloud cover kept the day at a perfect temperature. I found a bag of slumped glass pieces that I forgot about and I gave them out to the children, who I guess were surprised enough, not to say thank you. Susan helped. Monday the AMVETS will pick up the leftovers.

I am not very fond of endings. I would prefer the story to continue and continue. No finality. I would like to see a master storyteller, or in this case maybe a magician, at the end of the manuscript put in an addendum, a very short writing that discloses certain facts that will change the story line — say, when only the even number of chapters are reread.

You do wonderfully with your garden and meal preparation — It is always good to know what you are preparing and eating. Are chickens, at least hens allowed on the Island, and goats? — that would make your table autonomous, is that the right word? Chickens would supply good fertilizer and are excellent bug catchers with organic eggs supplied in addition.

LOVE,

Howie YPPYQQ=

MARTHA'S VINEYARD

Dear Howie: June 17th, 2012

Happy Father's Day with many, many happy returns. Does Susan live near you?

What triggered your yard sale? You have my sympathy about simplifying life. Material possessions do take over. Living on a boat was freeing. Every time I acquired something, something else had to go. In this great house, no one ever threw anything out, which means selectively culling and discarding and toting stuff to the Thrift Shop, and having to ponder over each little item — "Will a future generation want this?" I had to make room for my books in this house of generations of book readers. Agony.

A nice B&B couple left today after being here for the weekend. They'd never been to the Island before, so it was fun to see them discovering places. He's retired and is an artist and gardener; she's retired from being a librarian and now helps people with taxes. He was out early in the morning photographing everything in sight, and came back envying my compost bins, which, naturally, endeared him to me.

I got through my birthday in good shape. I've reached the reciprocal of the age I feel, at least mentally. My sister, Alvida, turns 89 next week, and said, "That's not true of me." Al and Johnny and Ann came over for drinks around 5:30. Ann volunteers on Fridays at Evan and Chris's (her son and daughter-in-law) Turkish imports store in Chilmark, and brought me a bottle of Turkish olive oil. Johnny printed out a card he made and said I should send it to you, which I will. It's to complement the photo he found of me at 18 and shows me at three.

Mark got the copy of *Victoria Trumbull's Martha's Vineyard* that I sent so he could anticipate his and Jennifer's visit next month. I look forward to their coming, a way to connect a bit more closely to you. Daughter Ann is urging me to visit San Diego this fall and says she will give me a trip to Santa Barbara and San Diego as a delayed birthday present.

The Sunday Writers will be here in three hours, and I haven't prepared anything.

Much love,

Cynner YYYYYp
yPPPPP
pyQ pyQ
QQQQQ

Chapter 25. Sitting Beside Me

CALIFORNIA

June 18th, 2012

Today I am not writing Cynner. I am talking to her as she is sitting beside me here in my bedroom at the computer desk. Finally we have a clear sky day, and look how majestic those palm leaves look as they sway in the breeze. I'll have to clean the windows on the outside —that last wind sure blew the dust around. Cynner, it is hard to type with only one hand — I'll finishing rubbing your neck later — ok?

It was nice that Susan came to help with the garage sale, she lives in Lakeside which is a 20-mile ride from here. The sale went well — not quite $400. Let's think about how we will spend it. Shall we give $100 to the Homeless Kitchen and you said we should buy more fruit trees and a mango would be nice. Fine with me — let's go tomorrow.

Saturday was the first time you saw Jim, he came over after finishing his shift — he works at the Naval Base SD, he is federal firefighter, classified as an engineer, he helped out a lot with the sale. While you were making lemonade he told me that he and Susan set a date for their marriage — November, but SWEETHEART, he said 2013. He told me he was taking early retirement and then with his retirement package and savings he would have $100,000 for a down payment on a condo in the Encinitas area. A condo with a view of the ocean and low payment so they could afford to travel.

Laura Hollister, the real estate lady, is so great in sponsoring these community garage sales. This is her seventh annual — she puts ads in the papers, makes fliers — 40 homes participated this year — 4352 Piper was listed as having graphic art, glass art supplies, books and photographic equipment for sale. The set up was the impetus to participate. We have some of the signs left over that we can use next year, and to top it off she brought us cold bottled water and macadamia nut cookies.

There is a lot of clover in our lawn this year. Seed must blow in or come from my gardener's shoes or his lawn cutting equipment. Darling, we have time — let's go get the fruit trees now!!

Love you,

Howie YQPQYQP

CALIFORNIA

Dear Cynner, June 18th, 2012

Daughter Ann in Santa Barbara, thank you for your beautiful offer to send your mother my way. Please keep a nice pressure on her to do just that — however, perhaps can you find another way to honor her? I am set on giving her more than words, feelings,and small packages. Allow me the privilege to care for her in this transport.

Love to Cynthia from Howie QYYPPQ

MARTHA'S VINEYARD

June 18th, 2012

... And this is Cynner talking to Howie.

Do you smell the new-mown grass? The big news today is I finally asked Arnie Fischer, who owns Flat Point Farm and raises sheep and has people who do mowing and gardening, to come and mow everything on the place. As you noticed, sections had grown up to hay. You and I were walking to the Mill Pond to check out the cygnets when Arnie's two brawny young men came at 8 am. They worked until 1, with a Gravely, a large hand mower, and a weed whacker. Another favorite scent of mine — new mown grass. With its nice short grass, the place looks like the estate of a wealthy retired dentist with a 75-foot yacht.

Well, we can look over the newly cut grass and pretend it's an estate.

How to spend our new wealth from your yard sale? Yes, a hundred to the homeless kitchen, another hundred to the battered women's shelter, and you need a new camera that will automatically give you three exposures more widely spaced. This has already taken us beyond the $400, but we can dream on. Off to that nursery near you. You will have to tell me about mango trees. Can we get an orange tree? And a grapefruit tree? And a lemon tree? None of those grow here, and the thrill of picking a grapefruit must be something special. How do the poor trees bear such heavy fruit?

You said you'd decided your traveling days are over, but you also said you wouldn't say never. Is there any chance I could talk you into paying a long visit to the Vineyard?

After weeding the vegetable garden all morning, trying to show those two brawny mowers I could keep up with them, it feels great to have my neck, and maybe my shoulders? rubbed. Might you scrub my back in the new Woodshed shower? It's tight quarters, but. . .

Much love,

Y Y
Y Y
Y Y
Y
Y
Y

Cynner

MARTHA'S VINEYARD

Dear Howie: June 19th, 2012

This afternoon is my weekly gig on the *American Star.*

Yesterday, with the new-cut grass making the place look like a park, I went around trimming plants that had made their spring presentation and now look bedraggled. An oriental poppy in one of the raised beds has sprawled out to a dense patch two feet by three feet. It's finished blooming, so I attacked it with clippers and vigor. As I was working on the densest part, I uncovered a little nest with four eggs. I backed off instantly, but I've been concerned ever since, thinking I've discouraged the parents from brooding. I didn't get a good look because as soon as I saw the nest, I covered it up as best I could and left. The

American Star **docked at Tisbury Wharf in Vineyard Haven**

nest was about three feet off the ground in the midst of the thickest part of the poppy plant. It was small, about the size of a small teacup, and the eggs were a sort of greenish blue with speckles of brown and were about the size of the end of my thumb. Two birds have serenaded me when I work in the vegetable garden, one a song sparrow who perches on the top wire of the deer fence and sings the theme from *Naughty Marietta*, La La lalalala la LA LA LA," and a catbird who perches in a wild cherry tree and sings a medley of bird songs. Now I'm thinking they were warning me to stay away, not intending at all to provide me with music. Would you know from my description what kind of bird nested there? And will it return to the nest? I feel awful about it. I hate to think of four less of whatever kind of bird the eggs would have hatched out to be. Funny that I never saw a bird anywhere near the poppy plant.

Much love, Cynner YYY PPP QQQ

CALIFORNIA

Dear Cynner, June 19th, 2012

Some speciesin the sparrow family lay 4-5 eggs, bluish green with brown spots and since you have seen song sparrows nearby it is very likely that it was their nest that you inadvertently came upon. The alarm sound that they emit is a hard, very high "tik," but maybe they were not alarmed at your presence since you are a familiar face in the garden. Hard to say if they will return to that nest, but do not dismay because it is early in the season and they can remain together, make a new nest and start a family over again. Happy days for all.

For Father's Day Mark sent me two books, *Gifts of the Crow* and *Bird Sense.* That one is about what it's like to be a bird. I seem to recall that when you were here we had a minor discussion on how to pronounce bird, burd or a higher sounding bird.

Love you.

Howie

MARTHA'S VINEYARD

Dear Howie: June 21st, 2012

Thank you for comforting me about the nest. I've been worried about it and what kind of trauma I'd vested on the little family-to-be and have been avoiding the poppy plant, but it's so close to the vegetable garden it's hard to stay clear of it.

Awfully short note for now, I'll try to make up for it later today. It's a gorgeous day, hot.

Much love,

Cynner YYYYYYYYYYYYYYYYYYYYYY
PPPPPPPPPPPPPPP
QQQQ
YYQPP

CALIFORNIA

Dear Cynner,   June 21, 2012

While going over some of my boxes in storage out in my studio I found a three quarter portrait of the man [Mark Twain] with his signature affixed at the bottom of the photograph. It says "With the kindest regards Stonefield? (he writes kind of sloppy) Oct. 7, 1909. This is a photograph of a photograph with his original signature copyright by J G. Gessford, I Googled him and he was a famous photographer and this particular portrait is well known.

An original sold at auction for near $11,000. The frame is very old and the backing has disintegrated but the man and his signature are in perfect condition. I would like to sell this item.

No, I am very much determined to trade for this item with you for six kisses and a very long hug. Place and time to be determined. If you agree **Sign here**________________________

You are a very busy beautiful lady. Email me on days that fit in with your schedule. I would rather have you breathe a little slower and have more time for yourself than pen me when you might be better involved in more critical avenues. You might say: Be quiet Howie!! I'll do what I want. I keep all your mail in a nice file box with a pink ribbon. I really love your messages.

Love and more love,

Howie YYYYYYP---------------P

MARTHA'S VINEYARD

Dear, dear Howie:

I'll trade you 60 kisses, a very long hug, and . . . place and time to be determined. But not for the Mark Twain photo. That's for your kids, not me.

My interest in Mark Twain is the voyage I'll be taking on the *Queen of the Mississippi* at the end of August. To that end, I'm reading all his books and taking the course on Mark Twain you gave me for my birthday. I'd always identified him with the Mississippi River as a river pilot and writer, and it's been an eye opener to read *Roughing It* and *Innocents Abroad* and *A Connecticut Yankee in King Arthur's Court* to realize he wrote on a much wider scope. His writing interests me. It's not uniformly well crafted or well edited, and some long dull sections I plow through out of a sense of duty.

As a person, I think I would have disliked him. He's self-satisfied, bombastic, pedantic, smug. He's very, very funny and modern in much of his writing, but not all. I loved his *Life on the Mississippi* and *Huckleberry Finn,* although the latter had an odd ending, almost as though he was tired of writing the book and didn't know how to end it and just threw a lot of stuff at the reader to be done with it. When he writes about the river, he's lyrical and perceptive. The river atmosphere is wonderful and real. I liked *Roughing It* with his sense of self-deprecation over the grand schemes and hoaxes and failures he got swept up in. I also liked *Roughing It* because I know Nevada and parts of California well, and spent a lot of time camping and canoeing on Lake Tahoe, which he brings to vivid life. His writing brought alive his trip out west by stage, and seeing the Pony Express rider pass in a cloud of dust. Wonderful.

Every woman who's ever lived has fantasized about being loved, truly loved, by a man who demands nothing of her, who understands her without her saying (or writing) a word, who is someone she can open up to without feeling any constraints. You are giving me what every woman dreams of, and I'm not sure you realize what a huge gift this is. By sending me that packet with the cryptic return address, you opened up emotions and feelings I had pretty much put aside. It was hard work to find you after I decoded your note. Thank goodness I did.

How many individuals do you know who own manganese nodules? When I ask people, they say, "What's a manganese nodule?" Such a connection. The Mariana Trench and the Antarctic Ocean.

It's been hot today, almost smothering. This is not at all typical of the Island, which boasts of an average summer temperature of 70 degrees with days seldom warmer than 80. The month of June usually means warm days, chilly nights with a fire going in the fireplace and a down comforter on the bed. Today it was in the mid-90s.

I haven't dared go near the nest in the poppies. I'd like to see what the nest looks like close up. The song sparrow was back on the fence today, singing.

Dear Howie, it's late, and I'd better shower and get to bed.

Much love,

Cynner ppYYpp
yPPy

Chapter 26. The Most Beautiful Place

MARTHA'S VINEYARD

Dear Howie: June 23rd, 2012

Five B&B guests are here for a wedding to the south, and another three for a different wedding to the north. In a way, it's fun to share in the excitement and the dressing-up, but in another way they're staying here simply as a convenience, not because this is the most beautiful and interesting place in the world. Most will never return. They come from far places like Chicago and St. Louis, and rush around seeing everything they can see in two days so they can say they've seen Martha's Vineyard.

We were supposed to have thunderstorms last night, rain today, but it was gorgeous, not as hot as yesterday, perfect for all the weddings taking place on the Island this weekend.

I started this when everyone went off to their respective weddings, then got distracted by the Polly Hill Arboretum summer intern coming home from a week-long conference in Ohio. I'm determined to make my next career horticulture. Plants are amazing. I don't see how people can be vegetarians. Plants do everything people and animals do, and can't communicate as well as animals when they're about to be eaten. Nevertheless, I like to eat both, and I try to treat both with the respect due them, and try not to waste anything. Parings go into the compost heap to start over, bones go to the crows to keep the crows coming back.

I peeped into the poppy plant today. I didn't look too closely, but the nest is still there and it seems as though the eggs are gone. I take heart by your saying the sparrows will nest again. Battles that go on around here take my mind off Afghanistan. Skunks, raccoons, hawks, guinea hens, Daphne and Diana, and snakes. The Island has no poisonous snakes. There's a resident corn snake living under the bulkhead doors of the furnace cellar and has, or his descendants have, lived there for 20 or more years. They take care of the mouse population.

I went out to water the garden, since the wedding people apparently have more psychic power than I do over rain making. And got involved in digging. Several years ago I must have dropped a daffodil bulb from the compost into the garden. Over the years, that bulb multiplied unbelievably. I decided to dig them all out this evening. There are at LEAST 200 bulbs. I probably didn't get them all, which is good, because I like the idea of daffodils growing in the vegetable garden. I never anticipate nightfall. Always assuming the day will go on forever, and I've done that for all eight of my decades — assuming night will never come. So I worked in the garden until I could no longer see and remembered supper and a quarter of a letter written to you. Supper is on the stove — my own potatoes. Here it is, 9:30. I'll be dining fashionably late.

The father and mother in the group of five just reappeared. He dropped his wife off, said three glasses of wine were enough for her but she'd added something else, tequila somethings, so he was tucking her in and going back for the fireworks. Fireworks? Did you have fireworks for your weddings? Maybe for the next one.

I am beaming great quantities of love your way. Catch it in a very large basket!

Cynner yyyyyyyyyyyyyyyyyyyyyyyy
pppppppppppppppppppppppppp
qqqqqqqqqqqqqqqqqqqqqqqqqqqqqqqqqq

This would be a longer letter, but I think I smell the potatoes running out of water.

My Dear, Dear, Cynner, June 24th, 2012

You remark on how you like the fragrance originating from your new cut grass. Your carefully coiffed turf does emphasize and is a part of what makes your home the most beautiful place to behold. Incidentally, when I was in the Army and taking Chemical Warfare instruction I remember that the very poisonous phosgene gas had the smell of newly cut grass or hay. Back to the mango tree in my yard. I do not remember planting the tree, so it must have started from a seed that was placed in the soil with kitchen parings. I never had much luck with it bearing fruit as I did not water or fertilize the poor thing as I should have. It is in competition with huge conifers and is losing. It did make a fruit on occasion. I understand that mangos give fruit one year and rest the following year and so if one wants a continual supply one needs two trees, one for each year. I will water and fertilize the tree now and see what comes from it.

You mentioned corn snakes and no bird eggs — perhaps a snake climbed to the nest, as they are excellent climbers, and one snake could swallow all the eggs and leave no remains, except later when the snake regurgitated the shells at another place.

I am not looking for another camera now that I understand the capabilities and lack of them in my camera and I know how to work around them. When I retired and became the photographer at Children's Hospital, I used to do weddings for the staff and acquaintances. It was difficult to get detail in the black tuxedos and the stark white wedding dresses at the same time, but now with HDR it is a snap. Fireworks at my weddings — no. First one was at a Superior Court Judges Chamber and it was on the dark side. Last one with candle light. In the future I prefer that she and I make our own internal fireworks but am ok with up-in-the-air pyrotechnics. Free, usual fireworks are available weekends at Sea World 9:50 PM to 10 PM. One that I like makes a large red heart and then it pops and silently floats away.

Aloe blooming in a San Diego yard

I believe I understand better about your B&B service. You are showing the participants your philosophy of life,your caring for the natural world, how to live, how to garden, the important items to cherish in a life, family, loyalty, compassion, helper to those in need and on and on. The way I see it to be with you just for a few days is priceless. You do it in a quiet, unassuming, criggs way, in that most beautiful place in the world. Your heart is there and you are not alone because your family memories are beside you. The bed and the breakfast are the least that should be taken away — what you impart is the treasure.

You Cynthia, you, YOU are loved,

Howie PQPPY

CALIFORNIA

Dear Cynner, June 24th, 2012

Photographed this aloe that resides down the street a few blocks away. I had hoped for a better outcome — but it's a least red and you can discern leaves.

Much love, Howie PPQYY.

MARTHA'S VINEYARD

Dear Howie: June 25th, 2012

Wow — this looks three-dimensional, and the color is magnificent. I've got pots of aloes in the kitchen and break off one of the juicy leaves if I pick up a hot pot by mistake. I had no idea they bloomed and were so beautiful.

Cynner Minding my Ps and Qs

MARTHA'S VINEYARD

Dear Howie: June 25th, 2012

Every one of your letters reveals another remarkable facet of you and your life. I look forward to spending time with you in person sometime soon and being able to ask you questions and then follow up questions. I want to hear more about you and plants, and you and your mountain village dental work, and more about your glass work, and your children, and your Tijuana Estuarine work, and all the other things you've done that I can't even imagine.

Ann wrote me to suggest I visit Santa Barbara sometime in September. How would you feel if I were to descend on you in San Diego in mid- to late September? Ann said she would take care of transportation costs from here to Santa Barbara and back, but she suggested it would be fun for me to take the train to San Diego. Here's what I wrote back:

"I think train from Santa Barbara to San Diego would be absolutely perfect. I'd love to do that, and will work it out with Howie. September looks good for a visit. The B&B calendar is open from Saturday, September 15th through Saturday, September 29th. During that period maybe I could stay with you for four days then head for San Diego for two days and thence home. What would be a good time for you? I'd love to go to that nursery again and get another tree — lemon or grapefruit or lime or whatever you'd like to have that I could plant. What is the orange tree doing?"

Do mango trees need another mango around for cross pollination in order to bear fruit?

We do need to talk in person. I think you have an inflated vision of me. When we get to talk in person, your opinion of me will plunge right down to earth where it belongs, and that would be a good level for us to be on.

I asked the B&B guests how the fireworks went, and they said only a few were shot off, which, they said, was a relief since the grass all around the place was tall, dry, and extensive.

I laughed out loud at your previous signoff. Q works beautifully as an O.

Cynner PQPPY to you, too!

CALIFORNIA

Dear Cynner, June 26th, 2012

Great news that you are coming. Anytime that is convenient for you is fine for me. Very much looking forward to September. Will post a letter today with a train travel stipend and some other items. Gosh! I will keep my compliments about you to myself. But Gosh! Gosh! Glory Be! Your know to make Happiness Happen.

As far as I know train schedules from Santa Barbara to San Diego and now few with most if not all leaving SB late afternoon or early evening for about a 6 hour journey. Some schedules allow transit straight thru to SD, others change at LA. SD has two stops, old town (OT), which is just a short distance from Piper street and thenthe main station downtown. You and Ann will decide what is best for you.

Frost free areas are needed for Mango trees. As far as I know insects do the pollination, mostly bees that are attracted to the Lily-of-the-Valley scent that the flowers emit. It is interesting to note that there is a connection between Mangos and Poison Ivy as they both contain the same chemical irritant that causes those skin reactions. Not as concentrated in the mangos, but in some individuals who eat mangoes without removing the skin but work around it, can get a severe reaction on the lips, tongue and nearby mucous membranes.

Love is here, Howie

MARTHA'S VINEYARD

Dear Howie: June 26th, 2012

Do you have room at your house for an overnight guest (me) ?

Cynner PYQQYP

CALIFORNIA

Dear Cynner, June 26th, 2012

YES, YES, YES, YES, YES, YES, YES

> Raise your G &T and listen as I say these words:
> Here's to me an unimpeachable and law-abiding man
> My only aim in life is just to do the best I can
> But I am not responsible for anything I do
> When my head is full of dreams and my heart is full of you.

Love feels so good!!!

Howie QP QP Q

Chapter 27. Tsilala

MARTHA'S VINEYARD

Dear Howie: June 29th, 2012

Roses are blooming now, all over the place. Asparagus is producing pretty fernlike foliage, the peas have finished. Yesterday was my sister Alvida's 89th birthday, and I went over there before supper for drinks. I gave her my last winter squash for a present.

Earlier this spring I got an e-mail from a woman in Bermuda telling me her daughter, a theater student at Carnegie Mellon, will be coming to the Vineyard to act in an outdoor production of *Romeo and Juliet*. She asked if the attic room where a fellow student of her daughter's had stayed last year was available. The room wasn't available, but I told her if she was desperate, the big attic — hot in summer, cold in winter, and totally rustic — her daughter was welcome to stay there. She thanked me and they made other plans.

I didn't think about it until a short black woman with cornrowed hair showed up with a tall gorgeous daughter and said the room they'd rented didn't work out. Was the big attic still available? The mother, Arlene Brock, is the Ombudsman for Bermuda and went to Harvard at the same time Barack Obama was there and was in one of his classes. Her daughter, Tsilala, is majoring in voice, dance, and theater. They were so thrilled with all the creative energy in this house that I immediately took to them. Last night was Tsilala's first night in the big attic.

Arlene, her mother, gave me a figure of a Gombey dancer, which I just Googled. The figure is made of copper and brass and silver and colored glass beads and ribbons, and is very ornate. It's about six inches tall and, I guess, is intended as a Christmas tree ornament. When she gave me the Gombey I was here at my desk and showed her Kokopelli. While they bear no resemblance one to the other, the Gombey has that same exuberance and feeling that he's urging everyone to go outside and dance and play. What a contrast! And yet they're so alike.

You realize I'm procrastinating. I've got to focus on that book summary. Trouble is, I don't write using an outline, I just start writing and stop when the book is finished, and have no idea what's coming next. My agent, said, "I know you're a pantser [writing by the seat of one's pants], but you'll simply have to make something up, and quickly. "

Much rather write to you. You are so very special.

Much love,

Cynner Qppqy (+ lots more)

CALIFORNIA

Hello Dear Cynner, June 29th, 2012

Summary time? Kokopelli does not mind if he is turned over face down. Seems I placed a very small logo on that reverse side — did you ever find it?

I was busy today doing a white, black, and colored wash today and the white wash is still on the line and needs to be retrieved.

Love, Howie Y
yQy
Y

MARTHA'S VINEYARD

Dear Howie: June 30, 2012

As soon as I got your e-mail I quickly turned Kokopelli over and searched and searched. Then I got out the magnifying glass and found it. There it's been, H YY, all this time, unseen and unappreciated. No longer. But I want him face up because I love his message — "Come out and play!" I heed it. Too often.

When you wrote about the white, black, and colored wash I thought, "Not only is this man of near perfection a scientist, a healer, a musician, a photographer, a sculptor in glass, a diplomat, a humanitarian, an aesthete, a lover, and a philosopher, but he's a painter of watercolors!" A blue wash for sea and sky hung on the line to dry. Then a green wash, for grass and trees. A black wash didn't fit, somehow. Then I re-thought the whole thing. Does a watercolorist paint a white wash?

Air-dried/sun washed sheets and shirts are in the scent category with lavender, baking bread, and new mown grass (despite the poisonous gas).

As you know, I should be writing that summary right now. Ah, procrastination!

This morning I was heading off to get some milk up at Alley's Store, started down the two wide stone steps, conscientiously holding onto the hand rail, when the hand rail snapped in half and I did a semi-somersault onto the stone (ouch!) step. I was in the middle of my tumble when Andrew materialized. Literally just suddenly was there. I don't know where he came from. I said, "I don't need help. I just want to sit here until I decide whether I hurt anywhere or not." Andrew said, "You probably hurt your dignity more than anything else" (true). Once I got up, dusted myself off, found a Band-Aid for a scraped arm, and looked for him to thank him, he was gone. No sign of him. He'd de-materialized. He and Sue have been getting manure from across New Lane, adding compost, rototilling that little patch of ground until it's like something out of a "How To Make A Garden" book. I got the milk then went on to Cottle's Lumber yard and got a seven-foot length of hand rail and propped it up where the broken one was. Chris of the Boat will take the hint and install it without my asking.

Summary, Cynthia ?!?! Get busy!

One more thing. I got the money for the railroad fare. Thank you. I look forward to the train ride and arrival in San Diego.

Much Love, Cynner P

YYY

QQQ

CALIFORNIA

June 30, 2012

Dear Cynner, I was surprised to find your mail on my computer as I thought you were giving your other writing a high priority. Love your mail, as when you have the time. Hope this means that you have a handle on what you were supposed to do. A white wash can be used as a beginning for some watercolor projects but you put a lovely spin on what amounted to my white clothes hanging on the line. I like your interpretation.

Found this photo. I must have been a senior in high school,18, likely. Thank you for telling me about your tumble and that you successfully walked away from it. You were careful and did the right thing, accidents happen. You are precious.

With tender love, Howie

Y

Y Y

Q

Howard Attebery as a high school senior

• • • • •

Cynthia sent Howie the nest from the poppy plant abandoned by the song sparrow.

• • • • •

CALIFORNIA

Dear Cynner, July 2nd, 2012

Nest arrived, after three days of travel, with the afternoon mail. I think the please on the address worked, as it arrived in good condition. I am wonderfully thankful that you did this. Quite a comparison between the dark base plants and the more delicate lighter lining. Amazing that the birds can do all this even for their first time — no one to help them — just what is in them — that inborn innate manual.

One of the first things I noticed was that small piece of bark. It had an area of green/gray that I put under the microscope and it was a lichen. Did you know that you sent me a fantastically gorgeous microscopic garden with sexual reproduction not hidden, but naturally displayed?

Do well Cynner. You sure brighten my lamp. I feel good writing you even though I may be leaving some of those participles dangling and other mistakes as well. But I do not have that manual within for writing — other things — important things seem to be working out just fine.

You are loved,

Howie Q
YY
Y

MARTHA'S VINEYARD

Dear Howie: July 3rd, 2012

You make the nest sound like an amazing receptacle. I'm glad I sent it. I knew there was a seed head from a black-eyed Susan incorporated in the lower part, and I couldn't help but think what an artistic little bird made the nest with its coarse under layer and nice soft bedding. It's so pretty and so delicate. At least some good came of the discovery in the poppy cluster. It's yours to dissect and experiment with. The extent of my knowledge of lichens is that they are a combination of algae and fungi in a symbiotic relationship. That's it. I love knowing that you put that tiny piece of bark under the microscope and found an entire world. It's remarkable that there is so much life on Earth given that so much of reproduction depends on happenstance.

Finished the summary of *Bloodroot,* not an easy task because I never know who the culprit is until I come to the end of the book and think, "Yes! Of course! The villain is So-and-So!" In the summary I have to let the publisher know that I am capable of putting an ending to my story.

Much love, Cynner pyq qyp

One Tuesday evening after my talk aboard the *American Star,* a woman introduced herself to me as Phyllis Dale, and bought copies of every one of the books I had available. While she waited for me to sign the books, Phyllis told about herself. She is a travel agent now, but for 14 years was an entertainer — a "Red Hot Mama," she said — aboard the paddle wheeler *Delta Queen* on the Mississippi River. Since I had been captain of the *Cherry Blossom,* a paddle wheeler on the Potomac River, we were soon reminiscing about boats.

"The American Cruise Line is building a new paddle wheeler called the *Queen of the Mississippi,"* Phyllis told me, "and her maiden voyage is this fall."

I thought for about two seconds. Then took a deep breath. "I'd love to sign up for that cruise."

Phyllis smiled. "The minute they announced the boat was to be built, the first cruise was sold out." Then, apparently seeing the disappointment in my face, she added, "If by any chance a single stateroom becomes available, I'll let you know."

And it did. There was a cancellation, and Phyllis called, Was I still interested?

Was I !

I wrote to Howie. In September, I was going on the maiden voyage of the *Queen of the Mississippi.* I sent him a packet of literature and the trip itinerary.

Chapter 28. No Lichens In My Yard

CALIFORNIA

Dear Cynner, July 4th, 2012

I enjoyed looking over the *Queen of the Mississippi* material and even went to the web site to fill in some of the questions that I wondered about. I believe you made a great choice in selecting that cruise for it's your home on water for seven nights with luxurious accommodations, the Mark Twain Library, and all those other activities. I crossed over the Mississippi river when it was at flood stage. I was on an Army Hospital Train headed for the VA Hospital in Battle Creek Michigan. That river is very impressive.

Love tonight and the tomorrows,

Howie YY

PP

QQ

MARTHA'S VINEYARD

Dear Howie: July 6th, 2012

Not exactly news, but I'm taking a break from my book deadline. I sent the summary and first hundred or so pages off, now have to finish by September 15th. THEN off to California! I don't have a date yet, but will as soon as I hear from daughter Ann.

Much love,
Cynner

YYYYY YYYYY
YYYY YYYY
YYYY YYYY
YYY
YY
YY
Y
YYY YYY
YYY YYY
YYYYY
YYY Y y
Y yyyy yyyyy
yyyyyyyy y yyyyyyyy
yyyyyyyyyyyyyyyyyyy
yyyyyyyyyyyyyy
yyyyyyy
yyy
y

That didn't work as I couldn't get the arrow to pierce the heart, but I think you get the idea.

MARTHA'S VINEYARD

Dear Howie: July 8th, 2012

I've made reservations for my sojourn to the Far West and will send my itinerary. My departure from San Diego is early, but that enables me to get the next to the last boat home.

You sent far too much money for the train, so I splurged and bought a reserved seat. I made the reservation to Old Town San Diego. We'll have a day and a half together, not a lot of time, but enough to sit in your backyard and watch the hummingbirds, the construction of the monstrosity across the canyon, the raptors soaring over it, and a lot of talk.

Much love,
Cynner QQyyPP

Dear Cynner, July 8th, 2012

Thank you for opening the door of your home and letting me in. I see you everywhere. You have a very lovely home and you have the goodness to share it. We have in common the kitchen tile, being of the same size and color but your grout is continuous and white and mine a little jagged and food stained. Your food selection is great, would not surprise me to see you write *The 130-Year Diet.*

I finished my senior year at Napa Union High in 1940 and did not do anything remarkable except I threw the discus 139 feet, which was a school record at the time but that's far surpassed by now. I keep thinking about your *Murder on C-Dock,* and believe it will make a great motion picture and that you can come to Hollywood during a winter season to work on the screen play, and divert yourself to San Diego on a weekend now and then. Wishes can frequently come true.

Your itinerary is now placed on my bulletin board. Good for you on the reserved seat.

A long time ago, I planted three rosemary plants and they did well. Recently, one just went crazy giving a superabundance of blue flowers and then it died. The other two are OK. Mystery?

For years I have driven by a Korean Church in the Clairemont area, not far from my home, and I used to marvel at the large number of cars parked for the Sunday service, and then all of a sudden no cars. Then a sign, CHURCH FOR SALE. I never before heard of a church for sale, then church for sale at reduced price. Then no church for sale sign, then a week later a big canvas type sign saying, "The Potter's House," with a schedule of activities. This morning I went to the 10:30 service, although I am not a Sunday service person, to find out what is going on. Jeremiah 18:3 "Arise, and go down to the potter's house, and there I will cause you to hear my words." It was interesting. Nice padded seats and back rests, open windows with a nice breeze blowing thru, lots of positive energy with the crowd, smiles, handshakes, printed Bibles, cell phones with Bible apps, pads with Bible apps, singing, good feelings. All in all, a positive feeling, but I am not a Sunday worshiper. The pastor talked too loud, and long. His talk was "Liquid Love" on the blood of Jesus Christ. I sort of study and compare religions. I am about a third thru *The Koran* which to me is a very hard read,with many beautiful passages but all too frequently it says, "Kill the Infidels."

Howard Attebery as high school discus champion

Back to earthly things. Seems that all is going well for you, I certainly hope so.

MUCH LOVE,

Howie YYQYY

Chapter 29. What We Haven't Touched

MARTHA'S VINEYARD

Dear Howie: July 9th, 2012

My daughter, Mary Wilder, was a discus thrower at the University of Washington! I have a photo of her ready to hurl it.

She was recruited by the women's crew coach to row, and was headed for the Olympics as a rower when President Carter cancelled the games over the Afghanistan situation. Much as I liked Carter, I always felt he was wrong to destroy the hopes after years and years and years of training of our young athletes for an essentially fruitless gesture.

Good grief, identical tiles, manganese nodules, church-going (I consider myself a lapsed Unitarian), music, birds' nests, grass, lichen, codes — a day and a half isn't going to be enough time to explore what we haven't touched on.

We haven't gotten into politics. I'd better lay it all out before I get to San Diego. I'd been a registered Republican ever since I registered to vote, and stuck with the party diligently, although the last Republican I voted for was Eisenhower. Since everyone on the Island is Democrat, I liked being the odd one out. Until, hearing on NPR an interview on the Diane Rheim Show with some respected Republicans essentially saying Rush Limbaugh was spokesman for the party, this in response to his saying he hoped Obama would fail. I was in my car, listening on the car radio. I did a U-turn, screeched to

Mary Wilder Stoertz practicing discus throw in West Virginia

a halt in front of Town Hall, pounded up the steps, and re-registered as a Democrat. I have a fluorescent orange shirt with OBAMA on it in fluorescent blue. Anyway, that's where I stand. I think he's doing the right things to turn the economy around, and I think he inherited a mess, and I'm really aggravated with the Republican Party that I used to belong to with pride, for not doing what the two-party system was set up to do, namely two differing viewpoints, debate and compromise, working for the good of we the people. Not this "our party and to hell with the public."

Well, Kokopelli is enticing me off to bed. To sleep, not to play.

Much love.

Wow — discus thrower!!!

Much love still,

Cynner

CALIFORNIA

Dear Cynner: July 10th, 2012

While turning on the computer just now 12 parrots flew by giving the chatter that always accompanies their flight. They are not rare here, but are permanent residents, inhabiting this coastal area and I see them at Point Loma, Ocean beach, and Clairemont. I do not know how many flocks, but I think not many.

I attended Santa Rosa City College for two years and was active with the discus and javelin. I did well so that I was invited to the state meet at UC Berkeley. I did not finish in the top 3, but it is a remembered meet in that Warmerdam set a world record in the pole vault and as I was walking off the field a gentleman introduced himself, he was Dr.Sproul, Provost of the university, and he asked me how I did and I said I was not a winner and he said "If you are here you are a winner."

Well this is an introduction to what I started to tell you initially. The Dean at SRCC called me to his office, he was a Stanford graduate, and wanted me to go to Stanford on an athletic scholarship for CREW. Just go down and enroll, tuition would be negated and work could be provided for room and board. I went to UC Berkeley instead. One of my life's big mistakes. I was thinking about Mary Wilder, discus to crew. Tall, thin, but muscular, great arm strength, coordinated —fits, doesn't it?

Ditto on your politics, I was born a Democrat. Rush Limbaugh is turning into an asset for the Democrats.

Love,

Howie YppY QQ

MARTHA'S VINEYARD

Dear Howie: July 11th, 2012

These connections are astonishing. Mary Wilder went to the University of Washington on an athletic scholarship, starting with discus, switching to crew. The first connection — actually, it probably wasn't the first — was your photo of Sedona and Mary Wilder's "Meeting My Father in Sedona." Her death, too young. Paul's death, too young. Mark's *Cactus on Mars,* Doug's critiquing of Mars research proposals and his panoramic photo of Mars showing a place that ought to have cactus. Manganese nodules — how many individuals in the world own manganese nodules?! On and on, now it's from discus to crew. How many individuals can claim that combination! What are we going to uncover when we meet again in September?

I can't remember whether it was pumpkin, squash, or cantaloupe that I planted over the propane tank. Whatever they are, they're bearing fruit, about tennis-ball-size right now, and I can hardly wait to see whether they end up orange, yellow, green, or tan. The song sparrow is back on the vegetable garden fence, singing. I don't know what's nesting in the bluebird box, but something's chirping in there right now. Should I clean out the nesting box at some time? Or just leave it alone?

Much love,
Cynner PPPPPPPPPPPPPPPPPPPPPPPPP

CALIFORNIA

Hello Dear One, July 12th, 2012

Have been reading *The Prophet,* and Gibran wrote: "And now you ask in your heart, 'How shall we distinguish that which is good in pleasure from that which is not good?' Go to your fields and your gardens and you shall learn that it is the pleasure of the bee to gather honey of the flower, but it also the pleasure of the flower to yield its honey to the bee. For to the bee a flower is a fountain of life. And to the flower a bee is a messenger of love. And to both, bee and flower, the giving and receiving of pleasure is a need and an ecstasy. People . . . be in your pleasure like the flowers and the bees."

Sending love by a messenger named,
Howie pPpPpPpPQ
******Goodnight Cynner*******

Chapter 30. A Raft of Careers

MARTHA'S VINEYARD

Dear Howie: July 13th, 2012

The DVD with your guided tour of your house came in today's mail along with a (small) royalty check from my publisher. A good day's mail. Before I did anything else, I hauled out my little DVD player and visited 4352 Piper Street. I love hearing your voice and picturing you cooking eggs, working on your computer, sitting in the director's chairs (they are comfortable), and dining on paper plates (paper plates? Oh, Howie!)

Yesterday's mail brought the account of your photography career. You continue to amaze me. I'd assumed, back in February when we first re-connected, that your career had been as a public service dentist. When I finally located you through the California Dental Association they listed you as getting your license in 1945 and giving it up in 1988. Then I find that you'd had a career, not only as dentist, but as microbiologist with a raft of publications including "Anaerobic Infections." Your interests in glass on a high technical level, grasses, plants, natural science guide, birds (I knew about that), photography, discus throwing (!) and now I find you had an entire career in photography, not simply a casual interest. What next? I look forward to grilling you in September. I love finding out layer after layer. Don't you feel sorry for people who sit in front of a TV set and vegetate! Think of all the remarkable things there are to see and do and learn.

The house is full of people this weekend. I overbooked by mistake. Downstairs in Aunt's Room are a mother and daughter from Poland, here for a week. The mother can barely speak English, but tries, the daughter is pretty fluent. When the mother apologizes I tell her I can't speak any Polish at all. An illiterate American with one language. In addition, Tsilala, the Shakespearean actress and student at Carnegie Mellon, is in the Big Attic, and the Polly Hill Arboretum intern is in the Porch Chamber.

I will be glad when I get the house back to myself again — this weekend is a bit much.

I procrastinate. Back to *Bloodroot.* Must finish by September 15th.

Much love,

Q to you, too!

And lots of ys and ps

CALIFORNIA

Dear Cynner, July 19th, 2012

Mark is doing a retreat this weekend, I think he said, at a Buddhist monastery and the monks make flutes which is a definite plus. [Grandson] Luke is having a great time in China with his work, night clubbing and he just sent pictures of his recent deep-jungle adventure and hiking in a remote region of the Great Wall of China, and he and his buddies slept in one of the towers. [Granddaughter] Sophia is at a summer camp just having returned from Peru? on a Habitat construction project. I guess Jennifer is at home/office taking care of her Pilates clients. Howie is at home doing what has to be done around the house and he prepared the air-conditioned room for sleeping as the hot weather has arrived.

I receive your e-mails of Cynthia's activities, and that is very nice of you, to see how she is involved in the community. She does well, with big ticket items and all those small but important things that take time.

Howie's wish is that while Daphne is on your lap you give him a thought now and then and that would be precious and all that is needed.

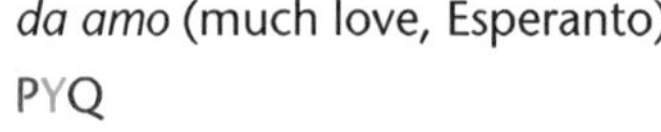

da amo (much love, Esperanto)
PYQ

MARTHA'S VINEYARD

Dear Howie: July 19th, 2012

Here's my review of Tsilala's performance.

In person, she is the most feminine of femmes, yet when she came on stage this evening — the very first character in the all-woman production of *Romeo and Juliet,* she opened the play — she was the most regal and masculine of Princes, striding with confidence, head up, a royal personage. The stage is a woodsy amphitheater. I am not influenced by the fact that Tsilala lives here at the Cleaveland House, so you can accept this as unbiased. She was the best of the performers in the play, and they were all quite good. She was totally believable, totally royal, you could hear every word she spoke, she was The Prince, she understood and respected the audience.

Her second role was in *Twelfth Night,* where she played Olivia.

Here's Tsilala as Olivia in *Twelfth Night.*

We celebrated back at the Cleaveland House with sparkling grape juice — Tsilala, Chris Cull (who lives on the boat), Lynn Christoffers (the photographer), and me.

She's a joy to have around, although she's not around much with rehearsals and productions for two plays.

I look forward to seeing her name in Bright Lights.

I promise to write and catch you up with all the activities around here. I would like a bit of peace and quiet!

Much, much love,

Cynner PPYYQQ
QQYYPP

MARTHA'S VINEYARD

Dear Howie: July 20th, 2012

It's much too late, but I've been so remiss in writing that I don't want to go to bed without saying goodnight to you.

This has been a busy week, and I'll be glad to have a bit of quiet. Sunday's program at the Vineyard Haven Library was great. About 60-70 people showed up, and it was one of those times when the audience was so receptive I could practically feed on their energy. Then Tuesday afternoon was my gig on the *American Star.* Wednesday, I went to Falmouth aboard the Island Queen for a talk at the library. It's the first time I've gone on that boat, as I usually go on the Steamship Authority ferries to Woods Hole. This felt more like a real vessel where you could sit and see the water spreading out from the bow. On the way back a storm was threatening, so they took off promptly and moved swiftly. Wonderful gray-black clouds behind us, whitecaps on the Sound, and a nice feeling of impending storm. Lightning. Wind. Lynn was at the dock to take photos.

I do have to get to bed. Despite how dreadful I'm being about writing, there aren't many hours when you're not in my thoughts. I look forward to Mark and Jennifer's visit when I will be able to talk to them about you and feel that much closer.

Good night, good night! Parting is such sweet sorrow,
That I shall say good night till it be morrow.

Much love,

Cynner QQQQQQpy

Chapter 31. The Attack Bird

MARTHA'S VINEYARD

Dear Howie: July 21st, 2012

For the past four days a bird has been hurling himself (or herself) against one of the windows in the Woodshed. He flutters up to the gutter, then drops down and whacks his head or his wings, I can't tell what, but it's a solid "thump!" and he does it over, and over, and over again.

What is going on? The bird is speckled brown and black, medium size, about the size of a catbird, and it may be a song sparrow, because I hear one singing nearby. I turned on the sprinkler to deter him, but that didn't seem to work. I tried to open the window, in case he wants to come in and build a nest in one of the plants, but the window is painted shut. I don't think it's because he sees his reflection and thinks it's a challenger he needs to attack. He does this pretty much all day long even when there must not be a good reflection of his rival. I'm afraid he's going to drive himself crazy. Do you have any suggestions?

Much, much love,

CynnerPPPPPP

CALIFORNIA

Dear Cynner: July 21st, 2012

Most likely that is a male bird, and as this is the season of love, territorial behavior is strongly displayed.

He sees a reflection and believes it to be a competitor and wants to rule the area. He has the inclination to keep making belligerent moves to keep the territory for his own. You can cover the window on the outside with paper or such, or if it is a big window tape some aluminum foil strips so that they blow around in the breeze making a disturbing noise and give off annoying distractions.

One day a mockingbird was repeatedly attacking the outside rear view mirror of my car. I threw a towel over the mirror to cover it upand that was the end of that behavior.

Hope your day went remarkably well and that oodles of nice things are happening at your home.

호위의 사랑 (Love from Howie in Korean)

PPYYQQ

MARTHA'S VINEYARD

Dear Howie: July 21st, 2012

Right on! I went out and taped aluminum foil strips over two of the panes, then took a picture, and what did I see but some female in a rose-colored shirt trespassing on MY territory. I guess I'd better cover all the panes. I had no idea they were so mirror-like. That poor bird! I think my camera needs another shot of WD-40, but you get the idea.

Much, much love,

Cynner pPP qQQ yYY (waltz time)

Daphne just stepped on a few other keys. Maybe she knows something?

Five windows, six over six panes + nine panes in the door = 69 (Hmmmm. . .)

CALIFORNIA

Dear Cynner: July 21st, 2012

I would hope that the bird will give up and let his menace reign.

Muito amor, Howie (Portuguese) YppY*******Q

MARTHA'S VINEYARD

Dear Howie: July 22nd, 2012

Quick note to let you know that blocking the window worked — I taped half-sheets of paper on each of the panes of the window the bird was attacking, and he seems to have given up. I hope he didn't suffer brain damage from the pounding he was giving the window.

Much love,

Cynner YPPY

MARTHA'S VINEYARD

Dear Howie: July 24th, 2012

You wondered about "Killer" In the sales report for our Martha's Vineyard guidebook that I sent. The translation is: I'm "Killer Riggs." Lynn, the photographer and Chief Financial Officer, is "TLC." Step came up with both noms de guerre. Since Lynn is mild mannered, TLC probably translates to Tender Loving Care. "Step" comes, of course, from Stephen.

Much, much love,

Cynner the Exhausted aka Killer Riggs

But not too exhausted to sign off with GGGGGGGPPPPPPPPPYYYYYYYYY

• • • • •

On July 26, Mark Attebery e-mailed that he and his wife, Jennifer, would be arriving the following afternoon on the fast ferry. "We'll be easy to spot," he wrote. "I'll be rolling a large, black road-case containing musical instruments and gear."

Cynthia wrote back: "I'll be there at the Oak Bluffs dock — I'm easy to spot, too, I'm six feet tall and have gray/white hair and am probably wearing a short-sleeved blue shirt and light-colored pants with dirty knees from weeding the garden."

Mark had agreed to play his flutes for an informal gathering at the Cleaveland House during their visit to the Island. So Cynthia invited a group over for Saturday evening.

• • • • •

CALIFORNIA

Greetings Cynner: July 26th, 2012

Again it is a thanks to Johnny, this time for making your birthday card, with the photo of a two-year old Cynner and a great appreciation to Cynner for sending it to me. It is a most endearing photograph and to speak plainly and truthfully as soon as my eyes saw her eyes and then took in the face, I automatically, and lovingly, placed two kisses on that photo.

I am much appreciative of you seeing Mark and Jennifer. You are a wonderfully generous person and a great asset to your community for all your good works and words. Might I say more — I am elegantly attracted to what is inside your head - your intellect — sounds better than brain, but it is your brain and what you have done with it, that warms me.

Howie *maite askoz* (Much love from Howie in Basque) QPYYPQ

MARTHA'S VINEYARD

Dear Howie: July 27th, 2012

Mark and Jennifer arrive this afternoon on the fast ferry from Quonset, Rhode Island. I've never taken that ferry, and look forward to hearing about it. He's going to have an enthusiastic audience on Saturday. I invited 30 people, and probably 15 will show up.

They will have a fellow guest, Neil Clifford, a sculptor from Toronto. He has an exhibit here at the Granary Gallery, a short walk from here. I traded his stay here for a sculpture of a horse's head named "Bronze Age," which I like a lot. His work is detailed and accurate, yet it's got a wonderful freedom to it. I'll send you a photo.

From me to you — your intellect, your humor, your ethics, your sensitivity, your romanticism are wildly attractive to me. I am awed by your brainpower, your interests, your accomplishments, your common sense, and feel quite humble compared to you. I wish I could keep up with you. I continue to be astonished by the multitude of our connections and interests, and feel reassured that when we meet, you won't be expecting either that cute two-year-old or a clueless co-ed. I'm marked by a pretty good life with wrinkles and folds where they ought to be.

I stopped this in the middle to make beds, and now I look at my watch, Mark and Jennifer have been on the boat for 15 minutes, and will be arriving in a little over an hour. Next time I write, they'll be here.

Much, much love,

Cynner PYQ. . . . .

• • • • •

Mark called his dad to let him know that he and Jennifer had arrived safely on the Vineyard. The three, Mark, Jennifer, and Cynthia, were sitting by the fish pond when they made the call. Cynthia and Howard had never talked to one another on the phone. After Mark greeted his dad, he handed the phone to Cynthia.

• • • • •

MARTHA'S VINEYARD

Dear Howie: July 28th, 2012

Your two kids, Mark and Jennifer, laughed when I was on the phone trying to think of something of great consequence to say to you in our very first phone call. I was tongue-tied. Really dopey! They kept saying "You two are like teenagers."

They are super people and I love having them here. They fit in as though they've been part of my weird establishment forever.

(Gotta run downstairs to check the cheesecake I'm baking for Mark's concert tonight — back in a second). . .

(Needs another five minutes)

Neil Clifford, the sculptor, is the same age as Mark and Jennifer, and the three of them are getting along famously. They took my rubbish to the dump this morning. Mark unloaded all my groceries from the car and he and Jennifer delivered a load of paper bags to the WT Library book sale for me. Jennifer came home with some books and ensconced herself in Chris Cull's new hammock under the maple trees. (Gotta check the cheesecake, the timer went off)

(Done!)

Galit, a B&B guest who is here for a yoga workshop, walked up to the Farmers' Market this morning and came back with an orchid plant that's now on the table with Bronze

Age and the Manganese Nodule. Mark is practicing something that sounds as though two musicians are playing. Amazing. And beautiful. This place is getting to be a musical/literary/ art salon. His flute playing is so beautiful to hear. He's downstairs in the dining room, where we have a sort of auditorium set up for tonight.

Now I really do have to get back to my writing.

Much love, and wish you were here to join us.

Cynner QQ PP YY
QQ PP YY
QQ PP YY

Chapter 32. A Magical Performance

CALIFORNIA

Dear Cynner, July 28th, 2012

Good to find that things and people are doing well at your home. I will miss your cheesecake and the comradery before and after the musical program.

Today I painted the front door and polished the brass kick plate. I walked along the San Diego River at Mission Valley and could only identify about half of the plants, that a few years ago all were known to me. Surprising no birds on the water or in the greenery, but I did see a blue darner, two sulfurs chasing each other, and a great number of ants.

Love,

Howie

y
y y
y y
y Q y
y y
y y
y

MARTHA'S VINEYARD

Dear Howie: July 29th, 2012

Mark's performance last evening was magical. About 20 people came, and were enthralled by his music, his performance, and his charm. They applauded vigorously with a few "Bravos!" thrown in. When he finished a magnificent concert with a wide variety of pieces ranging from Bach to his own compositions, from lovely, lyrical pieces to ones that had us tapping our feet, we demanded an encore. He performed a spirited piece with an engaging beginning, middle, and climactic end, a piece that sounded as though there were three or four musicians playing along with him. He told us later that the piece was entirely impromptu. He'd made it up on the spot. "That's what composers do," he told me.

Five of us, Mark and Jennifer, Neil, Galit, and I, sat around afterward reviewing Mark's performance and showering him with accolades. The thunderstorm that had been threatening all afternoon broke while we were sitting there, with lightning and thunder. A dramatic end to a superb evening.

Mark's mastery of that remarkable machine is astonishing. It repeats what he's played after a pause of a few seconds. He plays along with the repeated portion, and it's layered, the first portion with the second played along on top of it, and a third played along with the first and second, almost like a round. His ability to synchronize all the disparate pieces and have it come out as a harmonious whole is simply, . . . well simply amazing. I wish 50 people had been here to experience the music instead of a mere 20. Wonderful, just wonderful.

I'm enjoying their company and will be sorry when they leave. This afternoon we are going to walk to the Granary Gallery to see Neil Clifford's opening. Neil and Mark and Jennifer seem to have hit it off. We are all barefoot and are dining together on stuff we just somehow pull together.

You didn't need anything more to increase my admiration and awe of you, but Mark, as your ambassador, has opened up an entirely new facet of you that I love. What a joy to have such a son. What a credit to your upbringing. And just the right daughter-in-law, too.

I can't thank you enough for urging him and Jennifer to visit.

You are a most remarkable man.

Much, much love,

Cynner

P
PyP
Py yP
Py yP
Py Q yP
Py yP
Py yP
PyP
P

CALIFORNIA

Dear Cynner, July 29th, 2012

You paint a very nice picture of what living is all about. I am happy that peace, harmony, understanding, respect and fellowship is on one beautiful spot of land — wishes go for it to be infective and become world wide.

I have been in a reflective mood today. Did the minimal. Used my eyes in the backyard. My hands cooking.

Ears listened to music.

Do have a successful week writing.

Love and Thank You for Giving,

Howie PPPPyyyyyQ

MARTHA'S VINEYARD

Dear Howie: July 30th, 2012

Monday morning and a beautiful clear blue-sky day when all's well. Jennifer and Galit, the B&B guest in the downstairs room, went off to a yoga class. They thought it was to start at 7:30 and found out at 5 of 7:00 that it actually started at 7:00, so Mark drove them and got them there a few minutes late. They'll walk home, as it's only a mile from here. We were just sitting at the kitchen table, Mark and I, talking about creativity and the creative process. At the moment we have Mark, the musician; Neil, the sculptor; Jennifer, the dancer; Galit, the yoga soon-to-be-teacher; Tsilala, the Shakespearean actress, dancer, and singer; and Steve, a lawyer (B&B guest) who's taking a writing workshop called "Writing from the Heart." And me, of course, writing. Where does all this incredible creative energy come from? It all feeds into this house, which hums with it.

As we left the kitchen table, me to write, Mark to sit out by the fish pond, he said, "Say hi to my Dad," knowing I would come upstairs and write to you before I settled down to that looming deadline.

Funny (and embarrassing) comedy of errors yesterday. The Granary Gallery had a gallery opening for Neil and three other artists and he was getting ready to leave. Steve, a B&B guest, appeared on a bicycle. I'd booked him in the Indian Room, which has a small single bed, an ancient sleigh bed with solid head and foot-board. I'd put Neil in the West Room, which has a double bed. When Steve appeared, I realized the bed in the Indian Room would never accommodate him. He must be 6-ft 5-in and 250 pounds. Big. While I was cogitating about switching rooms, Mark appeared, and I introduced him to Steve as Neil. (I guess you can follow this. I'm not sure I can.) I said to Mark, "Neil, I'll move you into the Indian Room." Mark, ever obliging, just having awakened from a nap, already convinced that most of what goes on in this house has a surreal aspect that sort of appeals to him, said, "Okay," as he eyed the obviously too small bed. "I'll just tell Jennifer and we'll move." Whereupon I realized what I'd just done. "No, no, no!" In the meantime, Neil, still in his room, could hear himself being introduced to Steve, and was enthralled by the idea. Anyway, all are teasing me, of course. Mark and Jennifer sat in on my Sunday Writers, Neil came in late and introduced himself to Mark, saying, "Nice to meet you, Neil."

Mark, Neil, and I had supper after the Sunday Writers, about 10 pm. Oven-cooked rice and chicken, and beets and beet greens from the garden. Everyone else had gone to bed, and the three of us sat around the kitchen table talking and talking, a regular college dorm bull session on the meaning of life, touching on religion and love until I faded out and left. When I got up this morning, Mark and Neil had cleaned up the mess in the kitchen and Mark had already started the morning coffee.

It's so lovely out, it's tempting to put off writing, telling myself I'll surely be able to write a hundred pages before September 15th. After all, it isn't even August yet. And Kokopelli, who's holding down a stack of papers I ought to look through, is beckoning. "Come out and play!"

I'll resist both of you.

Much love,

Cynner QQQQQQQQQ

CALIFORNIA

Dear Cynner: July 30th, 2012

I do not want you to miss your train ride, so keep those pages flowing. I think this will be a great week for your literary creation.

I was digging in the backyard and sweet alyssum was placed in the holes.

I am so pleased to get that great feedback on Mark's performance.

Mark sent me a card not long ago that stated, "I AM BECAUSE YOU ARE."

I cannot top your rainbow Q's, so am sending it back by mental telepathy — real hard.

Ást frá Howie Love from Howie in Icelandic

PPYYQQ

PPYYQQ Good Night Sweet

MARTHA'S VINEYARD

Dear Howie: July 31st, 2012

A wonderful, wonderful visit from Mark and Jennifer. The time went much too quickly and I felt regret at taking them to the boat. They are two of the nicest people imaginable.

They both fit in with whatever was going on, whether it was quiet with nothing going on, or rowdy, which it was last night. Neil Clifford, the sculptor, decided to make dinner, and harvested beets and Swiss chard. I'd bought two steaks at half-price at Cronig's, Mark and Jennifer contributed a container of clam chowder. Neil was afraid he'd cooked too much, but Galit, the yoga person, joined us. Then Lynn, the photographer, joined us, too. While Neil slaved over the stove, we sat around the kitchen drinking Scotch and gin and tonic (not mixed together) and talked about I don't know what. We'd just sat down to eat when Tsilala appeared and we insisted that she join us, so we squashed ourselves around the table in the cookroom. A royal meal. I found a bottle of red wine in the east garden, the little garden outside the kitchen. The bottle was hidden among wild ginger and fern and the label was pretty much gone. So we had that. We discussed the meaning of life, I launched into my Lecture #14, titled "Jesus was Gay," and the rest listened politely and a discussion followed.

Jennifer claimed this morning to have a hangover, but I think that was an exaggeration.

I think they had a good time. I certainly did with them. I loved seeing expressions and gestures of Mark's that brought back memories of yours, long ago. Thank you so very much for having them visit. I hope they'll come back in the off season when things quiet down a bit. This was great fun and busy, the off season is more contemplative, with enough going on of interest, still.

Much love,

Cynner PY PY PY
QP QP QP
QY QY QY

MARTHA'S VINEYARD

Dear Howie: July 31st, 2012

I forgot to tell you about the finale to last evening's supper. Since neither Mark and Jennifer nor Neil could attend either of Tsilala's performances in *Romeo and Juliet* and *Twelfth Night,* we prevailed upon her to give us an al fresco performance. The moon was almost full, riding high. We turned on the outside entry light, Tsilala stood at the top of the steps, and we gathered on the grass below. First she performed her two soliloquies as the prince in *Romeo and Juliet,* then after we demanded an encore, she ducked into the entry door and came out as the silly and love struck Olivia in *Twelfth Night.* A magical end to our evening. Dark night, bright moon, dew-wet grass, cool evening, quiet. The entry light spotlighting her, the shingled wall her backdrop.

Much love,

Sweet Cyn yyyyyyyyyyyyyypq

CALIFORNIA

Dear Cynner, July 31st, 2012

I really appreciate your writings telling me what has gone on during M & J visit. I am glad that you enjoyed them both. I think that they are cool, but how could I think otherwise. Tsilala is a name I never came across before. Google says it means "celestial" and it came from the Georgian language.

I keep thinking about the rainbow colored Q's that you sent me. So charming and so beautiful and so sensual. I like to recall them in that magic moment between awake and sleep. And that block of colored P's, Y's, and Q's that you sent me today is outstanding and I can appreciate the thought and time it took to do this.

I gardened today, now have about 70 small plants in the soil and will finish it tomorrow.

Love. LOVE

Howie PYQQQQQQQ

CALIFORNIA

Dear Sweet Cynner: August 4th, 2012

I am sending you a photograph that is on the iPad and it is of Teddy, given to me 90 years ago as a birth gift from my uncle Henry. I busted the nose so many times that only the stuffing showed and my mother reconstructed it from a piece of clothing that I no longer wore and she sewed in the nostrils and smiling lips. She patched the worn-out feet and paws. The pants and jacket she made out of a my worn-out pajamas. The button shoe eyes are from my Grandmother's wedding shoe.

Howard with Teddy, the bear given to him when he was born

One day my neighbors Dot and Fred visited and Dot saw the badly worn body parts underneath the coat and she asked if she could take Teddy home with her and do some repair. She later returned with Teddy sporting a white turtleneck sweater. Dot and Fred are natives of MA, and are known for good works that they perform.

"Sometimes," said Pooh, "the smallest things take up the most room in your heart." A.A. Milne.

You introduced me to Pooh Bear

This is recent photo but I do not feel as old as I look.

Love, love, LOVE

Howie pppppYQ

MARTHA'S VINEYARD

Dear Howie: August 4th, 2012

You look superb! I am more than delighted to have the photo of you and Teddy. I love your looks and wouldn't want you to look a bit different. You're just the right age, both inside and out. I love your strong nose. I love your strong chin. I love your elegant forehead. You look perfect to me. Handsome and distinguished and with character. I love your battle scars. You'd hardly be human without them. Thank you, thank you for sending the photo! I've asked Lynn to print it for me because my printer does only black and white. I'm so pleased. (I wouldn't have minded if you'd looked funny.)

Much love,

Cynner q. . . .

p . . . .

y . . . .

MARTHA'S VINEYARD

Dear Howie: August 4th, 2012

This had to be a separate e-mail because responding to getting the photo of you deserved its own reply.

About Teddy. I had Bear. His paws wore out and my grandmother sewed socks over the worn out paws. I seem to recall he was stuffed with sawdust. He lost an eye, and all I wanted for Christmas that year was for Bear to have a new eye. Christmas morning, he was under the tree with a diagonal bandage on his head covering where his eye was. I can still remember the thrill of removing the bandage and seeing Bear's new eye. I don't know what happened to him and envy your still having Teddy. What a grand part of our childhoods.

I'd forgotten that I'd introduced you to Winnie-the-Pooh. One of my favorite poems is the one about the old sailor who was shipwrecked and lived on an island for weeks, and he wanted a hat and he wanted some breeks . . . and all the projects he started and didn't finish . . . and so in the end he did nothing at all, but bask on the shingle wrapped up in a shawl.

Me and my deadline, to a T.

Back to work.

I LOVE having your photo.

Cynner PPPPPPP

CALIFORNIA

Dear August 6th, 2012

Sweet, Sweet

Cynner:

From *The Yearling,* "I had me a 'coon when I were a young un," he said. "Hit were gentle as a kitten for two yare. Then one day hit bit a chunk outen my shin." He spat into the fire, "This un'll grow up to bite. Hit's 'coon nature."

I have had a good day and I hope you have joined me. It is my nature to try to have a good day.

Love, Love,

Howie ROYGBIV

YY

PP

QQ

MARTHA'S VINEYARD

Dear Howie: August 6th, 2012

You've stumped me! The best I can do with ROYGBIV is VIGOR BY BIG IVORY. Maybe that works? I had to double it, as you can tell.

Much love, and when I can figure it out, I'll reciprocate. (I think.)

I got it! Red Orange Yellow. . . Good heavens, I'm dense!!!!!

Much more love,

Cynner With VIGOR !

qpy pyq yqp

Chapter 33. Broad Shoulders

CALIFORNIA

Dear Cynner, August 8th, 2012

My Happy-Happy times are when I am reading your emails and when I am writing you. My thoughts used to be then, but it is now that and gives me tissue movement — heart rate increase and an important other, even now as I write.

Rainbows by Khalil Gibran

If I could catch a rainbow
I would do it just for you.
And share with you its beauty
On the days you're feeling blue.
If I could build a mountain
You could call your very own.
A place to find serenity
A place to be alone.
If I could take your troubles
I would toss them in the sea.
But all these things I'm finding
are impossible for me,
I cannot build a mountain
Or catch a rainbow fair
But let me be...what I know best,
a friend that's always there.

A friend for sure but I want to be more than that: an Admirer, Confidant, Helper, Soother, Spoiler,,,,...

....Lover.....

LOVE, It is 5 PM so you are getting a big hug now!

Some more PPPPPPPPPP

• • • • •

Cynthia was invited to give a talk on Cuttyhunk, the outermost island in the Elizabeth Island chain, less than a square mile in area. The Elizabeth Islands lie between Martha's Vineyard and the mainland. The occasion was a fundraiser for the island's tiny library.

• • • • •

MARTHA'S VINEYARD

Dearest Howie: August 8th, 2012

Just got back from Cuttyhunk, left my shoes by the door and came straight upstairs to my computer to report in to you. A perfect afternoon and evening. Everything went well. My Vineyard contingent was pleased with the boat ride and the visit to the far away island and the little golf carts that ferried us and the great audience — someone counted 34 people in attendance. Cuttyhunk has a winter population of 18 people. Summer swells to 400. I spoke in town hall for the library fundraiser. The library is next door and the school is next to the library. The library is 750 square feet and has 10,000 books. Amazing! The school is one room with two students, a sister and brother, 1st and 3rd grade. They're raising money to expand the library and shore up its foundation and have run into a bureaucracy that doesn't understand they don't need a separate reading room, they don't need toilets. They honestly don't need handicap access. With a winter population of 18 ?!? They put out nice refreshments afterwards, grapes, crackers and good cheeses, wine, and lemonade. And a pizza cut into small pieces. Where they got all that, I can't imagine. A boat runs there once a day from New Bedford. The ride back to Menemsha was spectacular. The sunset was behind us, and just as we pulled into the Menemsha fuel dock, dozens and dozens and dozens of people were gathered on the beach to watch the sunset. This happens every night in summer. They applaud if the sun does its thing in the right way. When we walked from the fuel dock to the beach, the sun was a half disk on the horizon, there was a great air of expectancy, a great hush, and the sun slipped lower and lower and then that was it, to loud applause and cheers of Bravo!. Perfect weather on the boat, coming and going. A great air of festivity. The audience was great and laughed at everything they were supposed to laugh at and asked good questions and said nice things afterwards. What a great experience! Cuttyhunk is about a mile and a half long by three-quarters of a mile wide. The boat trip was a little more than a half hour on fairly calm seas, and everyone had such a great time.

Thank you for the hourly hugs. That helped.

Much love, gotta eat something now, since cheese nibbles isn't quite enough.

Still more love,

Cynner the Fearless!

QQQQQQQQQQQQQQQQQQQQQQQQQQQQQQQQQQQQQQQQQQQQQQQQQ
QQQQQQQQQQQQQQQQQQQQQQQQQQQQQQQQQQQQQQQQ

MARTHA'S VINEYARD

Dear Howie: August 8th, 2012

Thank you for the poem. Thank you for being my friend, admirer, confidant, helper, soother, spoiler, and lover. I am in dire need of all and will do my best to reciprocate.

Much, much love, Cynner

All the Ys in the dictionary, all the Ps in the encyclopedia, all the Qs in the universe.

MARTHA'S VINEYARD

Dear Howie: August 9th, 2012

I'm third from the right, hands clasped on my knees.

I didn't want the spray curtains on the boat closed, so when I got home my face and hair were all salty from the spray. While I was eating a late supper I kept running my fingers down the side of my face and licked off the salt. A shame to shower it all away. On an occasion like this I miss the boating life.

More later. Much love.

The Cynner MMMMM
YYYYYYYYYY
PPPPPPPPPPPP
QQQQQQQQQQ

The M gives us more to work with.

Passengers on the ferry to Cuttyhunk were Wednesday Writers and friends, ***photo by Lynn Christoffers***

Chapter 34. A Program Called *The Moth*

MARTHA'S VINEYARD

Dear Howie: August 9th, 2012

A program on NPR called *The Moth*, where people tell stories about a life-changing event, is coming to Martha's Vineyard this weekend. Someone told them about our story, and of course *The Moth* decided this is a romance the entire world should hear about. On Monday, five of us will tell our stories at Union Chapel in Oak Bluffs. I wrote a script, with a bit of artistic license, and am sending it to you. I hope this pleases you and doesn't embarrass you.

Wish me luck.

Much love,

Cynner

Minding my ps and qs, and even my ys

CALIFORNIA

Dear Cynner. August 9th, 2012

I am familiar with the program. NPR is my favorite radio station, and the radio I have in my kitchen, is permanently tuned to 89.5. On occasion I have heard *The Moth,* a very touching segment that brings out bits of life in an inspirational manner.

I am pleased with your script and am in no way embarrassed. Any project that joins the names Cynthia and Howie comes to me with great favor.

Sure I wish you luck and always good wishes in all that you do, and you do a lot.

LOVE,

Howie PYQ's

MARTHA'S VINEYARD

Dear Howie: August 11, 2012

I wrote to my kids telling them about *The Moth* story. This back from William, the one teaching English in Korea. His wife, Fujiko, is Japanese, and they have two daughters, Masha and Sayaka, born in Russia, who speak Japanese, Russian, English, and now Korean. And I limp along in English, period. We are so illiterate in this country. I'm in awe of those two granddaughters, 14 and 11. I thought you might like to see what William, my eldest, wrote.

Much love, Cynner YYYYYYYYYYYYYYYYYY
You're far more than I deserve, despite what William says.

Wow, Mama! This is such a wonderful story! I never knew that you were sorting plankton at Scripps. Amazing how you met such a wonderful person, headed great places, with such a decent, caring character. Amazing... just 18! It makes a grand story, and a mystery, and, yes, a romance! I think you give hope to people in their "late teens."

It also makes me think on "destiny." Actually, I've come to believe in destiny, simply by seeing the way things unfold, connect, and later reconnect — as if they were being "led" by destiny.

I think many romances go somehow in a wrong direction, and a person somehow changes, and somehow sells their soul deep inside, or their "inner child" is somehow lost, repressed, huddling. All my life I've tried to make sure I never lost that, but stayed in touch with my own true inner self.

But of course, seeing me outside, people don't realize that. We can't know what people's souls, or inner selves, are like from the outside. Even if we know them for a long time.

Anyway, I guess this "destiny" or whatever it is (it's really not "God" — because that's something different — "destiny" is not providential or moralistic) allows for other stuff to come in between. It's kind of an "eventual" kind of thing, I guess...

Gosh, of course, I'm here, and that's very real, and of course there's Mary and James and Ann and Robert and all their lovely families.

You know, Mama, I think of Mary all the time. To me she's really "eternal." I always see her smiling face, feel her warm heart, her happy and uplifted mood. I don't think anything is somehow "lost." Mary has meant so much to me, and to so many people. The world is much more wonderful because of her.

It's so beautiful, how you and Howie found each other again. He's perhaps the man you really deserved. I hope you have a very happy time together! It makes such a beautiful, uplifting story. I wish you luck!

Sincerely, William

CALIFORNIA

Dear Precious Cynner: August 11, 2012

I looked out from my window at 1 AM this morning. I am up at this time briefly for pill time, and saw a crescent moon with Venus below and somewhat to the left. I did not stick around to see the Perseid shower which is to be at a maximum tonight — they say 60 an hour. I will look for it.

Getting back in bed I thought about the Valley of the Moon, I lived there for a year, I think it was in 1948 as I worked for the Sonoma County Health Department. Glen Ellen was the name of the little berg and my house was alongside a stream that was flanked by laurel trees. Maybe 50 people at most resided there. Raccoons were numerous and a sport of the natives was to go 'coon hunting with their packs of dogs. One good feature for living there was that a brandy distillery was just a few miles away and when distilling was in progress that aroma was self-satisfying.

On weekends I would hike about the area and I discovered Jack London's place at the end of a road. The place was deserted, the Wolf House had burned, the pool was green and slimy, the pond was overgrown with thistles, the pig sties were there — a lot of them but no pigs. The place absolutely empty of people and farm animals. I went back there many times as I liked to hike the oak-covered hills and watch the antics of the Acorn Woodpeckers. Jack London, it is said, did not type but dictated to Charmian, his wife, who prepared his manuscripts.

Thank you for being Cynthia. Today, Tomorrow and Always

QPY

MARTHA'S VINEYARD

Dearest Howie: August 13th, 2012

I had no idea what I was getting into with *The Moth*. *The Moth* team had all of us who are telling our stories meet at a huge house on the Edgartown Great Pond that a donor to WCAI (for Cape and Islands) loaned them for rehearsals. I thought the five story tellers would all be from the Vineyard. Turns out, I'm the only one from the Island. The four others flew in from various places including California. I hope you're not embarrassed, even though you said you weren't. I mean, it's national. I'd better warn Mark and Jennifer in case they listen to NPR.

After all the rehearsal yesterday we walked over to a big tent set up with tables and a couple of dozen people milling about on the grass. I was talking with some nice people, the guy who owns daRosa's print shop, and a man who was a communications teacher somewhere and their wives, and I was telling my story about how the editor of the *Vineyard Gazette* and I were having a feud and he refused to put my name in the paper and would delete any mention of me in the social notes column for West Tisbury, and, I said to these people I was talking to, "I determined to get even with the bastard and wrote a book about a narcissistic newspaper editor and called it *The Paperwhite Narcissus*. Wouldn't you know it, the wife of the communications professor is the new publisher of the *Vineyard Gazette*. There were all sorts of dignitaries from WGBH, the Boston NPR station, and from WCAI, our NPR station, and a swarm of people who are big donors to NPR. The sun set, we had an elegantly low-key catered dinner.

The program is tonight. I don't know whether they broadcast it live or whether it's taped for future airing. I'm pretty sure it is taped. It's at Union Chapel in Oak Bluffs, and we'll have an audience paying $35 each for tickets. I invited Lisa, Amy, and Cat to come, but Lisa is on an airplane going to Alaska to run marathon Number 46 or 47. Amy and Cat will be there.

I think I am now going to go outside, which I haven't done for two days, and see how many weeds I can pull.

Much, much love,

Cynner

Y P Q Y P Q Y P Q Y P Q Y P Q Y P Q

CALIFORNIA

Dear Cynner, August 14th, 2012

Thank you for your good work on *The Moth* segment and I see it is sold out tonight. I will try to find it on my local NPR station. I e-mailed Mark and told him about the event. Cynner, I am fine about this and anything that can continually bring us closer, is elegantly supported by me.

I like William and what he says. He may teach English but I feel it is also a course in Philosophy and Ethics.

Yesterday I could not find my glasses and I looked around for maybe half an hour and then I found them inside the glasses case, just where they should be. Today looking for the letter opener and it must have fallen off the desk and onto the chair nearby. What will it be tomorrow?

LOVE,

Howie YPPY QQ

Chapter 35. The Right Moments

MARTHA'S VINEYARD

Dearest Howie: August 14th, 2012

I'm ready to drop into bed but had to let you know about *The Moth*. Union Chapel was packed. Sold out. It holds maybe 350 people, and what a receptive audience! There were five of us presenting. A black guy from Brooklyn, a chess master who told about a significant chess match where he finally beat someone important in his life. Really dramatic, and then I came on with my quiet love story thinking this may be an anti-climax. Well! The audience laughed at all the right places, they cried, they were utterly silent, they groaned. It was magical! I had felt a tinge of discomfort because in a funny way, I'm a private person and don't like airing my private affairs, and I think we both feel that way. It seemed almost traitorous to tell an audience what you mean to me. But somehow, it was okay. If people laugh early, they'll laugh a lot. I told them "I was born on Island, [etc. etc.] But I got lost coming here tonight." And they laughed. They were just wonderful. When I finished, I got a standing ovation! The first time that's ever happened to me in my life! People came up afterward saying that meant a lot to them. That it gave them such encouragement. That this was a side of me they'd never known about. That it is such a touching and meaningful love story.

I had to tell you.

Gotta go t o b e d n o w.....

But thinking QQQQQQQQQQQQQQQQQQQQQQQQQQQQQQQQQQQQQQQQQQ

CALIFORNIA

Dear Sweet Cynner, August 14th, 2012

It is like you took the ball and ran with it and scored a touchdown! Congratulations for your effort and success.

The pause in your writing has probably ended, and with renewed enthusiasm and good spirits from your recent success you are turning out those pages.

The ravens are having a huddle in a tree across the street. I am looking forward to many huddles with you, trees not needed.

As much love as you can hold

Howie YYYYY
PPPPP
QQQQQ

Chapter 36. Connections

MARTHA'S VINEYARD

Dear Howie: August 15th, 2012

All the furor and hustle/bustle of *The Moth* is over, now. Apparently, the program won't be aired for some time, but they've promised to send me a tape, or whatever they use to record now, and I'll make sure you get a copy.

I am deeply touched by your e-mail. We have so many connections, some we'd rather not have. Our relationship has an extra-terrestrial feel to it. Same counter tile. Same mountain redoubt. Kokopelli and the Hopi connection. The Mars connection. Same wood stove. Discus throwing. And crew. Religion (or lack of it). Me trying to locate you two weeks before I got your packet. The manganese nodules — that is really, really weird! It's as though we are about to morph, one into the other. (Actually, on re-reading, that sounds quite nice.)

The *Queen of the Mississippi* cruise is coming up soon, but I am far more looking forward to my San Diego trip. We have so much to talk about and share and wonder over and laugh about and cry about and think about. A day and a half isn't long enough, I know, but I suspect we can cover a lot of territory in that short time. We are likely to be up all night, and you won't need to take the oxy pill at 1 am because we'll have better things to do than sleep. (Egads, everything seems freighted with meanings.)

Here comes a change in pace.

George, my husband, had a rigid, controlling mother, who tried to turn him into an invalid, although she didn't see it that way. She saw it as nursing him. He'd come down with a slight cold and she'd doctor him in truly inappropriate, invasive ways. He mentioned this only a couple of times to me. She was an awful mother-in-law, critical of everything I did or didn't do, and no matter how I tried to please her, nothing did. I suppose she saw this as protecting her boy from a bad influence. On top of having a mother being what we'd now consider sexually abusive, he spent all of his formative summers at a boys' camp in the Poconos. He told me once about the counselor who took groups of boys out to the woods, around a camp fire, and demonstrated with all of them how they should, for good health reasons, "exercise" their penises.

That was his background. From a seemingly caring and stable home, well-educated parents, active in the community, active in the Unitarian Church, extremely intelligent, but tied up in knots that couldn't be loosened. He was an inadequate father, abusive, inconsistent, misogynistic. Yet he loved the kids in his way and they knew it. He had a wickedly funny sense of humor, a violent temper, a grand sense of adventure. He was a hoarder — of rocks, of papers, of glass jars, of things, and once acquired, couldn't let them go. That included me. His intelligence was beyond brilliant. He'd been involved in an experimental test project for the Air Force Base in Dayton, Ohio, and the tester told me he'd "gone off the scales." I guess I already told you the best description of someone just like him is in the books, *The Mosquito Coast* by Paul Theroux and *The Poisonwood Bible* by Barbara Kingsolver. I don't know why you'd want to read either. They're both depressing. But the father in both books is George.

One can understand what made a person what he (or she) is, but there's no understanding why that person can't recognize what's happened to him and take positive steps to override that poisonous background.

I went to a psychiatrist toward the end of our 25 years. The psychiatrist said, "Why are you staying with him?" and my answer was that no one in my family ever got divorced. They worked out their difficulties and the marriage was stronger. And she said, he'll never work things out. He's always right. He's in control. These unbalanced, psychotic individuals seek out normalcy. You can feel reassured that you are quite normal and he's the sick one.

Well, I didn't mean to turn this into a couch session.

I'm going to end on a positive note. I told Liza, the post office clerk with the tattoos and multi-colored hair — black today with light green sides — when I mailed off a package to you this afternoon, that I'd mentioned her in *The Moth* story, and she actually blushed prettily. "You did?" "Yes, I really did. I mentioned you as 'the young post office clerk.'" "Wow," she said. "Awesome! You really did?" I nodded and handed her a large fistful of change I wanted to get rid of. She counted it out, still blushing. "Omigod! Thanks! Say 'Hi' to your boyfriend for me!"

So, "Hi!" from Liza.

And all my love, all my hugs, all my kisses, and most of my passion (I have to save up a bit for my writing).

Cynner

CALIFORNIA

Subject: Linus "I love mankind, it's people I can't stand." August 15th, 2012

Dear sweet, sweet, Cynner....you are a jewel, a precious, precious, one.

I wrote you a letter today but I need to go to the PO as it has a thickness that I need to have them check as I want to have the correct postage.

That counselor incident brought to mind the quote on the Subject line. I was a lucky one, I had no inappropriate stuff in my life. I recognized I had a penis when I was a Boy Scout due to poison oak bushes as I had bush to hand to it contact, and the itching was radical, and that is the time I learned it had a special purpose and also about calamine lotion.

About religion, I was born a Catholic and that was strong in my life, until I left home and then I went on empty. I follow Buddha, as a philosopher and a way of life, not as a God. I used to go to the Unitarian church for several years. Now when I have time I like to look around. I went to the Mormon church for a while. I am back on near empty.

We differ in that you act as an extrovert and I am doing the introvert thing. Maybe you were on the introvert side but overcame, but you certainly are a people person now and so beautifully done, that all that I know simply respect and take you to favor. I live a very quiet life, near hermit like. Not a good conversationalist. More than two in a gathering makes me uncomfortable Talking to you then and now by fingertip talk is fine, and I am anxious to explore your world and open you to mine as deep as you care to go.

You are probably asleep at this time, but by chance if not — Good Night!

LOVE,

Howie PYQ PYQ PYQ, on ad infinitum

MARTHA'S VINEYARD

Dearest Howie: August 15, 2012

I'm still up. Just came upstairs to see if HRARTEBERY@AOL.COM [sic] showed up in the In box and, joy! It did. It's thundering and lightning right now, so I'll shut down the computer, unplug it, and then, off to bed.

Howie, you are the gem. The diamond I can lean on, who grounds me while I flutter around.

Much love,

Your Cynner QYP PYQ

MARTHA'S VINEYARD

Dear Howie: August 15th, 2012

Oh NO! No wonder I didn't find you right away. I've done it again! My fingers slipped. (See previous message if you don't know what in the world I'm talking about — I spelled your name wrong yet again!)

PPPPPPPPPPPPPPPPPPPPPPPPPPPPPPPPPPPPPPPPPPPPPPPPPPPPPPPPPPPPPPPPPPPPPPPPPPPPPPPP
PPPPPPPPPPPPPPPPPPPPPPPPPPPPPPPPPPPPPPPPPPPPPPPPPPPPPPPPP

pppppppppppppppppppppppppppppppppppppppppppppppppppppppppppppppppppppppppppp
pppppppppppppppppppppppppppppppppppppppppppppppppppppppppppp

CALIFORNIA

My Cynner, August 16, 2012

For you to close yesterday's e-mail with "Your Cynner," brought me to a wonderful feeling of thankfulness, a point of arrival, and an important relief in that I have been with that essence of you all these years without your permission, and now you say, I am yours, which sets it all right for me. A heartfelt thanks. You know I am yours. For me to call you mine is with great pride and always means freedom of your spirit, and yourself. We will talk further when you are here.

It's as though we are about to morph, one into the other. (Actually, on re-reading, that sounds quite nice.)

I agree with what you wrote above and have been thinking about it for a long time. I have every reason to believe that some kind of oneness can take place. It is coming together now little pieces at a time and we have a following that is growing that wishes us to have some kind of, under the circumstances, perhaps an unusual climax that should remain. Forget others, let us do it principally for ourselves. Let us now, as we are at a distance, continue to come together in little ways. When we are together we will be side by side. I will transfer your essence into myself and make my being available for you to bring into yourself. We should succeed and become one, and have that oneness remain. What a Goal! Let's do it!

Good Night, Cynner
Much togetherness
Ho Η αγαπά Γ (H loves C in Greek)
PYQ QYP

MARTHA'S VINEYARD

Dearest Howie: August 17th, 2012

Totally yours. There's no one else. Hasn't been for a long, long time. You seem to have stirred up the embers.

Love, Cynner

• • • • •

Cynthia sent a DVD of an interview of her on MVTV, the Island's community access channel.

• • • • •

CALIFORNIA

Dear Cynner, August 17th, 2012

The DVD of your interview with Ann Bassett arrived and it was immediately played. Very nice, I even caught the mention of San Diego. You always do so well. I enjoyed and I learned more from it. You have a very distinguished look, remarkably beautiful hands, fingernails to perfection. You send, I observe. Your there, I like.

Am redoing my garden to some extent that will take place over the next few days. Nursery supplied me with enough plants, soil mix and fertilizer to keep me busy for those days. I was thinking of ordering some weed seeds and planting same so when September came you would have some weed pulling available, but I reneged.

This may be the time to pause gently. I am in a serene state and would like to meld all that you have given me and in so doing that would insure more freedom for your writing.You can erect my state at any time you wish with a few key strokes.

You are loved, which reminds me that you are surrounded by persons that do give YOU that gift.

Howie YPQ YPQ YPQ

MARTHA'S VINEYARD

Dear Howie: August 20th, 2012

You haven't been hearing from me because I blipped something on my computer that wiped out two days of work. Or a B&B guest may have logged onto my computer without asking or telling me, which I think is what really happened. That was on Saturday, when I couldn't reach Brian Athearn, who tends my computer. So I tried everything I could think of, spent too much time and psychic energy fussing about it, then finally girded my loins, so to speak, and reconstructed as best I could what I'd written. Done now and I can move on.

I missed writing to you. I would like to be able to grumble in person to you and have you console me and put things into perspective.

Now I'm getting stuff together for the *Queen of the Mississippi* trip, and am quite excited about that. Getting ready means putting the house in order. I donated lodging to a flute player who will perform for the West Tisbury Library's Troubadour program next Sunday — he and his wife and two children. Since I won't be here, I've been making lists of everything I can think of such as laundry (don't touch my machines! Go to the Airport Laundromat) and where to dump trash and how to reach the plumber. They'll be here for three days.

The weather has cooled off a bit. Down comforter last night and sweatshirt this morning. Good change because we've had a hotter than normal summer. No one on the Vineyard has air conditioning because there's usually a sea breeze. No need for fans, either. But this summer I put a fan in each room.

A little gray spider just scuttled across the top of my black computer cpu. I don't know much about spiders, but I've always liked them because my father used to tell us about Robert the Bruce and the spider.

This is a kind of utilitarian letter. You will just have to trust that I have a lot of nice things I want to say about how I feel and will tell you as soon as I can.

In the meantime,

Much, much love,

Cynner GGG PPP YYY

CALIFORNIA

Dear Sweetest Cynner, August 20, 2012

I miss writing you so, so, so much. What you can do is ask Brian to show you how to lock your computer. You will have to put in a password that you select to open it. In that way no other person will be privileged to your computer information or use.

My
Very
Excellent
Mother
Just
Served
Us
Nachos N is for Neptune

Cynner *Posterior nulli* (Second to None) Latin
Love, Love, Love
Howie

MARTHA'S VINEYARD

Dear Howie: August 21st, 2012

We made the editorial page of the *Vineyard Gazette*. I say "we" because it's your story as much as mine. It really is an amazing romance story in every way.

Tonight's gig on the *American Star* was just great. I like walking down the dock and up the gangplank, two crew members fetch my boxes of books, I like the audience, which is right around our ages and their experiences in life are something we all have in common, like poor eyesight, going down steps one at a time, and appreciating a microphone. It's fun to wander around drinking wine in the cocktail hour, and I really, really like the food. Very heady. Enough about me!

Lots to talk to you about, but it's going to have to wait.

Cynthia's Moth presentation made the editorial page of the ***Vineyard Gazette***

VINEYARD GAZETTE, MARTHA'S VINEYARD, MASS.

TTERS TO
E EDITOR

Drawn to the Light of Ms. Riggs

Illustration by Paul Karasik

Union Chapel is seated for now, but later erupts into a standing ovation.

Dear, dear Howie. Thank heavens you saved those cryptograms all that time and sent them to me. I loved the diplomatic way out you offered me with the latitude and longitude in case I didn't care to find you, and thank goodness I did. You are the best thing that has ever happened to me. I don't know what the future holds for us, but no matter what, you have given me so much. An understanding, a gentle love, a sweet passion. I treasure your love and friendship and look forward to our too short time together in San Diego.

Much, much love,

Your Cynner YYYYYYYYYYYYYYYYYYYYY
PPPPPPPPPPPPPPPPPPPPPPPPPPPPPPPPPP
QQQQQQQQQQQQQQQQQQQQQQQQQQQQQQQQ
(the lazy way out, to hold down the key, but I mean it)

Chapter 37. *Queen of the Mississippi*

MARTHA'S VINEYARD

Dearest Howie: August 22nd, 2012

There's likely to be a serious gap in my e-mail correspondence starting tomorrow morning, the 23rd and not picking back up until late the night of September 1st. I'll see what I can do aboard ship, but I'm not well versed in the remote stuff. Know that I'll be thinking about you and when I get back it will be only a matter of a few weeks before the train docks at Old San Diego station.

Don't worry about me — I have no intention of making any shipboard attachments. I wouldn't want to disillusion all the 20 million listeners we'll have when they finally air *The Moth*.

This will have to do until I get back:

Much love,

Cynner

The largest fond I could find. A deliberate typo.

CALIFORNIA

August 22nd, 2012

Dearest Cynner, Your adventure is about to begin. I hear that part of the river is closed due to low water and sandbars. That area is being dredged and is probably open by now. Enjoy everything and all. I will be taking the course, "Masterpieces of Short Fiction." Just finished Hawthorne's *Young Goodman Brown.*

I have the *Gazette* article that you sent, it came in OK.

Much LOVE,

Howie PYQQYP

MARTHA'S VINEYARD

Dear Howie: August 22, 2012

Here's the itinerary for the cruise and contact information if you want to get in touch with me for any reason. Phyllis Dale is the travel agent who befriended me on one of my gigs on the *American Star.* She's supposed to smash the champagne bottle over the bow. She arranged for a large bunch of her clients (I'm a client) to go to the Grand Ole Opry, and I said sure, I'd love to go. And a sightseeing tour of Nashville. All the tourist stuff, and it all sounds like great fun. I've never done anything even remotely resembling this before, never thought I'd deign to go on a cruise ship. However, this sounds different from a Carnival Cruise or one of those cruises with 5,000 passengers.

Did I ever tell you about being scheduled to be a speaker aboard the Carnival Splendor going from Long Beach to the Mexican Riviera a couple of years ago? My daughter Ann was going with me. About four days before sailing I got a message from the person in charge of the program, "Guess what!" along with a press release that the Carnival Splendor had caught fire and 5,000 passengers were without light, heat, air conditioning, running water, toilets, hot or cold food, and the navy was airlifting cans of Spam. That was the November 7 to14 cruise, ours was the 14 to 21. I'm relieved that it didn't work out. I don't like crowds, and 5,000 passengers on a boat constitutes a crowd. West Tisbury has a population of around 2,000, and we think that's a lot of people.

I've cleaned the house, left notes for everyone who's likely to be here, watered the plants, left cans of cat food for Lynn to feed Daphne, left money for the woman who cleans my house on Thursdays, emptied the compost bucket, taken the trash to the dump, done all the laundry (washed, dried, folded), all the dishes cleaned, all the flowers in vases emptied out and rhododendron branches stuck in the vases because they'll keep ten days or more, suitcase packed, couple of books, writing paper, camera, pens, glasses, what have I forgotten? Passport for ID, money — ah yes, address book. One small suitcase, one bag with books, papers, and toilet articles kit. All the stuff Phyllis Dale sent me about how to get from one place to another, boat, bus, plane tickets. My head is spinning. Cleaned the refrigerator and the drawer where I keep plastic wrap and aluminum foil and stuff, cleaned the cupboard and gave all the stale crackers to the crows.

I'm still trying to figure out the Neptune conundrum.

Much, much love,

Cynner ppp yyyyyyyyy
yyyyyy qqqqq
qqqqqqqq ppp

CALIFORNIA

Dearest Cynner August 23rd, 2012

Wow! You are thorough. What a list you went thru. What about a hat, and sunscreen — you are fair skinned and your face will be showered in actinic rays. Nice that you thought about the crows. That contact with the crows is to your advantage as they are harbingers of good times and a safe journey.

Nachosor N is for Neptune was hint that the list is of the planets Mars to Neptune.

It is sort of like, this is the first time you are away from home (the home in my head) — enjoy! enjoy! You deserve the best of everything.

Love, LOVE, Howie PYQQYP

• • • • •

There was a gap of more than a week, while Cynthia was cruising the Mississippi.

• • • • •

MARTHA'S VINEYARD

Dearest Howie: September 2nd, 2012

I'm home again after an even better time than I'd expected. Lots and lots to tell you in person when I see you in a little more than three weeks. I've got 350+ emails to go through, so I'll sign off with much love and a promise to write midway through the 350 for a nice break.

Cynner pppppp
yyyyyy
qqqqqq

Dear Howie:

This is cheating to send you a copy of an e-mail I sent to friends, who asked about the cruise, but I thought it might be better than nothing. Much Q many Ps lots of Ys.

Yr Cynner

• • • • •

The Mississippi River was so low there was concern about whether the *Queen of the Mississippi* could make the trip. As she came up the river from New Orleans to Nashville, where the boat was to be christened, a barge that had been only 30 minutes behind her ran aground and blocked the river for a week.

During the cruise, a "riverlorian" told about the river and its history, and Phyllis Dale, Cynthia's travel agent, a performer aboard the *Delta Queen* for 14 years, sang riverboat songs accompanying herself on the piano.

The *Queen of the Mississippi* would stop at some nondescript place on the river where a road ran down into the water for a boat launching site. The *Queen* would nose up to the road, the crew would lay down the stage, the long walkway that sticks out in front, and a couple of crew members would jump ashore and tie lines to trees. "Honest injun," Cynthia wrote, "they tie a 325-foot vessel to trees and stumps. The proper term is 'stump choking.' Even in St. Louis, which you'd think would be a place of wharves and docks, no, we nosed up a concrete slope, the crew clambered up the slope until they found a ring to loop the line through, and that was our docking for the night, despite hurricanes and tornadoes threatening."

Phyllis Dale, said Cynthia, "is worth the money just to see her in action herding her passengers like a sheepdog."

Chapter 38. Light My Fire

CALIFORNIA

Dear Cynner, September 2nd, 2012

Welcome Home! Tell me all about your happenings when you arrive in San Diego, In the meantime get plenty of the *M. vaccae* on your skin from digging and that will increases you serotonin that enhances good mood and it also increases the I.Q. The more you dig the smarter you get! The more you dig the happier you get! I like to dig and weed. I want to show you my favorite weeding tool when you are here — do not let me forget.

Good to talk this way to you again. I send you thought stuff on an irregular schedule. Till next time.

Love, Love, Love,

Howie YPPY......QQ

CALIFORNIA

September 3, 2012

Hello Cynner, this is the first time I have seen your books advertised on Amazon, right along with Gogol and Tolstoy......nice.

Love, Howie YYYYYYYYYYY

MARTHA'S VINEYARD

Dear Howie: September 3rd, 2012

Wow — and my books cost more than theirs!

YYYYYYYYYYYYYYYYYYYYYYYYYY C

• • • • •

Howie sent a new, government-issue paper towel he'd picked up at their former lab on Point Loma along with several hundred-dollar bills.

• • • • •

Dearest Howie: September 4th, 2012

I went to the post office and got my mail this afternoon, an entire week's worth, and was glad to see the familiar address. And the paper towel message — you're quite right, they're not made of the stuff they used to be.

And then the money. I need to scold you for that huge quantity of money. First of all, you have spoiled me enough. I wouldn't trade what you have given me over these last six months for anything. Rubies, diamonds, pearls, emeralds, sapphires are nothing compared to your constant, sweet, gentle, love. Few women are as privileged as I am. I realize what this means in this world. I'm saving the money — it's an awful lot, and I was aghast that you'd trusted the U.S. Postal Service to deliver cash safely to me. They did, but still. . . Anyway, I have an idea of the best way we can spend it and I'll talk to you about it in 20 days. Almost 19 now.

I'm a private person. Although I can stand up on a stage and talk comfortably about my books, my writing, or the Island, I usually keep my personal life to myself. However, this is the most extraordinary, most exquisite relationship I have ever heard of, let alone experienced, and I find myself, New England reticence tossed to the winds, wanting to share with everyone who will stop to listen to what must surely be the greatest love affair ever to have graced this planet. Words used in the right order are, to me, about as erotic as you can get, and you do know how to use them. You best the authors I most admire in stirring my blood.

I'm fully prepared, when we meet, for you to think (although you'll never express it) this isn't the 18-year-old I've held in my heart for 62 years. I've had all kinds of doubts about the physical me meeting the physical you after such a long time. You're new to me in your role of lover, you know. I've thought of you as the big brother I never had, as a protector, as a man I could look up to, as a man I admired. As a man I'm in awe of. Still there. You're all that. Now this new loving you.

With all your gentle hints about how I might spend that fortune you sent, it's too late. I already ordered a blue nightie trimmed with satin, ribbons, and lace.

Much love,

Yr. Cynner

ps I usually sleep in an XL T-shirt

QYP

PQY

YPQ

Now, I really do have to tend to that 15th of September deadline. Goodnight, Howie.

CALIFORNIA

My Dear Cynner: September 5th, 2012

Yesterday I mailed you a packet containing a summary of my last three doctor's visits and a record of my medical incidents over the past years. I did this because I have no future appointments and do not need to make them and I wanted you to know what has happened along the way. There is an extremely happy man in my body and he is riding high on a comfortable healing level. So no need to read that stuff . . . you can substitute your book thoughts instead . . . just wanted to be straightaway on every level with you.

Of course I remember the THEN Cynthia, but it the NOW Cynner that is with me. I read your first book and the last and have followed you thru Google.I copied a photo of you and the cat on your lap as you were seated in your living room chair, (I did not know at the time that it was your living room chair) and that was some time ago. Don't tell THEN . . . the one that is inside of you, that she has lost favor and that her big sister is the object of my affection. You are the one. NOW is the person I love and not the shadow of the past . . . but she sure set the stage and what a beautiful introduction. I know your physical self from all the videos screened. I can tell that you walk softly without seeing you walk. You may have some troublesome moment in viewing me but be assured you are all good and beautiful to my eyes.

Blue is my favorite person color and red I like for accents around the house. Good for you — You stepped right up and went in the right direction. With your 12 words you have made me and are making me turgid at this writing, I have about 30 white T-shirts, XLin my closet, a lot so I do not use the washing machine so much. I sleep in a T-shirt, when cold switch to sweatshirt, XL,

Russell's. I just thought about it . . . that I have some somewhat sheer Covington T-shirts that you might like to use around the house . . . that would be very nice.

You are so loved, You are doing that again Goodnight, Cynner

Howie Q

QQQ

MARTHA'S VINEYARD

Dearest Howie: September 7th, 2012

Just finished writing the finale to *Bloodroot.* Still have to spend a week going through it to make sure all the myriad loose ends are tied up neatly, and then I'll ship off the mss. Whew! This was more difficult to write than others, for some reason. I think I threw too many elements into the story and none of them fit until I twisted them around and force-fit them.

Andrew Nanaa, the fiber optic engineer, noticed the road gang sawing up a felled tree or trees, from the look of it, into firewood lengths. And somehow Andrew, who has contacts beyond contacts, found someone with a dump truck, and brought me two dump truck loads of firewood. The pile is as tall, wide, and broad as a small house, and what the road gang considered firewood-size chunks of tree are a size that will only fit in a Giant's fireplace eight feet wide and six feet deep. I'll send you a picture, now I have a breathing space. I don't want to look a gift woodpile in the mouth, but I do see a bit of wood splitting ahead of me in the future. Tilton Rentall rents splitters, and I may be able to con Chris of the boat, who likes machinery, to work the splitter on some nice cool day.

(17 days to go)

In haste

Cynner, with love

CALIFORNIA

My Cynner: September 8, 2012

We are about as far apart physically as we can be and still remain in the United States, yet I have this profound feeling that my mental state gives me . . . that you are besides me, near touching range. This is not a now and then occurrence but is continuous. It is most noticeable in the morning when I awake and your presence is very strongly felt and I need to bring you touching close but am unable to do so . . . a cruelty of life. I do give thanks for the experience that I have for the nearness of you. I need to have your goodness and self within me,you are so splendid, so outstanding. no person created, has that amazing group of characteristics that you possess that signify that rarity of your outstanding self and with your permission a little from you to me would be most welcome. I spoke of this before, that we will do this in, "ORE MAGICHE," the magical hours.

"I already ordered a blue nightie trimmed with satin, ribbons, and lace." I cannot think of a more powerful aphrodisiac than those words coming from you. Excellent purchase, and how could I be more pleased?

I hoped the pocket change would have reached you before your river trip so that you could luxuriate more and do things you might like to do, but needed a little push. I first thought of your safety, then well-being, then comfort and then the rest to follow.

Great for the news that you are on schedule. You make me feel so great, nothing can compare to it.

Love, Love, Love
Howie QQQ

MARTHA'S VINEYARD

Dearest Howie: September 11th, 2012

Got your doctors' reports, and although I couldn't understand most of it, I got the impression that your doctor is giving you a green light for whatever excesses you have in mind. A letter to you plus my own evaluation of my physical self, plus some reading matter is in the mail.

Much, much love,
Cynner Q Q Q Q
QP QP QP QP QP QP QP QP QP QP QP QP QP QP QP QP
Y Y Y Y Y Y Y Y Y Y
P P P P P P P P P P P P P P P

I was trying to make that swirly and wave-like and sensuous, but my computer is too literal and I ran out of time. Anyway, I tried, and the sentiment is there

CALIFORNIA

My Dear Cynner September 12th, 2012

I was out looking at my garden this morning and this is a summary: The most numerous plants are sweet alyssum and lobelia. I have one bougainvillea in a pot that has just lost all its pink blooms, three cordyline plants in a box that have long slender reddish brown leaves. String of pearls is by the entrance. Sage is coming up along the fence line. The peppermint plant is in bloom but alongside is the spearmint plant which has very tasty leaves to some insect as numerous holes are showing. Celosia, I call them red feather-duster plants, are alongside Buddha. Parsley and chives are also in the front garden. The showiest plants are the stands of lemon grass with the long thin leaves so green and waving in the breeze. The plant originated in Thailand and is an essential ingredient in Thai cooking. I use it on occasion to make lemon grass tea which is recorded as favoring "apoptosis." The word was coined by a botanist and refers to the biochemical process involved at the stem-leaf connection that takes place that allows the leaf to disengage from the stem. It is now used in connection of cells self-consuming themselves which lemon grass has been attributed to foster — so research has been going on to find the process and chemistry involved to make cancer cells apoptosisize themselves. Must not forget the one zucchini plant in bloom.

To the back garden . . . full of ornamental asparagus fern. Pear tree with some fruit; apple tree with rare fruit; mango, no fruit. Peach, much fruit but grunts. Rosemary, lemon verbena, euryops in a pot, celosia in pots, many plants with names I do not know. A juniper with berries that give that distinctive flavor to gin. A Torrey pine and two cedars, one of which I was told is a cedar of Lebanon. Benjamini along one fence is in bloom with a large translucent white flower that is glorious in the sunlight. Will tell you more about the houseplants another time.

I have no restrictions on my activities so excesses are allowed and will be pursued. I just do not like my walk, but am taking it in stride. HA! HA!

Thanks for all those graphics, I filled in those spaces somewhat mentally to get the waves and the sensual-ness. It is amazing how just one P, Q or Y from you is enough to light my fire. Real time, real you, experience you here in the flesh . . . what an honor . . . a privilege . . . nothing could be better.

As much love as you can hold,

Howie P Y

Chapter 39. Counting Down

MARTHA'S VINEYARD

Dearest Howie: September 13th, 2012

You should know that I have felt since we re-connected last February, that even if the doctor had said you'd have to sit still in your rocking chair, go to bed early by yourself, and go to sleep, that it would not have bothered me. Since that envelope with its erroneous latitude and longitude arrived, I have been titillated, charmed, enchanted, thrilled, and enriched by our correspondence. I love your mind, with its fascinating, erotic, sensitive, gentle, witty, brilliant, twists and turns, its erudition, its aesthetic appreciation, its love, its dips and understanding of my fantasies, its willingness to ride along with me.

I've thought often, what would have happened if we'd connected earlier?

I don't think I was mature enough to have appreciated you. I hope I am now. I will be fulfilled if I can snuggle up to you with my new blue nightie, you holding me and telling me everything you've said in your emails. It's likely to take all night, both nights, and you'd better not take your sleeping potion because I want to hear everything you have to say about how much you care for me. And I'll reciprocate.

Much, much love, and

Just as much of the following as you can hold:

QQQQQQQQQQQQQQ

YYYYYYYYYYYYYYYYYYYYYYYYYYYYY (Yellow didn't show up)

PPPPPPPPPPPPPPPPPPPPPPPPPPPPPPPPPPPP

Yr. Cynner

MARTHA'S VINEYARD

Dear Howie: September 13th, 2012

The Fishing Derby is in full swing, and Janet Messineo, the No. 1 fisherman of Martha's Vineyard, sent me a note that she had fish for me. I give her the Quansoo key every year in exchange for fish. I went to her house on Snake Hollow Road, got my car up her steep rutted road, marched into her house without a by-your-leave, went into her refrigerator, and pulled forth a five-pound bag of fish, newly caught during the derby, marked in Magic Marker with my name. I took the bag over to sister Ann's, marched into HER house, dropped the fish, except for a piece for me, in her refrigerator with a note, and returned home. For my supper, a small piece of bluefish, slathered with dill and mayonnaise, and baked just until it's no longer iridescent. Yum! With my own potatoes and Swiss chard. Tomato salad with my own basil. Ann will call in her troops for a feast and will let Janet know how she cooked the rudder fish.

Yours,

Cynner QYP

MARTHA'S VINEYARD

Dearest Howie: September 18th, 2012

I've been checking the weather in San Diego and it looks like balmy low 70s. It's dropped down into the upper 40s at night here on the Vineyard, in the upper 70s during the day. Perfect weather for sleeping and gardening. On Thursday at 6:00 am I leave for Santa Barbara.

Kokopelli is telling me to go to bed now and get some sleep. Knowing his penchant for play, I guess he thinks that's the way to go.

Much love,

Cynner PPPPP

YYYYY

QQQQQ

CALIFORNIA

Dearest Cynner, September 19th, 2012

Hello . . . it will not be long now and you will be here and we can exchange words and embraces and lots of Y's. I will very much need your help on three items after you arrive here. One is extremely important, one much less so and then there is the one I will explain below.

The female owner of the multimilliondollar mansion across the canyon has two dogs and one cat. Her cat is slightly beyond the kitten stage . . . has a long tail held as a flag pole and ruler straight. I would like a cat, not my cat, but your cat. Let me explain. I would like us to go to the Humane Society on Gaines Street, just a short drive from here, and if you would look over the selections of young and mature cats and pick out the one that you have that feeling for . . . then I will bring your cat home that you have named. We will need to obtain all the other things, litter box . . . why not the new self-cleaning one, plus the food you feed your cat and bowls, a toy or two, and I will feed your cat on a nice doily at the dining area, as you do. This would make me happy and I could send you a photo now and then perhaps showing you the first mouse caught or some trophy the cat left at the door. Could you do this? Your cat, my loving care.

You mentioned some time ago that you were mailing reading material plus other. It has not arrived yet.

See you soon with much love,

Howie PQY

• • • • •

A passenger on the *Queen of the Mississippi* cruise gave everyone a pin he'd made that had a tiny teddy bear on it. Cynthia sent it to Howie for his Teddy.

• • • • •

CALIFORNIA

Dearest Cynner, September 19th, 2012

I should have been a little more patient . . . your mailings arrived with the afternoon post. It took eight or nine days in transit.

You do so much. Your words, your writings. Ding! Ding! There Go My Heart Strings! It is you NOW.

NOW is my woman!

Teddy has the bear emblem from your cruise on the left side of his chest. I wonder if real bears do have their hearts on the left side of the chest?

Thinking about you all these years and now you are about to come to me.

What a wonderful life.

You NOW are very deeply loved . . . Howie ypQpy

MARTHA'S VINEYARD

Dearest Howie: September 19th, 2012

I'm relieved the reading matter and bear pin arrived — they took an awfully long time. I'm glad Teddy is wearing the pin. I wore it every single day during that wonderful trip on the *Queen of the Mississippi* so it carries great vibes.

My sister Ann is taking me to the 6:00 am ferry tomorrow morning, leaving here at 5:15 am to make sure I make all connections in time. I'll be in Santa Barbara at 6 pm and Ann and Paul will meet the Santa Barbara Airbus in downtown SB and we'll probably have supper at their home.

I'm travelling light with one small suitcase and a cloth bag with paperwork and toiletries, and, except for my new blue nightie, have my old, comfortable, usual jeans, cotton shirts, and boat shoes. I hope you haven't planned anything fancier than the Animal Shelter. That sounds like great fun! I like names from Greek and Roman mythology for our animals. I think we should respect their dignity. Any thoughts on names you like?

Don't plan any meals that differ from what you usually have. I like everything (except liver and raw shellfish), and I'm perfectly happy not to have a drink in the evening, and while I like coffee in the morning, I also like tea, and I don't have to have either, so whatever you have I will be pleased to share. I'm not a big eater. In the morning I sometimes eat cereal, sometimes toast, seldom bacon and eggs, but whatever you have will be exactly right for me. I'm not much of an eater-outer, because I like being able to converse and too many restaurants are so noisy one can't talk. But if you'd like to eat out and are willing to have me appear in boat shoes and jeans, I'll go along happily.

What else do you need to know about me as guest? I often wake up in the middle of the night around 3:00 or so, and read until I get sleepy. Not always. My hours tend to be irregular, so I'll fit in with whatever your schedule is. Sometimes (tonight after the Wednesday Writers left) I won't have supper until — eeks! Just noticed it's 11 pm!

You probably won't hear from me until I debark from the Amtrak train on Monday, the 24th at 12:17 in Old Town San Diego. Yippee!

Yours,

Cynner

With love and hugs and kisses and ypq

Chapter 40. When He Last Saw Me

It was pre-dawn when my daughter Ann drove me to the train station in Santa Barbara. After she made sure the train was on time, my ticket was in order, and I was okay (I wasn't), she left with hugs and many well wishes. Howie had sent me cash for train fare, too much. I spent part of the excess on the most expensive fare, business class.

The train pulled in to the station, I climbed on board. There were only two of us in the entire car, another woman about my age and me.

It was then that I began to have second thoughts. The last time Howie had seen me, I was 18. I had been gawky, gangling, and myopic, not every man's dream, but apparently I'd been his. But this was 62 years later and I showed it. Our correspondence had been safe. Thirty-five-hundred miles had separated us. I'd lived a contentedly single life for 34 years, and had never been tempted to change that.

What on Earth was I doing, heading south on a five-hour train ride, to meet this man with whom I'd become so very close — but at a safe distance. Was I insane? What was he going to think when he met me at the train station, visions of this 18-year-old dancing through his head, and an octogenarian descends from the business class car?

If I could have turned back at that point, I might have. For five hours my thoughts went back and forth. What was he going to think? True, he'd seen DVDs of me in action, so he was not going to be too surprised. Would we throw our arms around each other and kiss on the spot? My stomach hurt. What would he expect of me?

I chatted politely across the aisle and several seats up with my fellow passenger, and eventually moved to the seat next to her. We talked about our grandchildren.

The train moved on, the Pacific Ocean to my right, lapping gently on white beaches. So different from my Atlantic Ocean, and yet, with the familiar view to the horizon that went on forever to far shores. My Atlantic would lead to Spain. His Pacific, to China.

My fellow passenger told about her grandson's football. I told her about my grandson's hockey.

The train moved on.

I checked my watch.

Three hours to go.

In business class, you get complimentary coffee and sweet rolls and juice. And a newspaper. I walked back to the coffee machine and helped myself, then went back to my seat. I opened the newspaper and the print was nothing but black symbols I couldn't understand. I set the newspaper aside. I couldn't eat the pastry I'd taken. I opened the book I'd brought with me. I read the same paragraph on the same page over and over. I had no idea what I was seeing. I closed the book.

I looked out of the window at the ocean.

What will this first meeting be like?

Two hours to go.

At every railroad crossing, the train whistled its mournful warning — two longs, one short, one long. At every stop now more people boarded my private car. Our route moved inland.

One hour to go.

I checked the schedule to make sure I got off at the right stop, Old Town, San Diego. There were four more stops before then. I had just one suitcase. I lifted it out of the overhead bin and set it beside me.

A half hour.

"Old Town San Diego, next stop!"

My throat was dry. I stood up. The train stopped. The conductor helped me off. I was 81, after all, not 18. Would he recognize me? I ought to have a pleasant look on my face when he first sees me. Should I smile?

I stood on the platform as the train pulled away from the station.

No Howie.

Perhaps he's waiting where the taxis pull in. I walked through a gate and up a couple of steps to the taxi stand.

No Howie.

He must be held up in traffic, I thought. I checked my watch. Fifteen minutes. I hope nothing is wrong. Twenty minutes. Perhaps he had a heart attack. After all, he's no longer 28 years old.

A half hour passed.

I don't have a cell phone, but everyone else in the world seems to have one. I would need to ask a stranger to call Howie for me. I had my phone book with his number. I watched teenagers dart by, a woman with a baby in a stroller, two women chatting, a man in a wheelchair in a business suit talking on his cell phone.

He disconnected. Before he could move his wheelchair, I confronted him. "Excuse me, would you mind. . .?"

He dialed the number and handed me the phone. Would Howie answer? Was he all right? Had he been going through the pangs of uncertainty that I had?

"This is Howard." A sleepy voice.

"This is Cynner?" A worried voice.

"You're here already?" Now awake.

"The noon train." Relief.

"I'll be there in ten minutes." A strong voice. "I'd written midnight train on my calendar. I was napping in preparation."

Ten minutes later, a white truck with camper shell pulled up. I couldn't see the driver. He edged over to the passenger side holding a cardboard sign.

I can't even recall whether we embraced or not. I don't think so. We both felt awkward, I think, Howie because he'd miscalculated my arrival by 12 hours, me because I was glad to see him and didn't want him to feel awkward.

He maneuvered the camper truck around and we headed for his home and a day and a half of who knows what. He doesn't drive like a 90-year old, I remember thinking. More like the 28-year-old I knew so long ago with his Jeep and our camping gear.

He pointed out the landmarks. I made polite oohs and aahs. We came to the foot of a hill and he turned left and up we went, one block to a cross street, a second block, and then the circular cul de sac I'd viewed when I Googled his address.

We pulled up in front of the only black house. Gray, actually. He called the color Ansel Adams Gray. (I learned, much later, he'd taken a short course in photography with Ansel Adams.) Still awkward. We'd been so intimate in our letters. This physical presence was different. We knew each other's innermost thoughts, our hopes, our concerns, our histories, but at this moment, that intimacy seemed almost to have been a fantasy.

Face to face with the gray house with red stripe, it wasn't, as Howie had written, as bad as it looked in photos. It had a minimalist Oriental look. Off center was a bamboo screen that Howie parted to expose a front yard with bright green lawn, meticulously mown, nary a weed. Ahead of us to the right was his laboratory, the former garage. To our left was

On the sign was, "YPPY" in very, very large letters. Translated it read XOOX.

his house. Straight ahead was a walkway between house and lab and I could see, in the distance, a house under construction on the far side of a canyon that lay between Howie's almost conventional (behind the gray facade) house and the far neighbor.

He held the door for me. Feeling like a teenager on her first date, I entered his house. He was carrying the sign. He turned it over. On the back side was a very large Q and three subsidiary Qs.

He showed me my room and set my suitcase on a rack at the foot of the bed. On the bureau were at least a dozen candles, ready to be lighted. I wasn't quite sure what to make of that. Lighted, the candles would make the room look like a wake in progress.

"A day and a half isn't a lot of time," said Howie, leading me to his office/lab, where we sat in two black office chairs, facing one another, still awkward. "I thought we might like to see the Animal Shelter and pick out a cat for you to name, and for me to keep."

"I'd like that," I said. "Maybe just look. Not pick out a cat right away."

Awkward silence. Knees almost touching. Look at one another. Smile.

Howie took my hand and felt my fingers. Nice. He has huge hands. Gentle.

He reached for a small white box. "I know you don't like to wear jewelry, but I wondered if this might fit."

I sat very still.

He opened the small white box and took out a paper cigar band and slipped it on my left hand ring finger.

I laughed. Awkwardness gone. Vanished. "I do make an exception for rings," I said.

"Would you like to go to the jewelry store tomorrow?"

"Yes!" said I.

We'd been together for maybe an hour.

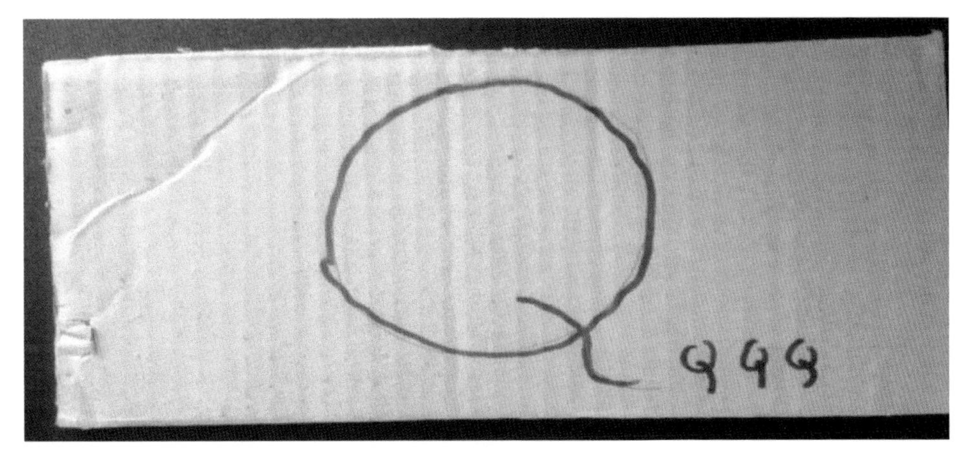

Q translated to P for Passion

We kissed. We laughed. We went to the Animal Shelter just to look. It would be unfair to Daphne to introduce a West Coast stranger to her domain. We went to the jewelry store and picked out a ring.

Howie has deep roots in California. A fourth generation Californian, he was born and bred in the Golden State and has always lived there.

"We can spend summer and autumn on the Vineyard," I suggested when we returned to his house, "winter and spring here in San Diego."

Howie smiled. "I'm moving to Martha's Vineyard. I don't intend to move again."

"Are you sure?"

He took my hand. "I'm sure."

He'd shown me around his lab, his house, his garden overlooking the canyon where his boys had played. His photos, paintings, his stamp and coin collections. Scrapbooks his mother had made of his athletic victories. He introduced me to his plants and trees, the equipment in his laboratory, his glass works, his metal works, his photography equipment and darkroom, his computers, microscopes, dental equipment, woodworking tools, cabinets full of special chemicals and papers and delicate glassware and boxes of photos and records . . .

How could he think of giving up any part of this full life, a half-dozen careers, and more than a dozen interests.

How could he think of moving?

We were sitting on his two-seater swing which overlooked the canyon and the plants, birds, and animals he knew so well. "Don't worry," he assured me, indicating house and lab behind us. "I won't take all of this to the Vineyard."

"There's room for everything," I said. "There really is."

He smiled. "It will be good to get rid of it."

"But it's your life," I protested.

"No it's not. " He took my hand. "You are."

• • • • •

September 26th, 2012

We called Howie's son Mark and talked to him on FaceTime. I don't think we told him what we'd just decided. He was left to figure it out. He e-mailed his father.

> Hi Dad,
>
> It was really great to see the two of you together on FaceTime. I like Cynthia very much. It makes me very happy thinking about you. So did she break you down and convince you to get up and go to Martha's

Vineyard? Are you engaged? All considered, I know you could do it (if you were so inclined) and would make the adjustment just fine. Her place is the most cozy, relaxing home, filled with great feelings, stimulating energy and kindness. Please give me an update. I'm here to help in any way that I may.

Love, Mark

September 26th, 2012

Dear Mark.

I botched Cynthia's arrival time but she turned it into an interesting event by borrowing a cell phone from a man in a wheelchair and let him dial my number after which I got the message she was at the train station, I apologized, she was beautifully composed and everything went well. She had no trouble in showing me the way to Martha's Vineyard and yes we are engaged. I am so honored and thankful that Cynner will be my wife, and that we will be together as one, her life style and writing undisturbed but enhanced by my presence. Even that this happened yesterday plans are afoot, the ring is to be delivered soon. Let me tell you about the selection of the ring. I first suggested a diamond engagement ring. She wanted a ring that she could wear all the time including gardening, one of her giving activities So we decided on a white-gold ring with a flower pattern that could be worn at all times even under Gardener's gloves. What a wonderful person she is . . . such goodness. I would like to be with her as soon as time allows and circumstances permit for a marriage on the Vineyard.

Love, Dad

September 26th, 2012

Hurray! Congratulations to you both.

My assistant band director will keep the ship on course in my absence, when you let me know. I say this because I would very much like to be involved in helping with any logistics in this great endeavor, even though I know you both are quite independent and capable. I'm very excited and just want to be part of it.

All my love, Mark

And so it was decided. Once Howie got his house in order, Cynthia's knight in shining armor would set off on his quest for his fair lady hoping to arrive about two weeks later.

• • • • •

PART 4: TO MARTHA'S VINEYARD

Chapter 41. Back Home

MARTHA'S VINEYARD

Dearest Howie: September 27th, 2012

Splendid! A perfect idea! Mid-March on the Vineyard is beautiful. The snowdrops are in bloom, and the crocuses and winter aconite are out. Everything is waking up. The redwing blackbirds arrive in the wetlands then and you hear them calling. Pinkletinks sound like sleigh bells in the swamps and marshes, and every year the *Vineyard Gazette* has an editorial about them. That would be a great trip in the camper. I had thought about your vehicles and it hadn't occurred to me that yes, of course, you could drive the camper cross-country to here. A great trip! I'll do my bit to keep you warm in our New England winters, but you truly needn't give up your beautiful California winters. We could spend cold months there, if you'd like. Anyway we can decide later. Such a great plan.

Daphne just this minute jumped up into my lap and is watching with interest our future unfolding. Exciting, world shaking. Daphne just reached up and licked my nose.

There's plenty of room for the camper to be at home, parked wherever it's comfortable, and there are electrical outlets in several places on the property. However, this house has so much room, I'm thinking you can have a working suite of your own so you can get away from too much activity and work in peace and quiet in the library with the fire crackling and snapping. All your computer equipment can be set up there, and if you need working surfaces, we can have one of our PhD carpenters install that.

Don't worry about reconfiguring anything in this place. It's been reconfigured to a fare-thee-well over the centuries. The library was once a bedroom where my grandmother was born. In 1930, my mother had a bookshop there and it was written up in *Publishers Weekly*.

I came along in 1931, and that was the end of the bookshop. When my dad retired, he turned it into a study. When I came back to live with my mother in 1988, it became a library again. I had the fireplaces in the library and Aunt's Room rebuilt from the ground up, so you don't have to worry about the oyster shell plaster in the chimney catching fire.

Kokopelli is facing me now and I can almost hear his flute. Good job, K.! March isn't that far away and he's leading us off, marching, I guess, toward frolics unknown.

Getting uprooted from your ancestral land is terribly painful. You are giving up an awful lot for me, Howie. Thank you. I hope I can live up to your hopes and dreams.

Much, much love,

Cynner QYPQYPQYPQYPQYPQYPQYPQYPQYPQYPQYP. . . . .

MARTHA'S VINEYARD

Dearest Howie: September 28th, 2012

I love the fact that you have a big, big heart. I will be tender to that heart and treat it with respect so it will continue its fine work for a long time to come. Ninety is no longer as old as is used to be. In fact, 62 years ago I thought you were older than you are now. I don't regard you as elderly and refuse to treat you as such.

A low-key wedding I promise you, Catherine (Cat) Finch officiating. She promises to come up with a ceremony combining Buddhist elements (for you) and Earthy elements (for me).

Dearest Howie, this is all slightly terrifying, bewildering, and an odd coming down to reality and practicality after our seven months of sipping nectar and a day and a half of sheer pleasure. Here we are, talking schedules and money and day-to-day living. It's a natural outgrowth of your 62 years and our seven months of romance, I suppose. We do have to launder our clothing and schedule appointments and deal with budgets and shop for groceries and pay bills and answer mail and wash our faces . . .

My parents had a lovely, comfortable relationship. My father was, like you, a romantic. He'd come home from his school, where he was principal. Always, "Where's your mother?" as though he was afraid he'd lost her during his absence, and he'd kiss her as though he'd never kissed her ever before; and I, the youngest, would think how mushy! How embarrassing! He'd often have flowers or candy or something small (it was the Depression and we were dead, flat broke), but nothing he did was as though it had become a habit, something expected. My mother always had tea ready and they'd sit and talk together, boring talk to me, who didn't have to sit in on it, about how his day went and how her day went, and the personalities of his teachers and her writing. I guess romance doesn't need to fade. That easy, comfortable relationship is something I want us to have. I want our home to be a sanctuary where we are safe from all cruelty and unkindness and selfishness and violence, where we can talk about anything without constraint. Where there are no secrets, no hidden angers or withholdings of feelings. Where privacy is respected. My parents

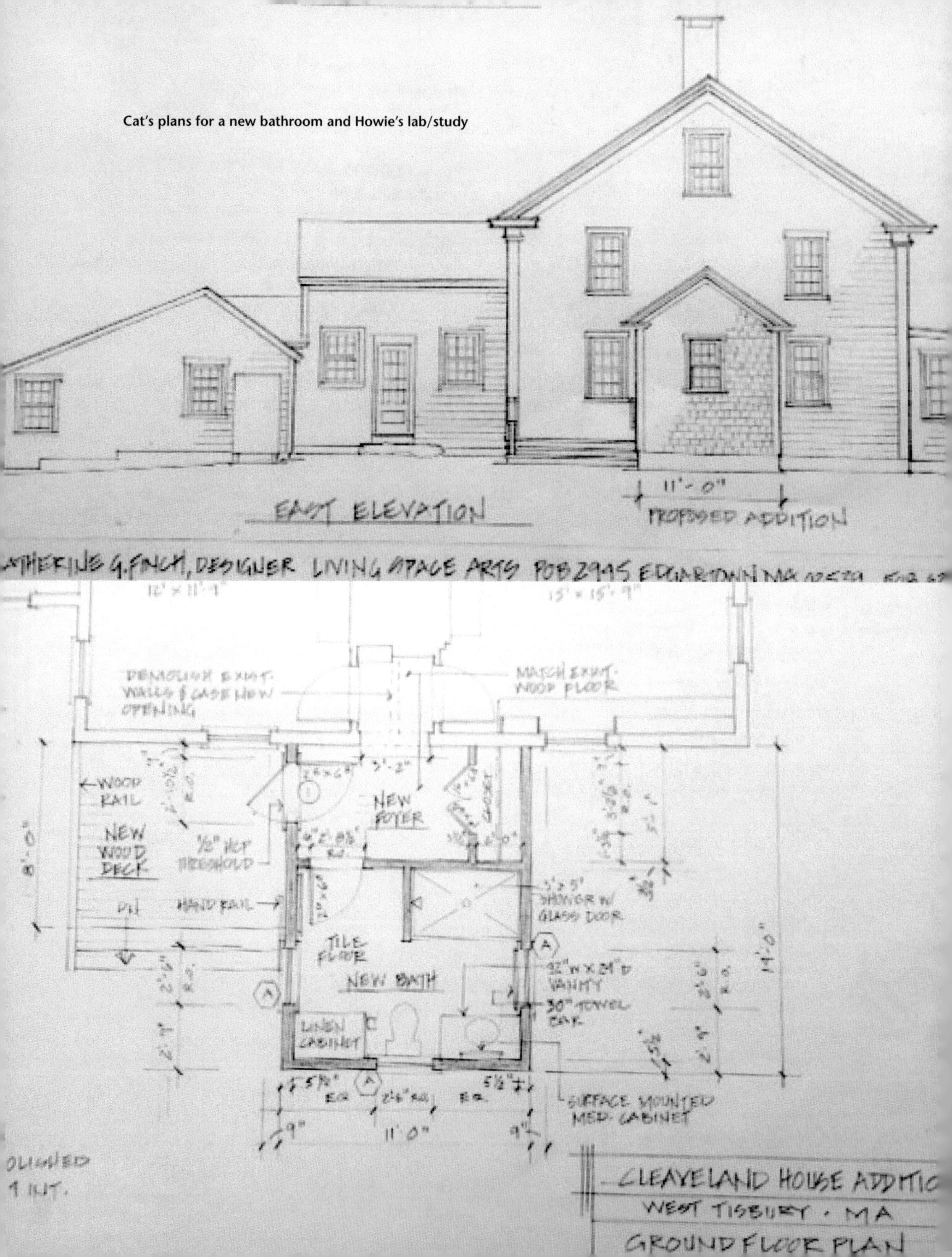

Cat's plans for a new bathroom and Howie's lab/study

would have arguments where my father would stalk out of the house and come back and sulk for much too long. And my mother would start out feeling abjectly apologetic, if she was to blame, and then would get angry all over again at his sulking. So I don't mind if we argue. Arguing is probably healthy, to some extent. Not healthy if we hurt one another.

Good grief — it's 9:30 and I haven't even turned on the lights downstairs and I've forgotten about supper.

Goodnight, dear Howie, my love, my own, my everything man.

Cynner GGG (Yes!)

MARTHA'S VINEYARD

Dearest Howie: September 30th, 2012

Cat and Lisa came over this morning for coffee and a debriefing on my trip to San Diego. After Lisa left, Cat stayed on. I guess I told you she is, by profession, an architectural designer. She went over every inch (lots and lots and lots of inches) of this house and we've come up with an elegant plan that will not disrupt my present activities in any way, that will accommodate future activities involving you, that will accommodate any activities you choose to do, will give each of us private space and common space, and at the same time will allow for the B&B to continue without having any appreciable impact on the two-in-one of us. How's that for magic!

We also thought, and this is really, really nifty, that we can add a deck sheltered on the north by the new bathroom extension, that will look out over the east garden and fish pond and to the south the kitchen garden. Not as spectacular as that gorgeous wild canyon of yours, but it will be sheltered and private and we can have a swing. And lots of bird feeders.

Let me know what you think about this. I'm going downstairs now to take pictures, which I'll send so you can see what I'm talking about.

All my love,

C /pyyQQQyyp/H

CALIFORNIA

Dearest Cynner: September 30th, 2012

It is as though you pulled the rug from under me . . . you are showering me with such good thoughts, words, plans, and such beautiful details . . . a deck with a swing! I am so humbled. I cannot think of words good enough to tell you what I feel, overwhelmed will have to do, thankful, your goodness and your desire to make me comfortable and taking care of all my needs is so appreciated. You show your love for me in many, many ways. I am in this extreme happiness mode and do not want to come down. It was that skin touch on Monday afternoon that again told me you were the one, the only one. I am still tingly.

It was my plan to present you with an iPad as a wedding gift and hook it up for you then, but I will have one sent to you now, so we can do exchanges quickly and more efficiently and you can show me what is going on at The Cleaveland House in real time.

You and Cat showed me a good solid plan for living and I succumbed, that is I do not at all resist. My present work room is 9 feet x 13 feet and is more than adequate. The scanner, printer and computer take up 6 feet of counter space, and I use 20 inches of space under the counter for an AV receiver. 3 feet of space is used for microscopes and related equipment. The desk is 4 feet long, but can be much smaller. The only thing important to me is the 6 feet of counter space. The rest can be configured to make good use of the remaining space. I will try to bring few books, less that 10 feet. I want to live simply. This will give me a chance to get away from the accumulated clutter. It is now Cynner and all that she holds dear that I want to take hold and cultivate and bring closer.

Much love as well,

Howie YPPY QQQQ

Chapter 42. Holding Tight

MARTHA'S VINEYARD

Dearest Howie: September 30th, 2012

I loved talking to Mark this afternoon. I'm not a phone person, but he made me feel comfortable and he assured me that it would be an enhancement for both of us to talk and see one another on one of those machines, like an iPad, and he won me over. I could nestle into my bed at 11 PM, hug my pillow and the machine, and sense you being with me even though you are 3,000 miles and a diagonal stripe away across the continent.

I am delighted that you and he decided to drive cross-country. What a great way to talk to one another, the luxury of having the time to talk about nothing and everything. I'm half-tempted to fly out and join you on the way East.

Thank you more than you can ever imagine and more than I have power to extend, for uprooting yourself from your home, your turf, the climate you know, the grasses and birds and plants you understand, to come to this alien clime, where the whole world is different. All I can offer you is Love and more Love. And beauty. Lots of that. Plus a good space in the Cleaveland House where you can have peace and quiet, if you want, and a share in the activity if you want that. Doors between you and too much activity can close, and your sanctuary can be shut off from it all.

I just got back from the Harbor View engagement. I casually handed them my bill for $1,000, and they just as casually said, "Thank you, we'll take care of it." That is a life with which I don't aspire to become comfortable. I hauled my white fleece jacket, the one I'm wearing in the DVD interview with Ann Bassett, out of the dryer. It's cool tonight. Then, wearing that and the striped cotton shirt and tan pants (my idea of dress up) hustled to Edgartown in time to join a small intimate group of multi-trillionaires who were considering purchasing small-house units. I don't think they call the units something as middle class sounding as time shares. Idle conversation. Talk about investments. Golf. Yachting. Then someone mentioned California. I mentioned San Diego. And then, Howie, you will be ashamed of me, I told my Howie story. All of a sudden, these dull trillionaires lighted up and stopped talking golf or *Forbes* or *Province* in little knots and all of a sudden turned into human beings and attention was on us and our story. Men and women, both. It truly is a glorious story. But I had no idea of the impact it has on everyone, man and woman. Everyone. I mean, I'm thrilled with our story, but why are the most cardboard-like people suddenly turned into caring human beings? Maybe we've got something worth spreading around.

We were in a private dining room of the Harbor View, seating an intimate 20 people at a long table and quiet enough so you could talk to people at either end. THEN the service started. Each of us had four different wine glasses lined up in some kind of order. A platoon of wait staff, sensitively divided between male and female, marched in and deposited a plate with a little dab of something on a big tablespoon in the middle, so everyone was served at the same instant. Then in marched the Chief Chef (he had a title), and he went to the head of the table and announced that what we had on the plate was something and something and crushed fennel and something and some special bleu cheese imported from a village high in the Pyrenees where the goats ate only some rare herb, and (you'll like this) mashed sweet potatoes. With balsamic vinegar. All on a tablespoon. The very rich doll sitting next to me who'd had at least two martinis in vases large enough for floral arrangements turned to me and murmured. "Do you like this shit?" I, who thought it was pretty cool, said an innocuous "Umph," and she said, "Me neither," and we became close buddies after that. Before we moved the tablespoon salad from our lips, the sommelier came forth and explained that the wine we were drinking came from the 19XX vintage of a small family run vineyard in Trouveau where they vint only X bottles a year. We ate our spoonful of salad. That was followed by seven more courses. Honest, I am not kidding you, and I asked them for a menu to send you, which I will. All tiny. All deposited silently at our places like Ali Baba's feasts. All accompanied by a dissertation by the head Chef. Soft murmurs of appreciation by the diners. All I can recall, without that menu in front of me, was a blur of delicacies including an oyster grilled over hickory charcoal with a touch of this and that and a dab of vanilla. The sommelier appeared and gave a little talk about why this wine was appropriate and where it came from. The four wine glasses were replaced with three more. I guess seven at a blow was considered gauche. Near the end we were served an ice cube size chunk of beef with an assortment of exotic herbs and spices. Conversation was gradually picking up so the Chef and Sommelier had to speak more loudly each time. Before the next to the last course materialized, someone on the other side of the table said, "Tell us the Howie story! We didn't hear it!" That was right in the middle of an explanation of the meadows where the sheep grazed in order to produce the most exquisite of cutlets. The Chef bowed out gracefully, I blushed seemingly, the diners hushed reverently, forks forgotten, eyes on me. I told them, Howie. Reactions are absolutely amazing. Love, interest, humanity, all pour out. Support. I said I was here to talk about murder, not the love of my life, but they wanted all the details I was willing to divulge. We did finally repair to the fire blazing in a sitting room and I did talk about my books. I signed a lot, without keeping track of them, and when I politely said that to the hotel staff in uniform handing me books to sign, he said, "Please, don't worry. We'll take care of everything." Which I guess they will. They had a minion carry my books out to my little inoffensive car, I got in, drove home, and thought I'd better unload that experience onto your broad shoulders. I did tell the woman next to me that usually on Saturday nights, I have baked beans and hot dogs. She nodded, eyes watering a bit, but I'm not sure she understood what I said.

I can't believe the time!!!!! To bed, with all my love in heart and soul and body.

Cynner

ps: I can't go to bed without telling you this. The head of the hotel , who was one of the diners, came to me and offered us, you and me, the hotel as a place for our marriage. "No, no thank you," I said, which would have appalled 99 percent of all the brides and grooms who settle on the Vineyard as their wedding site. "Well, then," he said, dusting off his vest, "We'd like to offer you a suite to stay in." "Er, ah," quoth I. "Please, think about it," said he. "Your story has touched the hearts of every one of us here, and the hotel would like to do something special for you and Howie." Nice, hey? I muttered a witty but dumb, "We're likely to mess up your room," to which he replied, "We should certainly hope so." You can Google the Harbor View Hotel and see what it's all about.

PYQ . . . . . forever!

CALIFORNIA

Dearest Cynner, October 1st, 2012

Apple will be sending you an iPad 3, wireless keyboard, dock for the pad, and a two-year extension with casualty insurance. A wedding gift a little ahead of time, but more to come. I have you now to do things for in a loving, my way. You are special beyond special.

I love Cynner.

Howie PYYP PYYP Hooray!

MARTHA'S VINEYARD

Dearest Howie: October 2nd, 2012

I wish you were here to hear and feel the warmth we seem to have generated on this Island. Congratulations. Hugs. Kisses. Well wishes. The nursery gave me a free chrysanthemum plant plus a discount on the plants I bought to brighten the border for my grandniece Sarah's wedding this weekend. He hugged me and charged me only $5 each for big bright mums.

It rained Saturday and Sunday, yesterday was sunny and pleasant, it's raining now and is supposed to continue tomorrow. All this is good for Sarah and Scott's wedding this weekend, because everything will be washed and watered. The grass responds almost instantly, sending up fresh green shoots.

Dearest Howie, I love you.

Cynner yyyyy ppppp qqqqq

CALIFORNIA

My Dearest Cynner, October 2nd, 2012

Chrysanthemum, what an honor to get one as a gift, good luck abounds with it being placed with you . . . it is a happiness flower. From Google: In Japan, there's even a "Festival of Happiness" to celebrate this flower each year. A symbol of the sun, the Japanese consider the orderly unfolding of the chrysanthemum's petals to represent perfection, and Confucius once suggested they be used as an object of meditation. It's said that a single petal of this celebrated flower placed at the bottom of a wine glass will encourage a long and healthy life. Howie says, do it!

You are delicious, and was that purring I heard?

Much, much love,

Howie It is still YPPY YPPY QQQ

MARTHA'S VINEYARD

Dearest Howie: October 2nd, 2012

If a single chrysanthemum petal will insure long life, I'm sending you a dozen along with some five-leaf clover leaves, some guinea hen feathers, and the foil from a champagne bottle Paul Magid brought to the Sunday Writers. Anita, his wife, wants to host a shower. I am deflecting most of the invitations that are being extended to honor us. We could live out our lives floating on the pleasure other people seem to be getting from our really quite simple love.

Dear Howie, I am very happy. I'll even promise to learn to use and like this machine you are sending me. Your instincts have been spot on, so far. I saw Brian Athearn at the Post

Office this afternoon (more congratulations) and he's promised to walk me through every step of learning to use it. He, as I guess I've told you, is my computer person, also my third cousin once removed. Discussing everyday necessities of daily life is something I'm having to get used to. Although March seems far away, it's not, really. And between now and then you may be able to soothe me into feeling comfortable with stuff that's going to happen in our daily lives.

Off to bed.

All my love,

Cynner QYP QYP QYP !

Chapter 43. Grandniece's Wedding

CALIFORNIA

Dearest Cynner, October 3rd, 2012

Grandfather's beard arrived and it was the first time for me to see this lichen. It does not grow in this county because of our poor air quality. It will be good for me to breathe your good air. This lichen is said to be edible and I wonder if is ever on your plate?

I miss you Cynner, your warmth, your skin, your goodness.

Much love,

Howie

Always, YPPY QQQ

• • • • •

Mark wrote his dad: "I must reiterate my hope that you don't get unnecessarily overwhelmed by myriad house details, " and promised to help in every way possible.

• • • • •

MARTHA'S VINEYARD

Dearest Howie: October 6th, 2012

I love the way our kids try to protect us. A funny kind of turn around. I'm getting this too. The plan sounds great. I'm glad you're not selling your house. That means you can store things in your laboratory, or if you have second thoughts about New England winters, the San Diego house will always be an option. Everything sounds so very right and so very positive.

I'm really not worried about your being overwhelmed. I know you well enough to understand that you are aiming for that 120 years and you're not going to jeopardize the minutes of that time we will be spending together by stressing out.

Now that Sarah and Scott's wedding is over, a grand all day affair, when I get my house and property back, WE can start planning.

Well, Yippee!

All my love,

Cynner

Chapter 44. Howie's Route Selected

CALIFORNIA

My Dear Cynner, October 6th, 2012

Did FaceTime with Mark this morning and our route has been selected with a detailed driving schedule from the ferry landing to Cleaveland House. The last sentence of the schedule says, "If you reach Tiah's Cove you've gone a little too far."

Love you Cynner. This is amazing (talking to myself). This beautiful, wondrous life happening is really happening. Wow! Wow!

YPPY YPPY QQQQQQQQQQQQQQQQQQ

MARTHA'S VINEYARD

Dearest Howie:

I'm glad plans seem all right to you so far. A very private commitment in March. A legal marriage in church for family and close friends in late May/early June. A big pot luck occasion in July for the entire Island.

When I saw Sarah and Scott's church wedding, I realized how much the family wanted and needed a traditional service so they could cry and laugh and share our joy.

All my love,

CynnerQQQQQQ

ypypypyp

CALIFORNIA

My Dearest Cynner, October 10th, 2012

In the packet you will receive, I wrote my words explaining the medical jargon that was sent to you some time ago. It was not easy telling you about my deficiencies, but I wanted to tell you why I do what I do. I want you to understand my medical situation and this is an example how we communicate freely. That said, I can tell you that a change is taking place within me. Since our eyes met and continuing, my walk has improved — not using a cane or wheeler and my gait has elongated. I feel more energized, alert, a happiness that I am not keeping all within myself, but giving to others. Thank You!

You make my heart throb . . . and my ear ring . . . and my shower stall . . . my door jam and my sun shine . . .

Much love,

Howie Y>>PP>>Y YY>>>>Q/Q

Chapter 45. Nest Building

CALIFORNIA

Hello Lovely Cynner, October 10th, 2012

You have sent me some great sites to explore which I have. We must be sharing the same wave length. I was thinking that when I got settled I would find a placement as a volunteer that would help the community, and which I would also benefit.

I will bring the hummingbird feeder — it will be all right, all the homes around here have feeders and the birds will not suffer from lack of sugar water.

Need to have the camper checked by my mechanic, so that everything is purring. Checked the power inverter that converts the 12-volt battery power to 110 volts so I can use low amp kitchen appliances, and it works fine. So am bit by bit getting things done — nothing to be left for the last moment.

I'm yours forever . . . you'll have to pay to have me hauled away.

You are still making my heart throb . . . and my drum roll . . . and my kitchen sink . . . and my birch bark . . . .

Much love,

Howie YPPY

MARTHA'S VINEYARD

Dearest Howie: October 11th, 2012

The UPS truck drove up, Lynn rushed out with her camera, the accommodating driver held out the package, Lynn snapped away, I pried the cardboard off, Lynn snapped, I took the nicely wrapped box out, Lynn snapped, opened it, took out the black velvet box, opened that, and — the ring fits exactly right. Slips on easily, is slightly difficult to get off. Perfect! I made my way to the Post Office to mail off the phone book to you that I'd promised earlier and Liza, the postal clerk, asked, before I even handed her the package, "Anything from Him?" I held out my left hand. Much squealing and shrieking, much congratulating, lined-up patrons waited, got informed about why the commotion, patrons joined in. I asked Liza, because her hair seemed unnaturally natural looking, "What happened to your hair? I wanted to tell Howie what color it is today." She turned around, and, Lo! the entire lower half of her hair in back is turquoise. She sends you her Love! In capital letters.

Gotta get this off quickly so you won't worry.

All my love, Cynner

Below in honor of Liza's hair today:

YPPY !!!

And this in honor of what I'm feeling today — please wake me up SD style:

QQQQQ

CALIFORNIA

Dearest Cynner, October 11th, 2012

Your happiness comes to me in so many ways. I am completely overtaken with joy and all those good feelings with every mail that you send me. I additionally fall more in love with you all the time, that is amazing — I must be growing taller, it has to be showing somewhere. You are truly the most of the most precious who abounds in goodness and loving kindness. I am overwhelmed with your concerns, your forward thinking, your plans supposed but ready to be modified if suggestions are to be made. Mark told me, "Dad all you have to do is show up." I wish it could be soon, no, sooner than soon.

I am now doing all to bring me up Maximum speed for our happiness and long life together.

Much love, Howie

You make my barn dance
and my ginger snap
and my teeter totter

YPPY!!! and all the Q's you can take

MARTHA'S VINEYARD

Dearest Howie: October 11th, 2012

You have to do more than just show up — you have to decide stuff along with me!

I haven't got your packet yet, but it sounds as though you're doing what I do when I get a call from a would-be guest. I try to scare them off: "This is an old house. The floors creak, the doors don't shut, baths are shared. If you're from New York City, the place is much too quiet. If you're from Vermont, there's too much road noise. Books and papers everywhere, no television, windows difficult to open and shut. . . " Then when they get here they think it's much better than expected. I know what to expect of you medically, and you're hardly likely to depress me. I'm no good at nurturing, but since you've been taking care of yourself, you can continue to do that. I'm just me, and I'm afraid you have an inflated opinion of what "me" is.

I haven't gone to Brian Athearn to have him show me how to work the iPad yet, as I didn't want to go too far from home before the ring arrived. Now that my ring is firmly settled on my left hand ring finger, I'll try to make it tomorrow to Brian's, and then you and I can talk face-to-face.

Much, much, much love

Cynner YYYYYYYYY

MARTHA'S VINEYARD

Dearest Howie: October 12th, 2012

I just talked to Rob Culbert, one of the Island's best birding people, and he is sending you my wedding present to you — a gift certificate for six private birding tours to take place when you and he decide it's a good time to view whatever birds are available. He knows you are well acquainted with West Coast birds and that you look forward to meeting those on the East Coast.

With all my love,

Cynner pyyq

CALIFORNIA

Dearest Cynner, October 12th, 2012

That was a very thoughtful and practical and wondrous wedding gift, the personal tours to introduce me to the ornithological wonders of the island. I Thank You! I Thank You!

Your Family chart will be most helpful. I should reduce the size down and carry it in my back pocket until I become very familiar with all.

Howie says, I love you more than yesterday, and more and more . . . by next week you will probably have to put me on a leash!

YPPY, it sounds good

Chapter 46. Tell Your Children

Dear Tsilala: October 16th, 2012

I think of you, rolling around on the floor laughing hysterically like a teenager, when your mother was insisting that I tell my kids about my long distance love affair with Howie and the likelihood that they might hear about it on national radio first if I didn't tell them soon. "Dear Children," your mother instructed me to write. "You should know that. . . "

The long distance affair has progressed to the point where I went to San Diego, Howie proposed, I accepted, we went to the jewelry store and picked out a ring, and now we have a date for our marriage. Howie's coming here to live. We'll have a private commitment ceremony by the fish pond in March, then a real church wedding in May.

The main reason I am writing is, might you be available (and willing) to sing at my wedding? I would be honored if you possibly can. Your mother, of course, must come!

The wedding is to be on Saturday, May 25th, the beginning of the Memorial Day weekend, here in West Tisbury at the Congregational Church. We haven't set a time yet, whether morning or afternoon. Plans are still in flux.

I hope school is wonderful and the agents are flocking to sign you up. I look forward to seeing your name in huge lights on the marquee.

Love, Cynthia

• • • • •

Cynthia and Howard exchanged a flurry of emails during October and November — wedding plans, house plans, travel plans. The iPad arrived and they talked every night. Cynthia wrote, "Over the air I could hear the echoes of possessions departing."

• • • • •

CALIFORNIA

Dearest Cynner, October 15th, 2012

"There is no passion to be found playing small, in settling for a life that is less than the one you are capable of living." N. Mandela. If I said that before, it is worth repeating again.

Good night Cynner, I had one dream about you so far, It seems like you were in a human-sized bird's nest.

Mama bird? I have no details — sort of a flash and that dream was over.

Love you much,

Howie YYYPPPQQQQ

MARTHA'S VINEYARD

Dearest Howie: October 16th, 2012

I feel honored to have you, the ornithologist of my dreams, dreaming of me in a bird's nest. I can picture me as an osprey with an untidy nest of sticks, the latest year's piled up on top of the last several years'. Soaring over the sea and plunging down to catch dinner. I would not be one of the more shipshape birds.

All my love,

Cynner YPPY !
QQQ

MARTHA'S VINEYARD

Dearest Howie: October 16th, 2012

I just got off the phone with Sean Gonsalves, a columnist for the *Cape Cod Times*, who wants to write a column about us and how we got together again. He may be calling you.

Last night the dishwasher flooded the kitchen floor. This happened once before with an earlier dishwasher, and it turned out that a mouse had gnawed the hose that led from the hot water into the machine. Probably bigger than a mouse, because the hose is reinforced with steel wire mesh, and whoever bit into it left a clear crescent chew-mark. Hart Plumbing is sending help. Hardly an emergency, but an inconvenience.

Another gorgeous day. Vineyard autumns don't have the spectacular colors of Vermont or upstate New York. Our colors are more subtle, except for the brilliant orange/red of poison ivy, the fluorescent red of burning bush (euonymus), and the purple-red of blueberry and huckleberry. I'm sending you samples in the mail (leaving out the poison ivy).

As soon as I post this, I'm off to MV Tech Inc to learn how to use my iPad. I'll let you know right away when I'm up and running. I think it will be good to be able to talk to each other and so you can see pictures of work that's getting done around here.

All my love,

Cynner YPPY
Q Q Q Q Q !

MARTHA'S VINEYARD

Dearest Howie: October 18th, 2012

Our story deserves the front page. But I'm afraid you captured a whirlwind when you won me. I hope you realized what you were in for. Please, please don't let me sweep you up in my enthusiasms if you don't wish to be swept up. You're entitled to rein me in and I won't take umbrage.

Everyone seems to be in love with us and our story. It's simply amazing the way it is spreading and bringing happiness to people neither of us knows. People say how we've brightened the day, how we bring hope. How we offset the gloomy and depressing world news. How the world needs us and our love. There are some great romantic stories in the world's literature, but I think ours tops all.

I hope I can bring to you all the good that you dreamed of and have earned and none of the not-so-good.

Hurry, March! Hurry!

But I am nest-building and it will take almost until then. What a pleasure anticipation is. Everyone wants to be involved. I can hardly wait until David Merry's sons come with their Bobcat and dig a foundation hole beyond the east wall.

love you, Howie.

Your Cynner

I can't even encompass in this note all the Ys and Ps and Qs I want to bestow on you.

CALIFORNIA

My dearest Cynner, October 18th, 2012

I feel splendid today, not because of the weather, which is cloudy, windy, unsettled, and promising rain, but because you are very near. You brought me to this state by your last e-mail which is making me feel very warm, and uncomfortably comfortable, because you are not near enough. You are the only one that has unleashed these primal passions that I have — it is like I am programmed to actions, that are at least equally fulfilling to me as you.

Yes our story goes on and on. I am so happy that you followed my clues, and put the story in its rightful place.

I just want to think about you and me. The blue Nightie. Keep it near.

Remember, I like you just the way you are. Continue to be free. Our marriage will not impose constrictions on your thoughts, ideals or activities. Do as you plan and have planned. Go for it all! If I can help, fine, be happy for the opportunity. I will be mostly around the house, the house of love. Passion is not to fade away. I want to court you every day, no insulated box, but a kindle, a warm flame, and then a roaring furnace to consume me.

I love you Cynner

Keep surrounding me with your love, a love that I always wanted.

Q's, in thoughts for the moment, in March a reality. As you say "Hurry up March!"

MARTHA'S VINEYARD

Dearest Howie: October 18th, 2012

Hart Plumber's Mark (#3 Mark in our lives so far) said he couldn't repair the dishwasher because a mouse had gnawed a hole in the drain hose, and the drain hose was a Maytag specialty item. However, his ex-wife's husband, Jason, was an appliance specialist. Jason came today while I was out gallivanting, and the mouse had not only chewed almost through the plastic drain pipe, but had made a significant foray into the metal-braided hot water hose. All fixed by the time I returned, bill for not too much on my kitchen table, the two chewed hoses on the captain's chair. The chew marks are impressive.

I took my iPad to Brian Athearn's, and he put me in the hands of Steve Jordan, who seemed to be the age of my youngest grandson, Wulfric, who's ten. Actually, Steve is a senior in high school, was extremely competent, understanding, courteous, serious, clear in his instructions, nice sense of humor, and together we opened up the boxes and he set things up and instructed me on its use. Gotta go downstairs. Chicken soup with rice, a tomato, and chopped parsley is on the stove. Lots more to say. Pause!

Back, and I've got the soup up here and it's yummy.

When I was at Brian Athearn's place, he said, "Saw the announcement in the paper. Congratulations!" "Wow, that was early," I said, knowing the *MV Times* deadline is Monday. I searched the *Times*. Nothing. Then I wondered if Sean Gonsalves, who'd called me from the daily *Cape Cod Times* saying he was working on a five o'clock deadline, might have been working for today's paper. On my way home I stopped at Alley's, and sure enough, we made Page 1. As well we should. When I read your quotes I laughed out loud. You are just plain wonderful. I'm so glad I love you! I'm putting the front section of the paper in the mail so you can get the full effect of a front page story about us.

In my autograph book that all 8th graders had back in 1943, some terribly clever boy wrote in all the girls' books:

> I love you much, I love you mighty,
> I wish my pajamas were next to your nightie.
> Now don't get excited and don't get red,
> I meant on the clothesline and not on the bed.

That came to mind recently. It occurred to me it would be good to have the blue nightie out on the clothesline along with your XL T-shirt as we snuggle under the new red blanket on the queen-size bed in the Howie Suite with the fire humming on the hearth and . . .

Before I get us into too much more trouble, goodnight, dearest Howie.

Much, much love,

Cynner QQ YPPY QQ

CALIFORNIA

Dear Cynner, October 19th, 2012

Glad to find that you are in the preliminary phase of exploring your iPad. FaceTime is not perfect and the screen will freeze on occasion and sound may be disrupted. Let's try FaceTime time tonight at 9 PM your time. With continued use we will find solutions to the problems and ease of use will be upon us.

You look well on my screen, any lighting will do.

Much Love,

Howie Always many YP's and more Q's

Chapter 47. Unfolding Events

MARTHA'S VINEYARD

Dearest Howie: October 25th, 2012

Mark Lovewell, the photographer for the *Vineyard Gazette,* and a reporter, Remy Tumin, came by on Tuesday to interview me about Our Story. As often as I tell it, which is a lot, I still marvel at the unfolding of events, the coincidences that have happened, great and small, the pleasure of getting to know one another, and the most natural of grand finales.

It was so pleasant out, I had lunch by the fish pond. Leaves were drifting down, dropping into the pond. The fish, about 13 of them, are big and fat after a season of grazing on delicacies that fall from the sky. They were standing on their tails, mouths open for more sky-borne morsels. I've brought in most of my plants now for their winter vacation.

My ring has become an integral part of me and no longer seems alien. It was the right choice. It's simple, yet the pattern of flowers and leaves is meaningful and decorative. When I went into the barber shop, Phil said, "Well, Cynthia Riggs! What's happening in your life?" I said, "Oh, nothing much," and held up my left hand. Bethany squealed. Phil said, "Does that mean what I think it means?" which is when I told them both and got hugged. And kissed.

NOAA hurricane reports we may get hit by Hurricane Sandy early next week. The projected path arcs to the north-northeast.

Mark sent me a copy of *Travels with Charley,* a beautiful 50th anniversary edition, paperback with deckle-edge pages. It looks as though you will be following some of Steinbeck's route, but not dipping down south, the way he did. What a great trip that is going to be. I imagine you as a knight setting forth with your squire on a quest to meet up with your lady love in unknown territory, leaving everything you know behind you. It must seem a bit daunting to you.

1963, right after *Travels with Charley* was published, was when we spent 14 months in desert areas of Nevada/Utah/California. For some time we camped out at Edwards Air Force Base at the end of the runway the X-15 used, and where we had parked a large trailer that we used as a soils testing lab. I worked as an unpaid soils testing technician. We were at Edwards when President Kennedy was shot. I was cooking bacon over a camp stove and we heard the news on the car radio and the bacon burned. At Christmas time we built a snowman of tumbleweed.

After that field season, we drove out west every summer for several years. George was brilliant, stubborn, persuasive, paranoid, psychotic, and toward the end, downright crazy.

I started this letter early this morning, and between various activities interrupting, it's now late afternoon and the light is pure gold and mellow and ephemeral.

I think back on what life has been like so far, and it wasn't all bad, although there were some pretty rough spots. Now I look forward to the future with you and it's bright and golden. Physical problems, we can deal with. It's this amazing, wonderful, exciting, stimulating, romantic, joyful, sensitive, appreciative, generous meeting of minds that is thrilling to me. To discover we have a lot more than mental compatibility was . . . !

All my love.

Your Cynner YPPY QQQ

MARTHA'S VINEYARD

Dearest Howie: October 28th, 2012

There's something about an impending storm that sets the blood flowing and the excitement level rising. I've filled a dozen half-gallon cranberry juice jugs with water, candles and matches are in place, flashlights have batteries, a B&B guest brought two cartloads of wood into the entry, and now we just hunker down. There are seven of us here now. The Steamship Authority is warning that boats may not run on Monday and possibly Tuesday. If so, my guests are trapped. The electricity is likely to go out, since it goes out whenever a zephyr knocks a dead branch onto the telephone wires. I have a dial phone, which works when no one else's phone works.

The branches on the maple at the end of the drive are tossing. A few patches of leaves have turned yellow-gold, but the tree is still mostly green, which means the wind is likely to do more damage because there's more surface area.

I'm not the only one who's comparing your journey in March to a knight and his squire embarking on a quest to reach his fair lady. Several people have commented on it. My knight even has a wide moat to cross before getting to the castle. Who knows how many dragons will be slain along the way.

Wish you were here. I would wake you up instead of this long distance stuff. Funny how I get inarticulate on the phone. You'd think it would be the other way around. When you're here, I hope I won't have to write to you to tell you how I feel. I guess I can always show you.

Much, much love, dear Howie,

Cynner

MARTIIA'S VINEYARD

Dearest Howie: October 29th, 2012

Not much so far, limbs down in places. The electricity is still on, but flickering. Andrew, who always shows up when someone needs him, showed up with a generator (!) Haven't seen him this morning. We're just hanging out. Biscuits in the oven, cooking what we need before the electricity goes out.

YYYYY C (wish you were here)

CALIFORNIA

Dearest Cynner, October 29th, 2012

Just to let you know that I will be at my FaceTime station 9 PM your time. With your weather situation, connecting is chancy, so no problem at all if I do not see you for several days.

Glad that you have company in the house while all this stuff is going on outside.

Much love,

Howie ````pp``yy``QQ

MARTHA'S VINEYARD

Dearest Howie: October 30, 2012

A writer associate in NYC wrote, "Woke up to incredible devastation all around me. The outer boroughs flooded, trees fallen on homes and power lines, some deaths. Homeland Security bringing in trucks to help out. "

Here, the NStar trucks and the West Tisbury police have been working on and/or guarding a pole on the Edgartown Road almost in front of the house. Something on the pole was shooting out sparks.

A lot of the branches that came down during the storm are festooned with different kinds of lichens or mosses, and I've piled some of the more interesting ones on the picnic table. I'll take a photo of them. It looks as though there's some kind of fruiting or blooming structures or something like that.

Much, much love,

Cynner YPPY — QQQ

MARTHA'S VINEYARD

Dearest Howie: November 3rd, 2012

Cat was here this morning measuring and sketching for the plans for the bathroom extension. She said we should get a new bed since our life together is new. So the new direction is this: She suggested I ask John Thayer, a Vineyard cabinet maker, to build us a bed. I like this direction best of all. Island designed and made. Cat sketched out her idea of the right feng shui bed. Queen size, absolutely plain. Solid wood headboard, straight across the top, no footboard.

Andrew, who, on his own, is a Public Utility, said our problem with the freeze frame is quite likely due to Comcast's method of sending data in bursts. The communication works for several minutes, then the data gets piled up waiting for the next burst. At least, that's what I gathered. He said he'd look into ways of getting around the freeze-up. It truly wasn't your being quiet. I love that quiet in you.

At this moment, the sunset promises to be spectacular, so I am going out to view it from the west step. Better hurry . . .

Worth rushing outside for — I'll send pictures, but I think the spectacular range of light, from dark vegetation to brilliant sky was difficult for my iPad to understand. This is where your camera with the multiple exposures would be perfect.

I've been thinking all day about you wanting to get in your camper and head East. I love you a lot.

Much, much love,

Cynner Qqqqq

Chapter 48. The Bee

CALIFORNIA

Dearest Cynner, November 4th, 2012

I am feeling like the bee who desires to go to his beloved flower, but should stay in his hive preparing for the journey, and needs to have the patience awaiting the flower's preparation.

Much, much, much. Love

Howie

MARTHA'S VINEYARD

Dearest Howie: November 5th, 2012

Your plans for Christmas sound about like mine, only instead of going out to a restaurant, I hide my head under the blankets until about 3 pm when everyone else is sated with festivities, and then I emerge thinking I've gotten through that. Once Christmas is over, the commercial blast is over, the days are getting longer, and things look bright again.

As a child I loved Christmas. My father and mother always sent Christmas cards with a block print of his, a poem of hers, and they got wonderful hand-made cards from other people. My father would take us out to buy a tree on Christmas Eve, when the trees were on sale, and we'd decorate it that night and keep it up until Twelfth Night, January 6th. We'd hang stockings, and in the morning we'd shake out the stockings and find nuts and a tangerine, things like Pond's cold cream or toothpaste or a bar of nice soap, maybe little animals to put under the tree. My mother thought every child should receive three gifts — a book, something to wear, and a toy. That was wonderful, and enough.

How would you feel if I flew out to San Diego where I could hide my head under a blanket at Piper Street until the worst was over?

All my love,

Cynner pypypypypy Q

CALIFORNIA

Dearest Cynner, November 5th, 2012

Most certainly you have engaged my mind again. Please do come as your schedule allows and stay on as close to ad infinitum as possible. Do it the first class way and permit me to do the honors.

Let me know the particulars when you have completed the arrangements. Happy Days! and Happy Nights!

Much love, Howie   Ding! Ding! QQQ=

MARTHA'S VINEYARD

Dearest Howie: November 7th, 2012

Good news about the elections — President Obama is back in and Elizabeth Warren won the Massachusetts Senate seat.

I was at the polls from noon to after 4:00, and West Tisbury's voter turnout was 83%. A steady stream of people and kids, and heaps of absentee ballots to process. Stimulating and exciting. After the polls closed, I went to Richard Knabel's (one of our three selectmen) for a get together and television viewing of the election results. I stayed until 11 pm, and the results seemed touch and go at that time, so I didn't learn until I got up this morning that all is well. Such a relief, both our president and our senator.

Wind warnings today, but I think all the branches that could come down have already blown down. The maple tree at the end of the drive is tossing and bowing and the wind is howling through its branches, still lots of leaves to act like sails. I just looked down onto the drive, and the four Guinea hens scurried across the drive, blown by the wind. I love this kind of weather. The steamships are not running because of the wind. Our power probably will go off. It usually does when branches fall onto power lines. You'd think the electric company would install underground wires. Much less vulnerable and certainly less unsightly.

I've been thinking about my visit to San Diego. I hope you see this as a working visit and will put me to work. I'm pretty good at organizing stuff and am sensitive about family treasures. In between bouts of work we can sit in your swing and soak up as much of your canyon life as we can to hold in your memory bank when our only view from the new swing will be the fish pond. Perhaps we can host a modest get together with your neighbors. I think that would be fun. I realized after I made the plane reservations that I won't have another chance to see them in San Diego. The next time will be their visits to the Vineyard, which I hope they'll want to do.

I've been grateful for the good gardening gloves you gave me. They're well broken in with moving fallen branches and stacking firewood.

West Tisbury has almost 2,400 registered voters. During the time I was on duty, about 800 voters picked up ballots. At least a quarter of them offered congratulations, which amounted to at least 200 congratulatory comments! At least half were people I didn't know. I hope you felt that energy — it must have pulsed its way to Piper Street! I just this minute fielded a phone call of congratulations. Can you believe how many people are interested in our story! The three most common remarks are "It gives us hope," and "What an incredibly romantic story!" and "How wonderful to hear good news."

Yesterday I was going over notes I'd made when I tried to find you after I received that memorable package. Early on, I got what I thought was your number and called, but got a strange recorded message that made no sense whatsoever, a robotic voice referring me to a new phone service. I just realized, in checking over the number I'd called then, that the area code must have been changed sometime within the past 20 years. The rest of the number is the same. I wonder now, if I'd gotten you right away, would we have connected the way we have with our written words? I'm not good on the phone and a short conversation might have been the end. I shudder to think what a narrow escape that was. What an elegant path we followed. Everything is promising and bright. We can simply drift on the well wishes we're getting from the entire world. Literally. Eleonore Biber, my friend in Vienna, called long distance to congratulate us.

I spoke about work, and I'd better get busy. I've piled books on the couch in your study, and I need to sort them out. What voracious readers we've had in this family! Whew! What a wide spectrum they covered. I like to think it will be your library, now, and what books would you like to have around you. I'm guessing a selection of everything. There's a full shelf of the Arthurian Legend, one of American Indians. Lots of religious history, lots of history of New England, settlement of the West, several books on the 49ers. I have a soft spot for those, given our trip along Highway 49. Biographies, world history, philosophy, not as much fiction as I'd expected. But autographed copies of books even I recognize, like *Advise and Consent* by Allen Drury. Lots of natural history, art history, creating art works. History of England. Castles and cathedrals of France. An entire bookcase of poetry books. All obviously read and well-worn. Well, you'll see when you get here. Upstairs, there's an entire bookcase filled with murder mysteries that I've added to the library. Daunting!

I procrastinate.

All my love,

Cynner PY PY PY PY and Q

CALIFORNIA

Dearest Cynner: November 7th, 2012

Lynn did a great photo of you at the firehouse voter check in station. I sure fit in with the predominately Demos who really turned out in mass.

I did a lot of window washing today. Theeight panes that face South from the Studio. Also moved stuff out there that will be part of a garage sale some day

Let's have a Romp on a day or evening when you are here, inviting those on the circle.

Jon Grant who plays the accordion and fiddle with a Cajun group may play. This would be a good time for you to meet the three families unknown to you. Children would of course be invited.

Much love, Howie

MARTHA'S VINEYARD

Dearest Howie: November 9th, 2012

Tomorrow I'll go to see John Thayer about making our bed. I think that is going to be the perfect solution. No impersonal factory will have a hand in making it, and it will meet the hundred-year plan requirements. I'll take my iPad and if he makes any sketches, I'll photograph them.

I've been working on the books today. I found a first edition of *Uncle Tom's Cabin,* and I think a first edition of a magazine story by Dickens. Loads of books of essays. It's almost like a down comforter that fluffs up when you shake it. There doesn't seem to be any more room in the bookcases, in fact, not enough room to put everything back, although I've now culled out eight bags of books for the book sale. Three and four copies of some books. This probably should be done once every 50 years or so.

Much love — much, much, much love,

Cynner

MARTHA'S VINEYARD

Dearest Howie: November 10th, 2012

I got up early this morning. Daphne had come into the Woodshed to snuggle up to me, but she had a tick attached to her eyelid, a job I couldn't deal with. So when I heard the shower turn on I quickly got dressed and presented Daphne and the tick to Andrew, as he came out of the shower. We wrapped her, growling and snarling, in a towel, and Andrew managed to pluck it off without putting her eye out. One last backward growl, and a good shaking and cleaning, and she doesn't seem to hold the undignified treatment against either Andrew or me.

Since I was up, I ironed all the bureau scarves that I'd laundered and piled in the top of the bathroom closet. Ironing is not something I do often. Maybe once every six months.

Then I went to see John Thayer about the bed. I had to climb a ladder to his office, which overlooks the Lagoon, a pretty body of water filled with boats. He understands we want simple, minimalist, traditional, solid wood, Vineyard made, solid headboard straight across, no footboard so we can sit on the foot of the bed and put on shoes and socks and watch the fire.

I'm impressed with Cat's renderings! I had no idea, when I asked her to work with Tim, that she was such a pro. More hidden talents around this Island. If you see anything at all that you think could be improved, be sure to speak up.

Today was gorgeous. About 60 degrees, cool enough for a sweater, perfect for being outside. I brought in two cartloads of wood — there's plenty of wood to burn, and raked up two large tarps full of leaves and dragged them over to the compost heap.

Tonight it's brisk, probably lower 40s, and the sky is black velvet and absolutely full of stars glittering and singing overhead and visible down to the horizon.

I am so sorry I missed all the good things you were saying to me before we hung up. I can imagine what they were, but I like to hear you say them. Don't forget what you were saying so you can tell me all over again when I'm there in person. And you know, it is I who should be bowing respectfully to you, not the other way around!

I love the plans for the Romp. Perfect!

Much, much love, much pleasurable anticipation,

Your CynnerQQQQQQQ

CALIFORNIA

Dearest Cynner: November 11th, 2012

Before going to sleep last night, I was thinking about writing you a personal love letter and I was trying to decide if I should use my usual printing or go to script. I fell asleep before I decided, but had an interesting dream. My entire body was sending you an e-mail like message, a soul baring, lucid account of my love for you. It was type-written, using only the middle of the page, such small type that I could not read it, no punctuation marks, just words after words, some capitalized. That Is all I can remember about it. It was like my body was acting like a computer. Mailing you direct.

Much, much Love, Howie

YPPY Q's abounding

• • • • •

Hi Dad & Cynthia, November 12, 2012

A colleague at Fieldston reads the *Vineyard Gazette* faithfully to keep in touch with her beloved summer home news. She was quite delighted to read your story then had a fit when it became evident I was the son in the saga. Apparently she began yelling excitedly to her husband who didn't understand what the hell was the matter with her. The story has certainly touched many lives. Love, Mark

• • • • •

MARTHA'S VINEYARD

Dearest Howie: November 13th, 2012

I'm listening to Jon's Cajun music and tapping both feet to go along with it. It's great, and I'll write him a note to that effect. What happy music. Even though I don't understand a single word, I don't think one needs to. In some places I laugh, not knowing whether I'm really supposed to or not. Such fun. I look forward to seeing him live in concert at the Romp. I realize my writing is probably repeating the rhythm of the Cajun Boys. When I went to the Post Office, two people I scarcely know hugged me and two other people congratulated me. This is all quite amazing and kind of fun. Now it's a waltz.

If I had two more feet I'd be tapping them. My fingers are hitting the keys in time to the music and I'm nodding my head too. What magic music is. How different the *Burnt Earth Ensemble* and *Cactus on Mars* is from Mozart's *Horn Concertos* and from this, and I like them all equally well.

Rained all day, and I got a lot done, errands and moving stuff around.

With this mood, all I can sign off with, is:

YPP Y! YPPY !!! YPPY !!!!

CALIFORNIA

My Dearest: November 14th, 2012

Today I am continuing work on the camper: Having the spare tire checked, getting a gauge for the propane tank, a port-a-potty, tape for the junction of the walls and the kitchen surface, and a small amount of painting on the ceiling of the camper. So that will take care of the camper except for an oil change and lubrication in March.

Mindfulness is about techniques to help one live in the moment. I reckon some people hardly ever do. Myself, I need to dwell in the moment more, but I do not want to give up my past essence of you, or my beautiful dreams of the future with you near.

I would rather not be so mindful, it is much more fun and pleasing having you in my mind and being with you, even closer than being in my imagination.

Much Love. Howie QQYYPP

Chapter 49. An Erotic Intelligence

MARTHA'S VINEYARD

Dearest Howie: November 29th, 2012

It was such fun to see — and hear — the three Wednesday Writers talk to you. They were really On. Amy said, "He's so Cute!" She's a fifth grade teacher and has picked that up from her students. I think it's supposed to be a great compliment. Lisa said, "He's so handsome!"

I think so too. I like your looks a lot. I like your hair and your forehead and your eyes and your nose and your chin and I like the strong angles of your face. There's nothing more erotic than a brilliant intelligence, and yours was everything that appealed to me. So it is a delight to find how physically attractive you are to me as well. Cat nodded and said to the other two, "I told you so."

Much, much love and everything that goes with it, Cynner   YYY

Dearest H:

This from son William. Nice.

YYYYY   Cynner

> Dear Mama,
>
> What I like about you (like choosing among tulips, geraniums, hyacinths, magnolia, hydrangeum and forsythia) is how you are such a positive possibility thinker!
>
> Who else would have given love, hope and serendipity such a window of opportunity, then carefully tended and nurtured the new green shoot?
>
> It is truly a beautiful and inspiring story.
>
> William

CALIFORNIA

My Dearest Cynner,   December 3rd, 2012

The nicest thing just happened. It has been a dark gloomy day and I had just downloaded your scene of the area next to the pond that you were considering as the ceremony site . . . and a burst of sunlight just came in the west window . . . I am at the dining room table and . . . that flick of a message from the sun on the iPad . . . I take as a solar . . . Yes. A down to earth, Yes from me also.

Thanks for all of your beautiful photographs. I could discern the slight green on the postmasters hair. I feel you getting nearer timewise . . . I wish it were sooner, but you did pick the correct time. Have patience Howie . . . which I will try to do.

Much Love, Howie

I love everything....really everything, about you.

MARTHA'S VINEYARD

Dearest Howie: December 4th, 2012

You would think three reasonably intelligent people — Andrew, Sue, and I — could outwit a mouse. When I called last night I forgot to give you the latest score as of 9 pm EST, Monday, December 3rd. It was CH 0; Mouse 5. With set traps, wads of steel wool, various baffles, food stored in critter proof containers, the mouse decided it might as well come out in the open and was devouring, or at least transporting to some cache, Daphne's food. I'd been pleased and surprised at her empty bowls in the morning. Sue recognized the empty bowls as another mouse victory. So last night, I put Daphne's food bowl in the Woodshed with me, thereby foiling the mouse. In the middle of the night, Sue woke to a great racket, came downstairs to find the mouse had emptied the compost bucket, strewing coffee grounds, egg shells, and decaying flowers all around the place-under-the-sink. The score as of this morning, then, is CH 0; Mouse 6. Andrew plans to go to the rat control officer today. He's talking about getting a Hav-A-Heart Trap. We are no longer calling the mouse a mouse. He (or she) is now The Rodent. I'll keep you informed.

Mouse out of the way. I want to say a lot of nice things to you, but I'll write them in a letter instead of lumping them with practicalities.

C YPPY Q

MARTHA'S VINEYARD

Dearest Howie: December 7th, 2012

The latest on The Rodent is no action on his/her part. I suspect it's planning something to up the score from 6-0 to 7-0.

Yesterday morning Andrew was leaving for work and was parked near a wooded patch by New Lane instead of at the end of the drive, when he saw a red-tailed hawk fly out of the woods with a squirrel. A murder of crows came after the hawk and he dropped the thoroughly dead squirrel into my fenced-in-against-deer vegetable garden. Andrew had to get to work and didn't see the resolution of the story, whether the crows came after the carcass, or the hawk retrieved it. Or whether I get to plow in a squirrel skeleton come spring. Andrew speculated on the possibility of The Rodent being that very squirrel. I don't think so. I think it's an R.A.T.

Guess that's all the news of the day, leaving only sweet looks when we talk tonight.

All my love, always,

Cynner YPPY QQQQQ!

• • • • •

Howie sent an astrological comparison of the Aries man and Gemini woman. A perfect fit. Here it is, summarized from Astrology.com:

> Aries and Gemini connect on a physical as well as an intellectual level. They love activity and stay optimistic even in the most trying of times. They enjoy excellent communication and a deep understanding of one another. Aries's independent, pioneering spirit is attractive to Gemini, who

also values independence. They create a good balance together:

Aries is ruled by the Planet Mars and Gemini is ruled by the Planet Mercury. These represent Passion and Communication, respectively. Because of their different approaches, Aries and Gemini work well in tandem.

Gemini helps Aries realize his full potential. She has the energy to keep up with Aries's fast pace. The combination of true, driving passion and intellectual prowess makes almost anything possible for these two. Both Signs have wide-ranging interests.

An Aries man and a Gemini woman will encompass variety, passion, and excitement. Every new challenge and mutual goals will bring these two closer and keep their relationship new and fiery. The Aries man has power but the Gemini woman can control her spouse due to her way with words.

• • • • •

MARTHA'S VINEYARD

Dearest, dearest Howie: December 12th, 2012

How fortunate that we're so compatible! I don't really take astrology terribly seriously, but when you see how amazingly close this is you have to wonder.

This world is so full of interesting things, I feel sorry for people who master one thing to the exclusion of all that's out there. I'm glad you've come to be who you are by the route you've taken. You are a fascinating man. I am privileged to be able to spend my life with you. I'm struck by how you understood what would attract me when you sent me that package. Had you used a real return address, I might not have answered. You intrigued me from the start. You are not only intriguing, you are stimulating and exciting, and it gets better all the time.

Just, Wow!

All my love,

Your Gemini YPPY QQQQQ

Nice to see that the Q part is confirmed by the astrology chart.

MARTHA'S VINEYARD

Dearest Howie: December 14th, 2012

The Cleaveland House Poets gave us a gorgeous bouquet. I've put a packet in the mail with the card telling about the flowers, but thought you might like to see what they are now instead of waiting for the uncertainty of the U.S. Mail. QQQ C

The Bouquet

Star of Bethlehem	Purity
Queen Anne's Lace	Fantasy
Red rose	Love
Phlox	Our souls are united
Calla lily	Understanding
Astromarium	Devotion
Baby's breath	Everlasting love
Pink carnations	Never forget you
Eucalyptus	Protection
Ivy	Fidelity
Tulips	Declaration of love
Rosemary	Remembrance

Chapter 50. Sandy Hook

MARTHA'S VINEYARD

Dearest Howie: December 16, 2012

Yesterday was a solemn day. Like most of the nation, the Island was stunned at the carnage at the Sandy Hook school. It's difficult to imagine what it must be like for the parents of those children. The wonder and excitement and bright promise of the Christmas season and the newness of it all for those six- and seven-year-olds. And then this. The Christmas season can never be the same for the families. It will never again be the same for their surviving schoolmates or their families. Or the entire town. At the Potts's supper last night, that was the main topic of conversation. It seemed unseemly to talk about anything of less consequence. One feels helpless to express the shock and horror and anguish. There's no way to even begin to ease the overwhelming grief of the parents. There's no way to make sense of the shooting. Those children were so little. Every one of them had such potential. Not much one can say about it.

Such a feeling of helplessness and senselessness and cruelty.

C

Much needed YYY

CALIFORNIA

My Dearest Cynner, December 16th, 2012

When I was a child I was never confronted with a world as it is today. There was a lot of unemployment, hunger, street crime, and people trying to get along with what they had, which was in our case was not much. I remember with a small amount of change, maybe, ten cents, buying a potato, some carrots, cabbage and the like to bring home to make soup. We seemed like a happy family and I guess we had hope that things would get better, and they did. Today too much hope has been put aside and depression has snuck in. We could handle natural disasters, but these man-made senseless acts are bewildering, disturbing, with the bottom line for prevention absent . . . In my childhood I was not confronted by man-made terrible actions . . . Why? Man has since changed, along with technology, some for the better, some for the worse.

I am so sorry to see the general state of mankind as it is today. I really want to live more minimally so others can live. I give a little for the food bank and try to help those thatI know to be in need. But this massive problem with the discontents and the mentally ill out in society, I would like to know of the solution.

I take your words at heart and feel your anguish. I am along side you. I feel with you. I am hugging you so that we both feel better.

H

MARTHA'S VINEYARD

Dearest Howie: December 16th, 2012

My mother used to send me out to get a free soup bone and ten cents worth of soup greens, and she made the most incredibly delicious vegetable soup with barley. She'd scoop the marrow out of the bone and divide it carefully into five pieces that we'd spread on a cracker for a very special treat. We would scavenge two-cent deposit bottles and with five bottles we could buy a loaf of bread. My mother made it seem like great fun, a wonderful treasure hunt, making something from nothing. Nothing wasted.

I attribute a lot of the nation's problems to television watching. It stunts creativity, it blurs the boundary between reality and fiction, it keeps people sitting and munching indoors when they should be out playing or walking, it keeps people from interacting with one another, it shortens viewers' attention spans, and I'm convinced that it alters brain function. The ads are designed to do exactly that. (Cynthia's soapbox lecture #43).

I guess all we can do is work locally, one on one, and hope decency spreads.

More hugs today, please — I can't think of us and joy when I think of those parents and the surviving children.

Doesn't lessen my love. Just increases it.

Your Cynner

• • • • •

Dear Cynthia~ December 17th, 2012

I want to wish you a wonderful journey to San Diego. You have added immeasurable joy to the small Attebery clan and I feel so fortunate that you are in Howard's life.

May we find peace in our hearts—

Love Jennifer

Dear Jennifer: December 17th, 2012

Thank you so very much for you good wishes. Really, I am the fortunate one. The three Wednesday Writers, Lisa, Cat (for Catherine), and Amy kept insisting that I follow up on that package Howie sent. They were so right. He and I have the most extraordinary things in common. Manganese nodules? Who'd have guessed that one ! I don't know whether Howie passed this on to you or not. Cat, who understands Buddhist things, is going to officiate at our very private service after you and Mark and Howie get here and have time to decompress. We'll have Howie and me, you and Mark, Lisa, Cat, and Amy, and Lynn Christoffers will be our photographer. Cat said trees are important. While this is Howie's affair, I butted in enough to say I'd like to plant a beech tree, and asked Jonathan Revere, a long-time friend, if we could dig up a beech tree from his property. Jonathan said, "Yes! Of course!" and on his own went to the Polly Hill Arboretum and asked Tim Boland, the director, what was the best time and way to plant the tree to insure its survival. Tim Boland said the best time to dig and plant is late March (you see?) and said he would like the honor of digging the tree and planting it. Amy has agreed to read my mother's poem, "Beeches," that begins, "If we could be, like Bauccis and Philomen, changed into trees, could they be beech?" Weather permitting, we'll have the ceremony by the fish pond, where you and Mark connected me with Howie by phone for the first time. Weather inclement, we'll have it by the parlor fire.

Much love to all of you, Cynthia

• • • • •

CALIFORNIA

My Dearest Cynner, December 19th, 2012

Soon you will be in the air and that brings excitement.

We had a big wind storm last night and early this morning but it is calm and sunny now. When you arrive tomorrow it will be sunny and 65 degrees and a promise of sunny or somewhat cloudy the rest of the week.

This is what memories are made. It will be better than good, good to see you.

Much Love, Howie A warm heart awaits you, and H. with Y's, P,s and Q's=

Chapter 51. A Low-Key Christmas

Howie met me at the airport, driving his white Hyundai. Less awkward than our first meeting in September, but still a feeling on my part, "Does he really know what he's letting himself in for?" Within minutes, all was well, a seamless transition from the passion of the abstract written word to reality. We shopped for an orange tree. We visited the museum, the waterfront, the botanical gardens, the Paradise Point Resort, where Howie introduced me to San Diego's birds. A low key Christmas, with brunch at his step daughter Susan's home, a long walk, a take-out lunch. Quiet talk.

• • • • •

On my iPad in San Diego was this message:

My Dearest Cynner,

This is a most happy day . . . When I woke up I remembered the ring box, opened it and now the ring is on my finger and I am exuding feelings of being totally with you...the togetherness that not only completes one dream, but now dreams that we will complement each other in a life that brings untold happiness to us.

A beautiful thank you to Cynner on this Christmas morning.

Howie=

CALIFORNIA

My Dearest Cynner, December 28th, 2012

A summary: WOW! WHAT A WOMAN YOU ARE!

I packed the scanner in its original box and am starting a pile of things that go in the camper. I made a list of things I want Mark to tackle. Finished a fish sandwich just before this. Will send this off now, but not before thanking you for the most extraordinary, beautiful days that I could not even have imagined, that just happened and happened and happened.

Your Howie Good night love, thinking about you in the most marvelous ways

• • • • •

Hi Cynthia, December 29th, 2012

Thanks for sending the handsome photo of Dad. Today we had our Saturday face-time. He was simply ebullient in the wake of your visit. Jennifer and I are so charmed and inspired by the both of you, as are so many. I must say thank-you . . . not only to the fates that brought you back together, but mostly for your influence on my father's life right now. He is so happy, open and in love. I am looking forward to celebrating the new year with Dad, and helping him with the final phase of his bi-coastal journey back to you.

—Love Mark

• • • • •

CALIFORNIA

My Dearest Cynner, December 31st, 2012

2012, a very wonderful year for me starting with emails to each other bringing together my dreams, hopes, and your love. September 24th you arrived, Howie proposed marriage, Cynner in so lovely a manner said yes, and the next day we were off to the jeweler. Two nights and a day and a half of bliss and you departed and we continued with emails and now FaceTime.

December 20 you arrived with perhaps your wondering if we could get along well for a week together. That notion was quickly dispelled as an effortless communion of togetherness occurred, and occurred, and occurred, bringing much joy and satisfaction for me. You are the one Cynner. I love you this day and all those past days and you have my love for all the days that will come.

The New Year will be the Happiest of all my years, for you and I will be together.

To the Loveliest, Howie=

MARTHA'S VINEYARD

Dearest, darling, Howie: January 1st, 2013

Happy New Year, Love!

It was good to see you last night. You were the one I wanted to see as the year closed and the first one I want to see, or at least write to, at the start of the new year. This will be the very, very best year coming up with even better ones to follow. I love you lots. I can hardly believe the depth of feeling I have for you. You've opened up an entire world of possibility for me, and I am grateful beyond mere thankfulness.

Now that I've tacked up a new calendar, I'm counting days until we are together again. The tasks before us both seem huge — you packing up or shedding an accumulation of a former life, and me building a nest for our new life. It really does seem like the knight in shining armor surmounting huge obstacles to get to his lady love waiting in her castle.

Dearest love, I can't begin to tell you how special you are to me, what a joy you are to me, what a perfect soul mate you are, what a perfect lover.

Your Cynner YPPY QQQ

CALIFORNIA

My Dearest Cynner, January 7th, 2013

Doing well in getting things outside. In March will have another sale of items in the house to clear all out and then rent it as unfurnished. Mark has done a wonderful job in organizing the sale. As soon as I am finished here will go out and price the items marking the larger more expensive items. Wanted to let you know what is going on, have been really busy, but this is all for us to be together as destiny beckons.

Much love, Howie YPPY......Q....Q....Q....Q=

MARTHA'S VINEYARD

Dearest Howie: January 7th, 2012

You may have fantasized at some point about being recognized as the world's preeminent microbiologist. Did it ever occur to you that you're going down in history as the world's greatest romantic? I'd agree.

Your Cynner PPY Q

MARTHA'S VINEYARD

Dearest Howie: January 13th, 2012

How beautiful the rosemary is. Rosemary for remembrance. We can grow it here, but have to take it inside for the winter. Do you have room in the camper to bring the plant with you? Along with lavender, lilacs, and lily of the valley, one of my favorite scents. Honeysuckle. Roses. Pine trees on a warm day. Wood smoke. Hot spiced cider. Bread baking. Boston baked beans cooking all day Saturday. Mud flats when the tide is out. I guess they're all favorite smells.

If you want to make a list of things you'd like us to grow, I'll order the seeds or plants or corms or bulbs or whatever. Saint Patrick's Day, March 17th, is the traditional day for planting peas here on the Vineyard. We can also plant lettuce, radishes, Swiss chard, kale, onions, and potatoes at that time. You and Mark will be on your way here then. You'll be here to see them emerge. Yippee! New life all around.

You looked so handsome last night, so vigorous and vital, so appealing. I love to hear you laugh. I wish I were as articulate as you are. I love to hear you say nice things to me. Funny, I can write okay, but I get tongue-tied in person. My mother wrote a poem expressing almost the same thought. The poem ends, "I have within, picture poem love, But no one knows."

Cynner PPPPP YYYYYY QQQQQQQQQQ

MARTHA'S VINEYARD

Dearest Howie: January 19th, 2013

I look forward to our evening talks. The other night when we didn't connect, I felt lonely too, as though a date to go for a walk had to be cancelled. I loved those walks during Christmas week. The walk around the lake where the vast city of holes marked where gophers lived, and then one peered out at us. And the walk around the Paradise Resort with the variety of birds, the trees and shrubs and flowers, and the beauty of the place . Irish coffee and that being your mother's choice of libation. The botanical garden and the fountain. The walk on the waterfront with the working boats, thinking about lunch and being reluctant to dine with the throngs and then you knowing the perfect small quiet place. You knew your way around that huge traffic jam. I felt safe and comfortable with you at the wheel.

All my love, CynnerQ

Chapter 52. Precious Possessions

• • • • •

Howie had a cherished collection of guns. When Cynthia told him how uncomfortable she was about guns, he sold them. The hand gun was his last.

• • • • •

CALIFORNIA

January 21st, 2013

Dear Cynner, Just had a visit with Jon. He bought the hand gun so I am relieved. Talk to you soon. Love, Howie QQQPPPPYYYYYY

MARTHA'S VINEYARD

Dearest Howie: January 21st, 2013

I went to the YMCA gym with my sister again today, and signed up for a membership. Actually, I signed up both of us, you and me, and the woman at the desk said, "Have your husband come in to have a photo taken." That sounded lovely. On Saturday when we went, I walked 5/10th of a mile on the treadmill while Ann walked a mile. The walking machines overlook a huge swimming pool where the high school swimming team was practicing, and it was fun to see. Ann is very diplomatic about my lack of prowess. She's 87 and I'm only 81. The place isn't at all gym like, it's immaculate, light and airy, and quiet.

It's dark out now. I'll go outside and see what the weather is doing. I love the anticipation of possibly being snowed in, maybe a major blizzard. Lots of wood in, I got the Versa gassed up and parked it nose out near the house, laid in eggs and bananas and half & half, charged up the iPad, put candles in the candlesticks for when the power goes out, and all's well. I would love being snowed in with you. My husband! I'm not used to saying that. We can set up the card table in front of the fireplace and have our dinner, heated over the fire, candlelight and linen napkins.

I would like you to be with me this minute, dearest Howie. There's so much ahead of us to do together, so much to do separately and discuss with each other, so many decisions to make together, so much to explore, so much of wonder in our future. I said the other day how comfortable I feel with you. It's more than that. I have a longing for you. I love the way you are interested in not only the big concepts in life, but the most trivial stuff I tell you. If I were to ask you what kind of paperclips you'd prefer in your desk drawer, you'd consider it thoughtfully. I never dreamed a relationship could offer so much.

I'll talk to you soon, my very, very own love.

Your Cynner YPPY — QQQQQQQQQQQQQQQQ

• • • • •

Dear Jennifer:

Howie may not have told you the tale of The Dress for Our Wedding, so just in case he didn't, here it is. I can't begin to tell you how much I loathe shopping and I was dreading the hunt for the right dress to wear for

Cynthia modeling her wedding dress at the consignment shop

our June wedding (what Doug Green, my son-in-law, calls Wedding Two after our Buddhist ceremony). I was on the mainland in Woods Hole at our local NPR station moaning to Mindy Todd, one of the hosts, and she said, "There's a wonderful consignment shop in Cataumet."

That was no help to me.

Then she added, "I just Love shopping there!"

A light bulb went off in my mind.

"Would you like to find a dress for me?"

"Yes!"

"I budgeted $500 for it. "

"That should be enough."

"A dress for my daughter Ann?"

"Of course!"

So here's a photo of me in my wedding finery. Yesterday I sent off a gorgeous lavender sleeveless dress to Ann. It's floor length and looks as though it was fitted onto her !

Love, Cynthia

• • • • •

CALIFORNIA

C. January 25th, 2012

You are the one that I first think about in the morning before my eyes open and it is you who is in my thoughts as I go to sleep at night. It is so great to have you by my side as I do my daily things. I have read about and have seen on cinema great loves . . . now I am the fortunate one to share with you this overwhelming hard to describe feeling, which is a mix of supreme gladness, happiness beyond happy, a splendid warmth that covers my body, contentment that echoes, a desire to make everyone happy and feel grand . . . and as someone said . . . OH! SWEET MYSTERY OF LIFE AT LAST I FOUND YOU!

I could not be more pleased in looking at the synthesis of you and the dress . . . what a delight, the color, the design, the detail, the fit, the charm in the way you two go together. Most beautiful and gorgeous. You look so happy. You are to be the beautiful bride . . . and mine . . . Thank You! I appreciate the effort of all those involved in the finding this ideal dress. Again an example of community wanting to be there and to be a part of the theme of delightfully bringing us together.

Yes, Beautiful One, You are my love for all my days...and nights

YYYYYYYYYYYY PPPPPPPPPPPP QQQQQQQQQQ

MARTHA'S VINEYARD

My dearest, dearest love: January 25th, 2013

What a wonderful letter! I'm so glad you approve of the dress. It looks even better in real time. The dress for me and the dress for Ann, that beautiful lavender one, came to a total of $103.50. How amazing to get exactly what you want with minimum effort on my part and what I would pay for three pairs of jeans.

That makes it sound too bargain-ish, but you understand, I know. When someone at WCAI called Mindy on her cell phone at the consignment shop and asked if the dress fit, Mindy said, "Of Course!" and the person at the other end said, "That figures. Everything in this relationship is so right."

It is, isn't it!

Gotta run.

Everything Plus !!!

Cynner

MARTHA'S VINEYARD

Dearest Howie: January 26th, 2013

Lisa, Cat, and Amy came over today and addressed and stamped wedding invitations, and I took them to the P.O. Closed, of course, on Saturday afternoon so I put them in the outside mail drops. It was great fun. My list has about 150 names on it, including people's children, but I think a large number of them won't be able to attend but will be pleased to be asked.

Weather is warming up, but it's still only around 20 degrees. Next week is supposed to be up in the 40s and 50s, so I've got my fingers crossed that they can finish pouring the concrete.

Talk to you soon, you wonderful, special guy. I look forward to our talks. I treasure your emails. You are so articulate. Fresh, sweet, loving, kind, decent, and romantic, and you are able to convey it across the wires and airwaves in a way that makes me feel as though you are here and brings tears to my eyes. Thank you for being all you are to me.

All my love,

Cynner PPPPPPPPP

On January 30 I went to the YMCA gym again with my sister Ann with new sneakers I'd bought. I planned to get into shape for our wedding. After I did a mile on the treadmill, I dismounted, tripped over my new shoes, staggered, and fell heavily with a tremendous crash onto the mountings of a nearby machine. The sound of working machines stopped and people came running. I lay there, hardly able to breathe, horribly embarrassed, and not sure what hurt and where.

A crowd gathered around me.

"Are you all right?"

"Can you get up?"

"Do you need help?"

I could only shake my head and gasp, "I'm okay. I just need to wait a minute."

Someone brought me a wet towel and held it against my forehead.

Eventually, the well-wishers went back to their machines. In horrible pain, I struggled to my feet.

"I'll take you home," said Ann.

Pause. "I don't want to," pause, "to keep you from. . ."

"We're going home," said Ann.

Somehow she got me down on the elevator, walked me to her car, eased me into the passenger seat, and drove me home.

"Will you be okay?" she asked.

"Yes, yes, " I mumbled. "Just shaken up. Just want to lie down."

I grabbed my iPad, the wedding present Howie had given me, and eased myself onto the couch at the end of the dining room.

As minutes ticked by I felt worse and worse and decided I'd better call Ann and have her drive me to the hospital. I couldn't move. I couldn't get up to get to the phone.

But I had my iPad. I knew that Lisa, of the Wednesday Writers, checks her emails frequently. She has a teenage daughter. I stabbed out a message on my iPad, "Please call my sister Ann," with her number.

The next thing I knew, Lisa was there, at my side, with her fiancé, Charlie. They sized up the situation and called 911. Within two minutes, literally, two West Tisbury police officers were there, checking to make sure my situation wasn't life threatening.

"The ambulance is on its way," they assured me.

"Is Jim Osmundsen on?" I mumbled. Jim, an EMT, is a friend.

"He'll be here."

Within another three minutes, the Tri-Town Ambulance arrived with three EMTs including Jim. They eased me off my couch onto a stretcher, strapped me in, and wheeled me out through the front door, which is used only on grand occasions, into the ambulance.

A communications center with everything needed to have the hospital physician prepared for whatever injury was on its way, the ambulance sped me to the emergency room.

Lisa and Charlie were there for me.

I'd fractured four ribs in my fall.

I spent the night on a gurney in an emergency room cubicle because the hospital was full of flu cases and no rooms were available.

From my gurney, I e-mailed Howie, who told his son, Mark, what had happened. "I left my FaceTime on all day so she could call me if needed," Howie said, "and I sent her a video of a flower, an oxalis — and the citrus we planted and the cutup pink flesh of the orange from the tree we planted. She takes her iPad everywhere."

• • • • •

CALIFORNIA

Dearest Cynner, February 1st, 2013

I have been listening to *The Point* with Mindy Todd so I have bookmarked it and will tune in at the appropriate time.

It is good to hear your voice over FaceTime and you always look splendid.

Glad to know that you are on the mend. You are tough but you have the right amount of feminine allure that gets me.

Interesting sky. Sun has set and the clouds are various shades of grey and what makes it striking are jet contrails, stark white, as the planes are headed to Texas.

Love my lady Friday and all the days, Howie No P's but lots of Y's and Q's=

CALIFORNIA

My C February 5th, 2013

Every night before I turn the lights out over my bed I kiss the ring that you bestowed on me and I am thankful that we are forever forever together.

Every night when I am in your presence, I will always kiss you good night and remark what you mean to me.

Every night and throughout every day . . . I love you.

Y'r H=

CALIFORNIA

My Dearest Cynner, February 6th, 2013

The Bed

At my stage of life the bed assumes a more prominent role that it has ever had before. It used to just exist, but now it calls. It is more than a place of rest and a means of regaining lost energy. It is now more than ever a desired time between the place where day ends and the starting point for the next day's beginning. It now has a life of its own. Our bed now is that most important place which gives the time spent there, results that are most wondrous, bringing forth the dearest, sweetest, warmest and fulfilling moments imaginable.

The bed is a very special place to be respected, honored, even altar like for the sacredness of the togetherness taking place there. Can you now imagine the feelings generated in me when my betrothed asked me to participate in the designing of our own bed, to be made on this magical island. She handpicked the bedding and even towels with CH, for Cleaveland House, but secretly meaning Cynner/Howie. This is one mighty and exceptional woman full of endearing love of which I am honored to be on the other side (of the bed) with her.

Cynner you make me feel exceptionally good. You are the loveliest of the lovely. Thank you for saying, "Yes" . . . sometimes it seems our two hearts beat as one, in perfect time . . . your breath and mine.

All my love, Howie Infinity of Y's

• • • • •

The Moth program taped in August on Martha's Vineyard was aired nationwide shortly before Valentine's Day.

• • • • •

CALIFORNIA

Dearest C February 8th, 2013

Heard *The Moth* presentation from the Vineyard rebroadcast today. You did a splendid talk and I heard all the applause.

Thinking of you I need you C. Be well I am sending a large number of kisses =

• • • • •

Cynthia was invited to tell her story again on *the Moth*'s NYC Mainstage on Valentine's Day. Although she was in great pain from the fractured ribs, she was determined to go to New York.

• • • • •

MARTHA'S VINEYARD

Good morning dearest H: February 10th, 2012

I'm upstairs on my computer, feeling more and more normal as each day passes. I think it's advisable on Tuesday for me to have someone from WCAI in Woods Hole drive me that one block up the hill, even though right now that seems overly indulgent, and then to have someone from *The Moth* meet my train at Penn Station at 4:45. Might as well play my sports injury up for all it's worth.

Much love,
Yr C

• • • • •

Mark and Jennifer, who live in Nyack, not far from New York City, invited her to dinner. Mark wrote his dad, "Jennifer was driving on errands yesterday and Cynthia's voice miraculously issued forth from the car radio!"

• • • • •

MARTHA'S VINEYARD

Dearest Howie: February 10th, 2013

Funny about Jennifer hearing *The Moth* on the car radio. That happened to a B&B guest driving from Boston to Vermont, and also to my daughter Ann and her husband Paul who had just parked at the hardware store in Santa Barbara when the announcer said something about a romantic story coming up, so they waited, just in case, and sure enough!

Your Cynner

Chapter 53. Mainstage *Moth*

Catherine, from *The Moth,* met me at Penn Station and escorted me to a cab and from there to the hotel where they'd booked me. I could barely walk, could hardly breathe without pain, and was determined to not let anyone know how much I hurt.

The hotel room was a disaster: too small, too stuffy, too dark, and with a bed so soft that I had no support for my fractured ribs. During the sleepless night, I e-mailed Valerie, one of the Wednesday Writers, who had once offered me the use of her New York apartment.

She responded with a warm welcome.

I learned how many friends I have. Lynn Christoffers, who was in the city, relocated me to Valerie's seventh floor penthouse apartment, airy, roomy, comfortable, with two window walls overlooking the city, a large kitchen along a third wall, and a wall of books on the fourth wall. I was about to write "fourth dimension." It seemed that way — a retreat into an otherworldly dimension.

The Moth rehearsal was to be at their third floor walkup office that afternoon.

"I can't do stairs," I said.

"You can come up slowly," they said. "We'll wait."

"Not even one stair," I protested, my side screaming in pain at the thought.

Valerie, hearing about this, offered her apartment for *The Moth* rehearsal. Three TV cameras, five storytellers, a half-dozen *Moth* staff members, and a dozen supporters of *The Moth,* fit into Valerie's apartment with space left over.

Howie had no idea of the drama going on in NYC. He was busily organizing and packing boxes for shipping to Martha's Vineyard. At the end of phase one, he noted in a February 13 e-mail, he had 11 boxes weighing a total of 350 pounds. The heaviest box was about 70 pounds, he reported, with most in the 25-40 range.

CALIFORNIA

My Dearest Cynner, February 14th, 2013

You give me strength, please use all that I can give you.

Much Love, Howie YYYpQ=

• • • • •

Dear Family: February 24th, 2013

Here's a photo of Howie, practicing his ferocious expression. Peter Dunkl, of the Vineyard Classic Brass, felt that Howie needed some form of protection against villains on his cross country trek, and loaned him a vest: NEW BEDFORD PISTOL TEAM in bold letters. Given New Bedford's reputation as one tough town, Howie's obvious ferocity, and the pistol team — not merely a club — the combination should ensure that some would-be brigand will not mess with him.

Cynthia/Mama/G'c

• • • • •

CALIFORNIA

February 25th, 2013

Dearest Cynner, Camper was at the RV Service Center today to get its final service. It is now fit and ready to go. I suppose it had a good time visiting its big brothers (RV's are all masculine). Never did name my camper, maybe will do so on completion of the trip.

Beautiful sunny day . . . just spent an hour there for the service. It is full of gas and anxious to start the trip but not more than me.

You are loved by Howie.

Y Y
YY
Y
Y pQQQQ

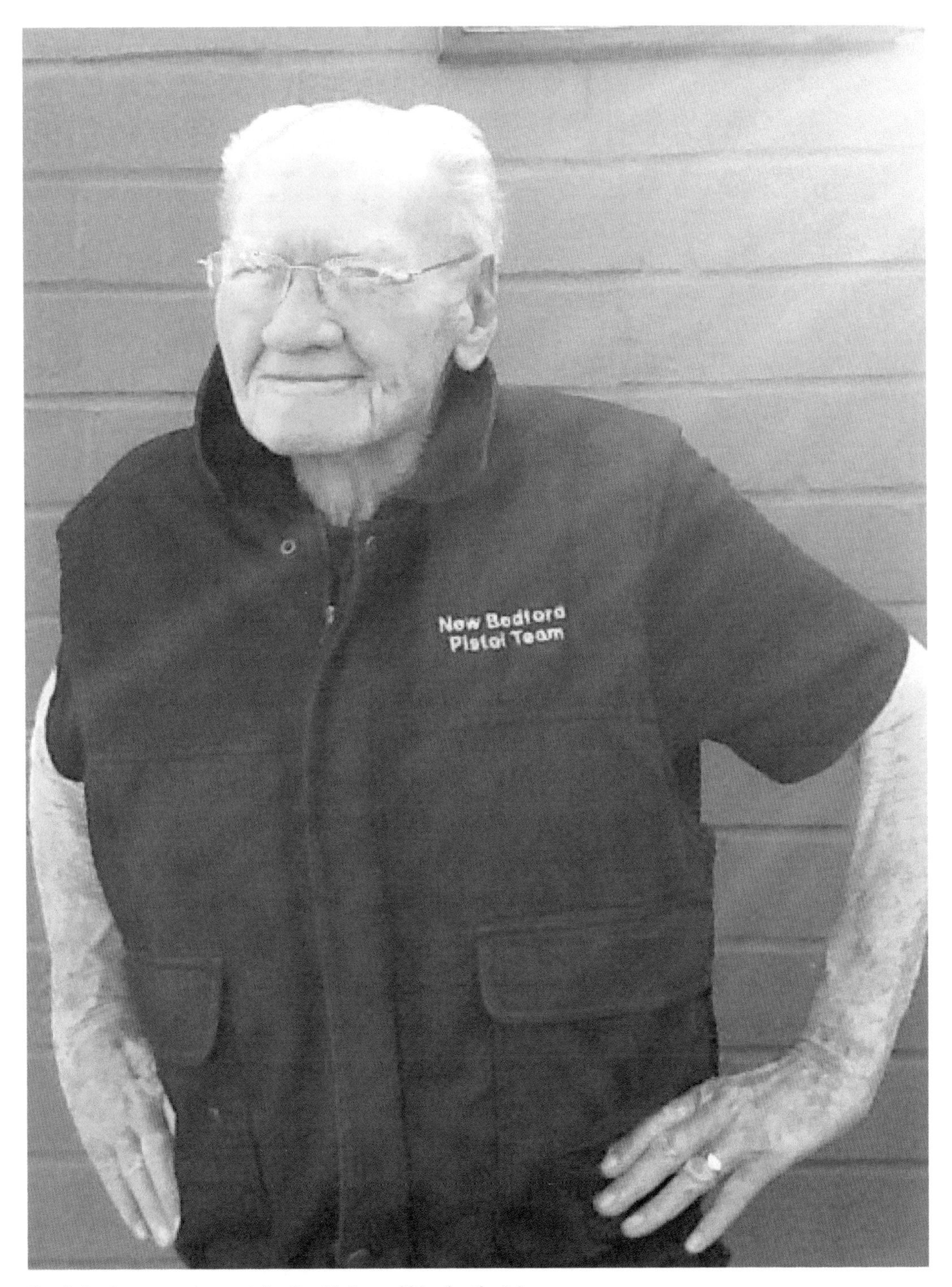

Howie in the protective vest the Dunkls loaned him for the trip.

MARTHA'S VINEYARD

Dearest Howie: February 26th, 2013

That's a great photo. Your camper looks almost like the tender for the Queen Mary.

ALL my love, Cynner YPQ

• • • • •

For the next week or so their emails involved plans for the cross-country trip. Howie wanted to leave no later than March 20th, writing, "In that way it will give us extra time that may be needed as we may be slowed by road conditions or weather." In the meantime, weather had held up construction of the new bathroom, and Cynthia assured the carpenter, Tim, that Howie was "perfectly okay with the present bathroom for the nonce, especially since the study is all put together as is our bedroom."

• • • • •

MARTHA'S VINEYARD

Dearest Howie: March 6th, 2013

I went to Bert's Barbershop to get my hair cut today, and Rob Culbert was in one of the two barber's chair and Shelley Christiansen was waiting. Of course there was a spirited conversation about the best time for you to start birding with Rob. Both Phil and Bethany, the two barbers, got involved in the conversation about birds and birding. Apparently migrating birds are arriving now and will continue through early April, so any time you're ready is fine with Rob. He said the redwing blackbirds are here now, as are the starlings and grackles. Susan Whiting, author of the bird book you purchased, is birding in Texas, according to Rob.

Shelley, an NPR commentator, is the one who urged me to tell our story on *The Moth*. I may have sent you one of her newsletters that really capture the essence of the Island.

The propane people wanted me to run out of kerosene before they installed the propane heater in the Woodshed so we wouldn't waste the kerosene. I think we've run out. The Woodshed has reached the ambient temperature of the out-of-doors. Invigorating.

I love our evening talks about such consequential things as eggs and WD-40. So much more to talk about! Did I ever tell you about my shipwreck?

All my love, Cynner

PPP (I'm mending rapidly), YYYYY (yes!), QQQQQQQQ (oh, my!)

CALIFORNIA

My Dearest Cynner, March 7th, 2013

Visited the WD-40 plant today and talked to a young lady at the desk, who, by the way, is a transplant from MA. The kind, thoughtful gentleman who showered us with gifts was Robert Ramirez, who is their accounts chief. I gave the company a copy of your presentation in *The Moth* program. On the back of his card it says "We live under the sink, in the garage and in the toolboxes of the world." I Googled WD-40 and found they have a very active fan-club, also something about a list of 2000 uses for WD-40.

You are my love. Mark will be here this day next week and then in possibly five more days we can be on the road. YPPY Howie QQQ=

CALIFORNIA

My Dearest Cynner, March 17th, 2013

Just finished getting back from FedEX and dropping off five boxes, for certain the last of the boxes. They should arrive around Friday. Another 150 pounds to stress your floor. Signature needed, in that way the driver can bring the items inside your house and place them where you desire.

All is going well. A painter has been contacted and he will paint after we leave. Cleaning crew will come tomorrow. I will make a final visit to Kaiser Medical for leg bandaging and pharmacy pickup. Load the camper, gas-up and also change addresses and do little things that have to be done, Jon gave me a security deposit and he is coming tonight to pick up the keys and get a rundown on the house which is to be empty except for the personal camper items to be placed tomorrow. Also tomorrow at 7 PM going to John Trapp's for the party.

Mark has been going nonstop in getting things ready for the painter, caulking the bathroom skylight, removing brackets from unwanted shelves, having duplicate keys made and hundreds of other things.

Good to see you near the beech tree with the planters. I was expecting a very small specimen and the one presented is a towering one.

Talk to you tonight. Take your time getting to FaceTime, we will be here.

Much love, Howie YPPY QQQ=

Chapter 54. En Route

My Dearest Cynner, March 19, 2013

Just about an hour left and we will be on our way. My dream is in its final stage of becoming true. What a wonderful life!

Love you the most, most. Howie kisses, hugs, and all the other good things in abundance.=

My home was now empty of furnishings, goods . . . everything . . . and it was ready for the new occupants to move in and it was glad times for me to move on to the much anticipated road trip across the country and a new beginning on an island in the Atlantic Ocean.

Started off in my camper, a Kaiser mounted on a 1986 Toyota truck that was packed with clothes, computer, and other electronic items. Mark and I were to share driving and we had preplanned our trip inch by inch selecting motel spots every 400-500 miles. I said let's forget the plans and go as far as we can each day. I started the driving . . . it was early in the morning and I honked the horn to say goodbye to the neighbors. I drove nearly to Arizona and then Mark took over for the rest of the day and evening.

We planned to go the mid-country route for the shortest mileage but heavy rains and snows were forecast so we ended up going a southern path. I was amazed in seeing so much construction of motels, a hospital, a convention center, and homes on our travels through Arizona, New Mexico, and Oklahoma. The railroads were busy, long trains with 100 plus cars were going across the country day and night. The semis hauling freight were numerous and annoying, but well driven. Campers and recreational vehicles were few in number. We stopped each night for lodging rather that stay in the camper so we could take prolonged showers and have a good meal and then use the wi-fi so we could message our loves to what had occurred during the day and tell them how far we had progressed.

• • • • •

I was getting closer to Cynner and all had been going well until we went thru Tulsa on our way to Oklahoma City and then the motor blew. We had been running the Toyota long and hard trying to make as good a time as possible to get to our destination quickly. We ignored a red light on the dash that came on just for a few seconds after most stops for gas or food or in the morning startups.

A cell phone to Geico, my auto insurance carrier got me a tow into Tulsa. The tow truck driver was a character and it was a welcome relief that his jokes and remarks provided, especially about the lady giving directions on his map locator wi-fi.

The truck was towed to a Toyota agency where it was pronounced dead, new motor needed. That would have taken several days which we thought we did not have and it was an old truck, etc . . . but considering what was in store I wish we had fixed the truck.

• • • • •

So we were down to a camper shell and no vehicle. Tulsa is called the truck capital of the United States so it should have been easy to find a truck for the camper. We looked, old trucks, new trucks: despite the best efforts of Tulsa-area truck dealers, none of them had the right bed dimensions for the usable but obsolete camper.

Giving up after a long search we decided on a new Ram truck. We would leave the camper behind. This was real sorrow as my camper was in pristine condition and I was full of travel memories with it but most of all it was an efficient and comfortable living module.

Since the new Ram had a flat bed unprotected from the weather we rented a U-Haul trailer, moved my belongings into it, and set off after this two-day delay, keeping in mind that we had a Buddhist Commitment Ceremony scheduled for March 28. All seemed to be going well. It was raining a lot but we were putting on the miles using toll roads, which were new to me and required stocking up on change to make transitions doable.

• • • • •

When we stopped for the night just past Memphis, we went to get some items from the U-Haul. We opened the door — and water rushed out. The roof had leaked badly and it was a mess inside. We salvaged what we could and early next morning bought large plastic bins to transfer everything into. We sort of merrily went along in the snow and the rain secure that all would not get further damaged and most of all we were getting closer and closer to Cynner for me to be joined with her in a few days.

The new Ram was cozy and luxurious and had a lot of electronic stuff for the driver to admire, use, or just wonder about. The ride was very comfortable but on occasion we felt a power loss and put this to patches of ice on the highway. It was in Nyack N.Y. that this power loss was complete. The transmission failed and the truck was towed to a dealership who provided me with a new loaner truck while my truck was being repaired. I reached the Island on March 27, the day before the Ceremony.

PART 5: HAPPY ENDING, HAPPY BEGINNING

Chapter 55. A Buddhist Ceremony

HOWARD'S STORY

I, Howard, am a Buddhist in the sense that I am a spectator and follower in the philosophy of the Buddha. To me he is not a God but a man who lived and a light went on and he made known his way of life for those who would like to use it and I choose to use it. Buddhism complements all religions and no person has lost a life in its efforts and because it is just there, no one is making you a part of it or getting angry because you are not with it.

Cynthia and I decided that I would be responsible for the Buddhist Ceremony and she would do the Church Wedding details. Since I was a long way from the Island, Catherine Finch, a member of the Wednesday evening writers group, was an ideal person to help with the planning and performing the ceremony.

• • • • •

This is what happened on March 28, a rainy Wednesday, so that we were in the parlor of the Cleaveland House. Assembled were Catherine, ringing the Tingsha bells to start the Ceremony, the members of the Wednesday Writers Group, my son Mark and his wife Jennifer, and granddaughter Sophia. Lynn was present as guest and photographer.

There were lots of flowers everywhere. Two chairs. one for me and one for my love, and a small table which held my Mala Beads, four candles, sandalwood incense, small Buddhist bowl for the incense sticks containing Pacific Ocean sand that I brought and Martha's Vineyard sand, Tingsha Bells, Cat's White Quan Yin and my Buddha.

Cat lighted a large candle and three incense sticks. The members were quiet and Mark played on his flute, a lyrical piece that he composed for this ceremony. I thanked Mark and offered an explanations as to what was to follow:

This is a ceremony that uppermost is the exchange of endearing words between the two of us, what we are giving to each other, what we mean to each other, and how this coming together enhances each of our lives.

Howie lights his candle and gave his declaration:

Cynner, I will love you and will share with you all things, for all days that time will allow. I am living a dream that started then, many decades ago, and is being realized here today.

I am to be your husband but am now saying I will share responsibilities in all things — our home, family, endeavors and others.

I want to brighten your grey days by giving you my support . . . I will be there for you.

What do I want from you? I want to feed on your words which are very important to me. We will talk together on matters small and large.

I will give you warmth, kindness and unending love as I want to make you happy and secure. My object is to make you really feel grand . . . for you are Cynner who is very deserving of all that I can give. I just want your presence . . . for you to be near. I thank you for joining with me this day binding our love and life together in this union of commitment.

Cynthia lighted her candle and gave her declaration, short, heartfelt, and unprepared. She told of her growing love, of her determination to live up to my vision of her, of her joy in sharing her life with me, of her feeling of completeness.

Together Cynthia and Howie lighted the third candle.

Cat used my Rosewood Mala Beads and wrapped them around Cynthia's and Howie's wrists for Handfasting while declaring:

As this knot is tied, so are your lives now firmly and lovingly bound. This togetherness is secured by the wrapping of the Mala around your wrists, along with the wishes of your family and friends, and of yourselves, for your new life together. With the tying together of this knot, here in this family parlor I tie together the desires, dreams, happiness, expectations and love to your lives for as long as life endures.

You two entwined by love, bound by commitment, you can now face, sadness and joy, hardship and victory, all of which can bring strength to this union.

Remember it is not the physical binding, but what it represents, that will keep you together with respect, goodness and love

Go with love . . . Continue to bring forth goodness.

Cat rang the bells signaling the completion of the Union of Togetherness. She then un-bound Cynthia and Howie's wrists.

Congratulations took place. All participants brought a small stone with them and one at a time they placed their stone in a small basket saying out loud their support and blessings. Then in the misty rain all went by the pool where a Beech Tree was recently planted and Amy read "Beeches by Our Door" by Dionis Coffin Riggs. All joined hands and circled the tree shouting what they liked. Howie said, "Thank you Cynner for being here now and forevermore at my side, thanks Buddha, this is happiness, we are going to live HAPPILY EVER AFTER."

BEECHES
By Our Door

If we were to be,
Like Baucis and Philemon
changed into trees

Could they be beech?
How lovely our spring
in pale green.

In summer how cool
with comforting shade
and the chirping of birds.

In autumn
a wealth of gold coins,
a rustle of silk

Strong boles and gray boughs would defy
the rough wind, and hold
winter-bronzed leaves to the sky.

—Dionis Coffin Riggs

Then back into the house for meaningful food and drink to celebrate the glorious occasion with the centerpiece being a Buddhist cake that Lisa had ordered made for us. Three layers for the three paths. Mocha frosting symbolizing mud from which the Lotus grows unstained and Buddha and our candle from the ceremony. proudly displayed on top.

Dear Mark: April 3rd, 2013

Your dad sailed through his Registry of Motor Vehicles encounter and emerged with a Commonwealth of Massachusetts driver's license with a good photo of him on the front. He and I have done the following, with him driving this behemoth of a truck down narrow lanes to get to hidden destinations: to Maciel Marine, where John Thayer's cabinetmaker's shop is located, to thank John's son, Nate, who made our bed; to our financial advisor, Jen Adamson; to Cronig's a number of times; the post office; The Tisbury Printer; Bunch of Grapes bookstore; C.B. Stark Jewelry, which engraved our rings with initials and dates in just a couple of hours and got the rings back to us on Saturday afternoon before Easter; Easter Service at the New Ag Hall; Cottle's Lumber Yard; the Gay Head cliffs, Menemsha, and Fielder and Fielder Imports (our nephew and niece Evan and Chris Fielder's shop), where there was barely room to turn the truck around; Shirley's Hardware in Vineyard Haven; Phillips Hardware in Oak Bluffs; to the Airport Laundromat (my washing machine broke down and your dad tried to fix it, in vain); Easter dinner at our niece and nephew's with 18 in attendance and names to remember, which he did; to the Howes House (Up Island Council on Aging) to talk with Joyce Bowker, the director, about Massachusetts Health Insurance; returned (with regrets) the New Bedford Pistol Team protective vest to the Dunkl family at their water bottling plant. What have I forgotten? Omigod! To the West Tisbury Town Hall to apply for a marriage license.

We're going to Polly Hill one of these days to thank Tim Boland for the beech tree.

Your Dad is the most amazing man. He met and charmed Arlene Bodge, the defrocked Catholic nun and Methodist minister who will perform our marriage ceremony at the West Tisbury Congregational Church. He's almost mastered Scrabble after two games. He meets and greets all the myriad people who flow in and out of this house and grounds. He sharpened all my shamefully dull knives. At the moment, the poets are meeting downstairs and he's working on sorting and organizing things in his study. He no longer walks with a shuffle, it's almost a stride. The cat sneaks up onto our bed in the middle of the night. We keep the door open a crack because we've had the fire in the fireplace the past two nights and want to make sure we don't get asphyxiated. He's set up his study/office/lab so it looks as though he's always been there. He's ordered his new microscope. We're working on meals, since his idea is five small meals a day, and mine has been one huge meal late at night. We seem to be settling on four meals, which is probably healthier. Speaking of healthier, I should tell you that he ate all the rest of that cake, all by himself.

Love to all, Cynthia

Howie's 91st birthday was on April 9th, 2013, a quiet birthday we celebrated by ourselves, in the pleasure of our own company.

Now came the plans for Wedding No. 2. The small intimate church wedding for family and close friends seemed to be morphing into a world class production. The West Tisbury Congregational Church holds only 150 people, so we had, of necessity, to limit our list of invitees to that. Not easy.

The day dawned, Saturday of the Memorial Day weekend. Cloudy and chilly. The dress fit, and Howie helped tuck in and pin stray straps. The sandals Lisa found on eBay were perfect, gold with a big pink flower that might show as I walked down the aisle. Amy decorated the wreaths I'd made from wisteria vine with ribbons and fresh flowers that trailed down my back. Howie was dressed in a suit that made him look like something out of *Gentleman's Quarterly.*

Mark Wright, a longtime friend, agreed to play the organ to accompany whatever music we wanted. Ed Rodgers, retired from the U.S. Navy Band, volunteered to play trumpet for our processional. Peter and Frank Dunkl, knowing my favorite instrument is the French horn, prepared a piece for two horns and piano, with Mark to dash downstairs from the choir loft to play the piano and then rush back upstairs again for the processional. My sister Ann and Mark had adapted a vocal piece from Handel for her to play on her cello with organ accompaniment. Tsilala promised to come from college in Pittsburgh to sing "The Prayer" with Mark again clambering down the steep choir loft stairs to the sanctuary's piano.

The church service was officiated by the minister of the Chilmark Methodist Church, the Reverend Arlene Bodge, a member of the Sunday Writers' Group.

I don't recall how either of us got to the church, but when I got there, cars were lined up as far as I could see along State Road and Music Street. My tall, six-foot-eight son Robert, enlisted last minute to escort me down the aisle, was splendid in his sports jacket. I forgot that I was to carry a bridal bouquet, forgot my glasses to read a poem to my beloved Howie, forgot the papers with the poem printed in 16-point type.

Robert and I waited in the vestibule while Peter and Frank played their French horns with Mark on piano. It was so beautiful, I cried. And then, Mark's footsteps pounded up the choir loft steps, and — Oh My! The trumpet and organ blasted out the processional. My beautiful six-foot-two-inch daughter Ann, gorgeous in the lavender gown Mindy Todd had miraculously acquired, strode down the aisle hand in hand with the flower girl, my youngest granddaughter, four-year-old Skye Willow.

Robert and I followed. The congregation stood. I saw Arlene and Kathy, long-time friends from Vermont, and bent down en route to the altar to kiss tiny Arlene.

And there was Howie, handsome and standing tall with his son Mark.

We'd thought to borrow bar stools from sister Alvida so we could sit and be seen during what we knew would be a long service. All was perfect. At what seemed like the proper time, Howie and I seized one another in a grand embrace and a long kiss, that we'd practiced. The congregation cheered. The service went on. The Reverend Bodge came to a pause and announced, "NOW you may kiss," to more cheers. We'd been too eager.

CBS News covered the wedding. Since the entire crew couldn't make it over on the ferry, it was left up to one handsome young man. Since I was in the mood for matchmaking, I tried to pair him up with Tsilala, and got as far as a "thumbs up!" from Tsilala's mother, who'd flown in from Bermuda.

The rain held off until we'd accepted congratulations from the last of the 150 well-wishers from our bar stools, moved by a nephew to the church lawn. And then it poured.

All 150 crammed themselves into the Cleaveland House. Ed Rodgers blasted out a joyous fanfare when we appeared in the tightly packed dining room. Tsilala sang. Mark played his keyboard. My granddaughter Rosemary and husband Jay had baked our small wedding cake, and 150 chocolate cupcakes with butter cream frosting to go with it.

Howie had ordered two luxury outdoor porta-potties, and they were never used.

• • • • •

Steve Hartman of CBS's *On the Road* interviewed Howie and me the next morning. The segment appeared the following Friday, and again on the *CBS News, Sunday Morning.*

Chapter 56. New Beginnings

It's a rainy Thursday , late afternoon. Maria, our Brazilian cleaning woman, has left us with a clean, sweet-smelling house. Howie has put the guineas and chickens to bed, safe from raccoons and owls, and he's checked to make sure the skunk hadn't slipped inside their coop. I'm in the kitchen, standing with my back to the sink. Howie eases himself into my great-grandfather's chair, a real captain's chair made a 150 years ago. He takes off his boots, the ones he wears to tend our flocks. Tomorrow, Brian Lawlor is coming to talk to us about having his goats clear the brush in our wooded area, a new project for him and for us. Howie puts his boots aside and slips on his sheepskin-lined slippers. That done, he sits back, looks up at me and smiles. Life is good. We don't intend to misuse a second of it. He eases himself out of the chair and stands. We look at each other with the hunger of an 18- and a 28-year old. He takes my hand. We walk from the kitchen through the dining room and into our bedroom, the room we have always called "Aunt's room" in honor of Great Aunt Alvida. He shuts the door. It has no lock, so he props a chair against it. He's accustomed, now, to neighbors walking in unannounced. There's no need to say anything.

The bed John Thayer's son Nate built for us takes up most of the room. Hidden on the headboard he carved our secret code letters for hugs, kisses, and passion.

Howie draws the sheer curtain closed to mute our unacknowledged imperfections. He folds back the quilt. We sink onto the bed, as close to each other as we can get. Rain drums softly against the ancient window panes.

"Love," says Howie, "is a beautiful place to spend the rest of your life."

—THE END—

About the Authors

Cynthia Riggs has authored 13 books in the Martha's Vineyard Mystery Series (St. Martin's Press). As a journalist selected by the National Science Foundation, she was the seventh woman to set foot on the South Pole. She held a USCG 100-ton Masters License for 20 years, taught sailing at the Annapolis Sailing School, and was tour boat captain for the Washington Boat Lines. She made numerous boat deliveries including two trans-Atlantic crossings in a 32-foot sailboat. She has a degree in geology, Antioch College (1953), and an MFA, Vermont College (2000). She and her husband, Dr. Howard R. Attebery, live on Martha's Vineyard.

Dr. Howard R. Attebery has published numerous papers on microbiology, and is author or co-author of four books, one of his own photography. He served in the US Army from 1943 to 1947. He has a degree in dentistry (College of the Pacific) and was public health dentist for Sonoma and Santa Cruz counties, California. As National Institute of Health post-doctoral fellow he did research at UCLA on anaerobic bacteria and lectured at UCLA Medical School. After retiring from pediatric dentistry, he served as photographer for San Diego Children's Hospital and Sharp Hospitals, was on call by the San Diego County Sheriff as forensic photographer, and was expert witness for numerous court cases.

Made in the USA
Charleston, SC
12 November 2016